Extraordinary Thoughts About *Thunderbolt Thinking!*®

❝ *Inspirational and transformational! It will change the way you use your brain. Concrete recommendations and exercises will enhance your creativity and increase your success. I'm buying a copy for everyone on my staff!* **❞**

> —Jack Canfield
> President
> Self Esteem Seminars
> Coauthor of *Chicken Soup for the Soul*

❝ *I found the book thought-provoking and it allowed me to focus on my specific thinking skills—one of the most useful tools for me.* **❞**

> —A. V. Ramamurthy, Ph.D.
> Corporate Fellow, Union Carbide Corporation

❝ *An invaluable resource that we've used time and again, not only to think 'outside the box,' but also to turn our ideas into effective strategies.* **❞**

> —George Dramowicz
> Director, Supplier Quality Assurance, Honeywell

❝ *An inspiring collection of practical ideas that will awaken you to new possibilities in every arena of life. Wonderfully whole-brained and rich with paradox. The T•N•Ts are great ideas, easy and fun to use.* **❞**

> —Ann McGee-Cooper, Ed.D.
> Author of *You Don't Have to Go Home from Work Exhausted!* and *Time Management for Unmanageable People*

"Interesting and provocative approach to getting the most out of your precious creative thinking time and opportunities."

—Ron Zemke
Coauthor of *Managing Knock Your Socks Off Service*

"Just the jolt your brain needs to get jump-started."

—Rieva Lesonsky
Editor-in-Chief, Entrepreneur Magazine Group

"It's terrific! Required reading for any business that wants to survive in the next century."

—Mary Del Brady
President
TissueInformatics, Inc.

"I know well the source of Grace McGartland's inspiration. Its authority leads directly to the bottom-line focus of her book."

—Ned Herrmann
Author of *The Creative Brain*

"One of the freshest approaches to the creative process since Whack on the Side of the Head. *It gives the 'What' and the 'Why' to getting unstuck— as well as the 'How.' BRAVO!"*

—Carolyn Warner
Carolyn Warner and Associates
Author of *The Last Word*

Grace McGartland

SECOND EDITION

THUNDERBOLT

THINKING®

Electrifying Ideas for Building an Innovative Workplace

Grace McGartland

Bard Press

For more information about quantity discounts, write or call:

Bard Press
1515 Capital of Texas Hwy. South, Suite 107, Austin, Texas 78746
512/329-8373   Fax 512/329-6051
www.bardpress.com

ISBN: 1-885167-42-3

Library of Congress Cataloging-in-Publication Data

McGartland, Grace.
    Thunderbolt thinking : electrifying ideas for building an innovative workplace /
Grace McGartland.--
    2nd ed.
        p. cm.
    Subtitle differs from 1st ed.
    Includes index.
    ISBN 1-885167-42-3 (pbk.)
    1. Creative ability in business.   I. Title.

HD53.M38 2000
658.4'03--dc21   00-025238

First Edition
First Printing: March 1994
Second Printing: November 1994
Third Printing: December 1997

Second Edition
First Printing: May 2000

A BARD PRESS BOOK

A U S T I N ,   T E X A S

Copyediting: **Helen Hyams**

Text Design: **Suzanne Pustejovsky**

Jacket Design: **Suzanne Pustejovsky**

Composition/Production: **Round Rock Graphics**

To Dunc,

with love,

for your gentle strength,

courage,

and absolute faith

in me

CONTENTS

The Author 12

Preface: Deepening the Thunderbolt Thinking Experience 13

1 When the Thunder Struck Me 17

PART ONE: THUNDERSTRUCK

---

2 Thunderbolt Thinking: Why Now? 21

3 Do You Need Thunderbolt Thinking? 31

4 The Thunderbolt Thinking Model:
   What It Is and How It Works 49

5 Thunderbolt Innovators:
   Building an Innovative Workplace 67

PART TWO: THE THUNDERBOLT SPIRIT

---

6 Spirit: The Stuff That Makes Thunderbolt Thinkers 79

7 Flexibility: Another Name for Change 87

8 Awareness: Inside and Outside 93

9 Courage: Risk and Vulnerability 99

10 Humor: More Than the Frosting **103**

11 Action: A Can-Do Attitude **115**

PART THREE: THE FIVE "HOW-TO" THINKING STEPS

---

12 Step One: Expand Your Perspective **127**

13 Step Two: Rachet Up Your Brainpower **147**

14 Step Three: Turbocharge the Environment **167**

15 Step Four: Master the Conversation **179**

16 Step Five: Be a Catalyst... **195**

PART FOUR: THUNDERBOLTING: WHEN AND HOW TO USE IT

---

17 A Zero-Based Meeting Attitude—Here's How **205**

18 On-the-Job Thunderbolting **223**

19 Do It Now—With Action You Get Results **239**

Chapter Notes **241**

Glossary.. **246**

Index **248**

THIRTY POUNDS OF
T·N·T

TIPS AND TECHNIQUES
TO PUT THUNDERBOLT THINKING INTO ACTION

1. The Art of Brain Flossing

2. The Birth of Bun-Huggers

3. Brain Fantasy

4. Brain Jolts

5. Brain Stretch

6. Brain Transformers

7. Breaking Through Conditioned Responses

8. Corporate Portraits

9. Develop Your Sense of Humor

10. Draw-a-Brain

11. The F.I.S.H.™

12. Flexible Focus

13. The Garbage Bag Dump

14. Head Bowling

15. Hidden Communication

16. Idea Hatchery

17. Image Storming

18. A Name Tag Is a Name Tag Is a Name Tag

19. One Picture or One Thousand Words

20. Regressive Introductions

21. Spill the Beans

22. Theme and Tools for Thinking

23. Thought Walk

24. Thunderbolt Show and Tell

25. Total Immersion: Using Sense

26. The Shape of Things to Come

27. Eggs-straordinaire

28. Reel to Real

29. Sing-a-Song

30. The Flash Cap

THE AUTHOR

Grace McGartland has coached thousands of leaders and teams inside Fortune 500 companies, as well as in national trade and professional associations, showing them how to harness brainpower and drive innovation inside their organizations. For more than eighteen years, she has influenced leaders by helping them to build a strategic foundation for innovation, integrating it into their business strategies, procedures, and workplaces. The organizations with which she has worked include AT&T; American National Bank; Bristol-Myers Squibb Australia; BB&T; Ernst & Young; Honeywell; IBM; Motorola Canada, Ltd.; Owens Corning; SmithKline Beecham Pharma, Inc.; U. S. Steel; Royal Bank Financial Group; and US WEST Communications, Inc.

As the founder and president of Thunderbolt Thinking, Inc., Grace has the vision of building thinking organizations worldwide that sustain innovation. Her mission as a strategic innovator is to help visionary organizations achieve market dominance in the new economy by systematically integrating innovation at every level.

Grace developed her positive and fresh approach to life through a series of professional and personal experiences, including a successful battle against cancer. She has since used her ever-abundant energy to create the F.I.T. (Fearless Imaginative Thinking) Foundation, a nonprofit organization focused on erasing the fear of cancer reoccurrence for other survivors.

PREFACE

Deepening the Thunderbolt Thinking Experience

In this revised edition we've enhanced the Thunderbolt Thinking Model by adding the Innovation Formula. This formula emerges from a direct discussion with a group of global leaders about their quest to learn how to build an innovative workplace. The formula shows how innovation results when change is leveraged with a combination of creativity and analysis and has become the backbone of a set of thirteen strategies for fostering an innovative environment.

Building on this foundation for innovation, this How-To Guide includes a collection of new tools and techniques that we've developed while working with strategic innovators inside our client organizations. Some of the new how-to components we've added include six *new* TNTs (tips and techniques) in our "yellow page" section, as well as a new Lucky 13 strategy assessment tool and a new Change Lab Planner. All of these are concrete supports to help you step into the role of strategic innovator and move into action quickly.

Since the first edition was published, I have watched leaders harness Thunderbolt Thinking to drive the innovation process through their organizations. These strategic innovators, through their power to influence, drive innovation by aligning it with their organization's vision, integrating it into their business strategies, embedding it in their procedures, and bringing it alive in their workplaces. But most important, they discover their own innovative core and learn how to nurture it with their own brainpower.

Unpredictable, chaotic, experimental—all describe the impact our clients, the leaders within organizations, have as they step outside the boundaries and, through the power of influence, experiment with Thunderbolt strategies, tips, and techniques. Over the past six years, they have learned and, as a result, we have also learned.

This new edition reflects the discoveries and feedback from our teachers, those influential leaders. I thank them for making a difference within their organizations.

Thunderbolting entered my life in 1984, but until I met *Gillian Rudd,* I didn't understand its magic. She revealed it through her vision and insight. I thank Gillian for the difference she made in my life. And I thank my husband, *Dunc Morrison,* for the opportunity to celebrate Thunderbolting power every day. This year marks the fifteenth anniversary, for both of us, of being cancer-free!

Reminiscing about Thunderbolt Thinking's early years brings to mind memorable images of the initial Thunderbolters. *Rick Malis* urged me to investigate the displayed thinking process taught by *Jerry McNellis;* Jerry's support helped me to develop my skills as a facilitator; and I remember *Wayne Smith*'s brilliant but serious face when he said, "We need some concrete way to capture this process." I thank each of them.

A hilarious meeting with *Lorraine Fink, Donna Drew,* and *Nena Pavlik* trailblazed innovative service promotions and birthed several Thunderbolt concepts. I offer a heartfelt thanks to these colleagues.

Mentors make entrepreneurs. In my case, I'd like to thank *Virginia Littlejohn* and, though I didn't know him, *Albert Einstein,* for their courage to break the rules, give beneficial advice, and provide valuable thoughts that strengthen this book's fabric.

As a lifelong friend, *Edie Turna* continues to steer and focus my efforts in the right direction. *Marcia Wieder*'s conversations of possibilities encouraged me and opened new aspects for transformation. The editorial talents of my sister, *Nancy McGartland,* drove me into despair as I heard "To be a good writer you need to *eat your own babies*" and sparked many late-night rewrites; for this, I thank her.

Thanks also go to the Bard Press team for excellent guidance though each step of the process. In particular, *Ray Bard*'s ongoing commitment to Thunderbolt and his business savvy were invaluable. *Suzanne Pustejovsky* and *Helen Hyams* also added a special quality to the entire project.

Finally, in various periods of my life I've experienced a rich confluence of individuals and a rich blending of collective talents. My years in the leadership of the National Association of Women Business Owners were one instance; another has been the last two years in my own business.

The current Thunderbolt team, *Maura Farrell, Susan Fung, Catrina Colme, Ailene Deaville,* and *Grace McGartland,* didn't just happen—we made it happen. With playfulness, ongoing commitment, and trust in each other, this team put flesh on the bones of Thunderbolt Thinking. Whether we were cooking up new ideas as "Bowling Queens" at our annual retreat or stretching ourselves in the role of "Black Belt Babes" as project leaders, these four women made a difference in my life.

Maura Farrell's breadth of skills helped me to transform difficult, unclear ideas and plan new ways to present information and encouraged me to penetrate further into my own experiences. I thank her for her willingness to walk into the unknown. *Susan Fung*'s unwavering loyalty provided the constant in a turbulent environment of questioning. Her attention to detail as our Administration Czar created the support system that kept Thunderbolt charging. I thank her for the courage to stretch. *Catrina Colme*'s fresh talent and untested experience were just the juices needed to challenge me to take concepts one step further; her writing style strengthened the pages of this book. I thank her for the openness she brings. *Ailene Deaville* brought balance and depth to my thinking. Through her years of experience she added the value of reflective thought to yet-unproven ideas; for this, I thank her.

From our exploration ideas flourished. Our conversation of possibilities expanded and previously uncharted courses were tried; thus the Thunderbolt Thinking presented in this revised edition offers deeper, more mature thinking about how we can connect new patterns of thought and transform them into insights and opportunities.

I've been blessed, and I am grateful for the opportunity to play, discover, explore, create, and make a difference through the Thunderbolt Thinking experience. I invite you to do the same.

Grace McGartland
March 2000

When the Thunder Struck Me

It was the summer of 1984—a hot, humid June night that's really atypical in Pittsburgh so early in the season. Because of the new moon, my room was dark as I lay there awake. It was 11:30 P.M. My cat's purring was noticeably soft compared to the pounding of my heart as I thought—*I'm going to die.*

The previous two weeks had been filled with waiting, wondering, and tests. Actually, as I look back, they didn't seem real, yet that night reality set in. I came face to face with the biggest challenge of my life.

I usually think in pictures and on June 23, 1984, the images that rushed through my brain were ones I wanted to erase. At my age, death should have been the furthest thing from my mind, but that's what I was thinking about. That's the message my brain was sending: *Grace, that's what happens when you are diagnosed with cancer.* I was stuck in one thought: *I'm dying.* As tears streamed down my face and disbelief filled my heart, the sounds of my creaky 1908 Victorian house drifted through the room. Kitty stirred a bit, but I lay still—which was highly unusual for me, a woman of action. I lay still, frozen by my fear, trapped by the frightening pictures in my head, and resolved—*I'm going to die.*

By 3:15 A.M., I had collected my thoughts and started preparing to die. That's the only thing I saw. I had only one vision . . . no options . . . I was stuck. I began to recap the memorable snapshots of the past thirty-two years, the people and events that had been crucial parts of my life.

And then it hit me. I sat up, switched on the light, and said to myself, *Wait a minute!* An overwhelming feeling flooded into my being and I heard myself say aloud, *Grace—yes, you have cancer, but you don't have to die.* In a flash, I realized that the real challenge was not dealing with death, but creating a life that was worth living. Even if I had cancer. In an instant, my brain was shaken. A wild flurry of pictures flashed by again, but this time, they were pictures of the future. As I watched them fly by me, I realized that I was still scared—not of dying, but rather of facing the challenge of living. I knew I couldn't face it alone. I needed help. I reached for paper and a pencil and composed a letter to my family and friends. I asked for their support in dealing with my Hodgkin's disease. Then I closed my eyes and went to sleep.

Thunderbolt Thinking was born that June night.

PART ONE

Thunderstruck

CHAPTER

Thunderbolt Thinking: Why Now?

You don't need a life-threatening experience to get unstuck. What you do need is the flexibility, awareness, and courage to risk rearranging your thinking so you can make a transformational shift: the shift from one answer to a multitude of alternatives, from inertia to action, from resisting change to welcoming it.

We lose opportunities because we don't embrace change. Stuck in the status quo, we miss the warning signs of major events. This shortsightedness stunts our growth, our vision, and our possibilities. We know this. Yet we are starved for that fresh flash of energy that can break our fixed mind-set and build our enthusiasm.

"Everything that is really great and inspiring is created by the individual who can labor in freedom."

Such flashes occur all the time, jolting freshness into our thinking. Occasionally we can taste its invigorating flavor, we can feel its exhilaration, all the way through to the marrow of our bones. But many times we miss it. Why? Because there's no time to think. There's no system in place, no direction to guide our thinking. We move at such a rapid pace that we miss the freshness. Life blinds our vision, deadens our taste, and numbs our touch. We're stuck on a daily treadmill, running faster and faster—and don't even know it.

Think about this for a moment: We operate on only one-tenth of our potential brainpower 90 percent of the time. Therefore, even though thinking is our most precious asset and it's the primary source of innovation, our brainpower often remains an untapped resource. Why? Because most of us don't know exactly how to harness it or use it to our best advantage. So how can you tap into your innovative potential?

The answer: by managing your thinking. Thunderbolt Thinking is a way of managing your thinking by being alert to how you think, being aware of your brainpower, and being agile in your thinking. While most people only use 5 to 10 percent of their brainpower, by focusing on *how* you think, you can raise that percentage. Being alert, aware, and agile in your thinking allows you to think on purpose and with a purpose instead of coasting day-to-day in a mindless state.

In an age when innovation is a key business driver, we can't afford to let our minds stagnate and we can't afford to get stuck. We need to be able to welcome the changes we face on a daily basis. Thunderbolt Thinking helps you to respond to the signals, those daily events that represent both challenges and opportunities, by leveraging your thinking. By being deliberate in your thinking you become more effective, so that you can make a difference not only for your organization but for yourself, your family, and your community in how you:

- Approach tasks each day
- Think about problems or challenges
- Take advantage of opportunities

The Transformational Shift: Picking Up the Signals

Paying attention to the signals, those daily events that flag both trouble and opportunity, keeps us from being caught. The trick is sensing which signals telegraph the most danger as well as the greatest possibility, providing us with kernels of insight about our future. Crafting a sensible response to alarming symptoms while recognizing the importance of constant improvement and satisfaction of our customers' needs calls for a keen sense of awareness. And, at times, bulldozer action to let our flashes lead us to a better tomorrow.

Are you picking up the signals? Is your organization? Your family? Your community? Managers ask for help. Workers look for action steps. No one wants to be stuck.

SIGNAL NO. 1
"Stuckness": Getting Stuck in Your Organization

I believe that as we move into the future, "stuckness"—the "don't buck the system" attitude cemented into the corporate pillars of too many organizations—presents a real threat. However, we rarely identify it as a threat—it's unseen. Many organizations will stagnate. Continuing to operate as they have for decades and lacking the tools to change, they will be unable to move forward. They won't keep up with the world's increasingly fast pace. They'll be gone. Just one look at the faster-growing segments of the world's economies reveals enterprises com-

prised of technology links rather than traditional brick-and-mortar-type industries.

This accelerated, globalized environment challenges obsolete management practices, demands fast-paced, but not quick-fix, innovative thinking, and erodes the orthodox models of the past. As Rosabeth Moss Kanter states, "Fine-tuning is no longer enough. . . . Nothing short of transformation will do." [1]

Yet many organizations don't hear this message or even see the consequences of falling behind in competitiveness. A "that's not us" attitude blinds them, hindering their thinking. Their "stuckness" threatens their future. Sometimes they fall in love with an approach, a product or service, or a target market. This is what sealed the fate of the Cabbage Patch Kids. These dolls were made by Coleco Industries, an American toymaker. Each had unique features as a result of production techniques that made trivial variations in every doll. In America, Cabbage Patch Kids were the hottest toy of Christmas 1985. But with no new hits, Coleco went bankrupt in 1988 as real kids went back to their old favorites. [2]

When companies slip into a myopic state, they find themselves unprepared to deal with change, sometimes to the point of being vision-less. Failure to build in a mechanism that responds to change leaves many organizations stuck and lacking in versatility.

SIGNAL NO. 2
Lack of Insight: A Barrier
That Inhibits Your Options

To many, the very idea of change is threatening. People resist change when they don't understand its implications and perceive that it might cost them much more than they will gain. It doesn't matter whether we're a seasoned manager or a budding entrepreneur; we all tend to rely on past experience to set our future direction. Yesterday this ten-dency was okay. However, today a lack of insight into the future causes stagnation. Without it we are limited, seeing only confusing symptoms, not the causes of the problem. Too often we react and don't stop to think about the problem; we tend to go for the "here it is" solution without piercing to the core of the situation.

Richard L. Nolan, co-founder and past chairman of Nolan, Norton and Company, points out that "getting the transformation message is hard because transformation involves 'creative destruction'—destruc-tion of the old ways of doing business in such a way that business can be done while new ways of doing business are being formed."[3] Creative destruction dismantles the outer facade, questioning every aspect of an organization starting with its basic purpose. The questioning process requires a constant reconceptualization of how an organization will meet its basic purpose along with continual reassessment of that pur-pose as it relates to changes in the world. In the end, we want this cre-ative destruction to facilitate a rebirth from the ashes of current reality into fresh, innovative insights.

We are not used to shifting our frame of reference. We are not used to recognizing the value of a less familiar point of view.

SIGNAL NO. 3
Shrinking Time Frames:
No Time to Think

A company that can bring out new products three times faster than its competitors enjoys a huge advantage. At Tivoli Systems, Inc., an IBM company, production cycles move quickly. Initially, when she was asked to design a demo for a new product within five days, Lynn Wilczak's jaw dropped. The demo ended up taking ten days to finish, and six months later the product was shipped. Now, Wilczak, vice president of enterprise R&D, says, "I love this fast pace. Let's make decisions and go." Today Tivoli is the fastest-growing segment within IBM's $14 billion software division.[4]

From a static environment to a speed-driven marketplace, this transformational shift, which is shaking our entire society, requires a heightened sense of awareness about the accelerating rate of change and its impact. For instance, in the fifteenth century, it took a long time for people with little control over their day-to-day lives to come to grips with the idea of a round earth and the heliocentric motion of the planets.

The impact of change really took hold in the 1980s. The destruction of the Berlin Wall started one evening and at 6:00 A.M. the next morning we read, in detail, the whys and hows in our hometown newspapers. Within days after the bombing of the World Trade Center in New York, security tightened in airports across the country. And when authorities suspected that Tylenol had been laced with poison, thousands of bottles were stripped from grocery store shelves within hours. In each case, the domino effect was felt at once. We run the risk of getting stuck faster than ever before because in our more complex, time-sensitive, interdependent world, we have no time to think.

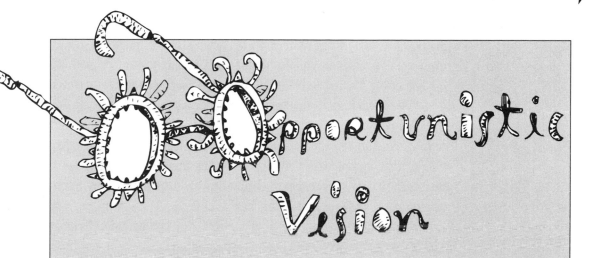

An adhesive with very low sticking power . . .	*3M creates Post-it Notes, a $100 million product.*
A flight program off-course 90 percent of the time . . .	*Apollo 11 flight mission reaches the moon and gets back home.*
A falling apple . . .	*Sir Isaac Newton discovers gravity.*
An oversight by a factory worker who let a stirrer run too long in a soap vat . . .	*Ivory Soap is invented (and floats!).*
Coors Brewing Company finding itself with spoiled beer . . .	*Multimillion-dollar sales of "food" are made to Japanese farmers for their beef cattle.*

SIGNAL NO. 4
Globalized Trading:
The Blurring of Borders

Global players, global rivals, and global experts dominate the basis of our production cycles. For instance, a book idea originating with a New York publisher, printed on paper processed in the northeastern United

States, and made from pulp imported from Canada might be printed on German presses using ink developed in Japan. Afterward, the book is shipped to Mexico for binding, then returned to Chicago and New York for distribution throughout North America.[5]

However, years of immunity from international competition have created an arrogance in some organizations, a type of competitive barrier that immobilizes thinking and traps them in old logic. Xerox Corporation came back from the brink only by dismantling their matrix organization and accompanying bureaucracy and restructuring into product teams. In order to outmaneuver the competition, Eastman Kodak Company eliminated 24,000 jobs and changed from a centralized organization by structuring the front line to handle key daily decisions. Millions were allocated toward a competitive global strategy that linked Kodak to existing foreign business partners.

We are not used to thinking in terms of global competition, which is played by different rules. Now is the time to take a tough-minded look at the risks we are running, to think "on purpose" about enduring in the global village.

SIGNAL NO. 5
Declining Returns:
Poor Investment in Human Capital

Garry Berryman, who ran American Honda Motor Company's training center in Marysville, Ohio, sums it up this way: "An organization, with all its greatest muscle—machinery, equipment, money, facilities—can't do anything unless it's got a brain. The brain is the people."[6] Too often, the brain of the company is simply overlooked.

According to Faith Popcorn, futurist and author of *The Popcorn Report,* "The trouble in corporate America is that too many people with too much power live in a box (their home), then travel the same road every day to another box (their office). They rarely turn on the TV, because they're swamped with paperwork. And they rarely even scan every page of their newspaper, because they're too consumed with yet a third box, their In-box."[7] With all this brainpower locked in a box, the corporation's vision remains limited and its experiences sterile. Looking for the future, managers don't know enough to take off the lid and stick out their noses. Imprisoned by their own traditional mind-sets, they aren't even aware that they are stuck.

In short, corporations have been scrimping on human capital. After trying to become competitive by pouring hundreds of billions of dollars into capital equipment, they're discovering that they have been blindsided when it comes to workers. During the Industrial Revolution, one of the most momentous concerns of capitalism was that the division of labor, its key principle, turned people into nothing but their hands. It stunted individuals, smothering their most human faculties of heart and brain.[8] However, the evidence is overwhelming: people, not machines, are the driving force behind our new economic realities. The principle organizations must follow today is the creative use of workers' full abilities, as they purposefully develop strategies to ratchet up the brainpower within the corporate vault.

66 The whole of science is nothing more than a refinement of everyday thinking. 99

The Thunderbolt Model: A How-to-Think Process

In today's rapidly changing business environment, we can't afford to ignore the signals. That is why as organizations and as individuals we need to focus on *how to think*. By deliberately instituting a how-to-think process, we can facilitate a shift that will help to overcome automatic, ingrained behavior. The Thunderbolt Thinking Model is a tool to help you make a shift in how you think by combining the specific challenges you need to work on with a proven five-step thinking process. Working through the five how-to-think steps, you will blast through the rigid walls of traditional thinking, feel safe when you step out of bounds, and cause enough of a shift so that effective thinking emerges.

The Thunderbolt Thinking Model prepares you to:

- Smash through thinking gridlocks by breaking traditional mind-sets and reshaping thinking so that you, your organization, your family, or your neighbor don't get stuck

- Let go and change your focus from WHAT you are thinking to HOW you think

- Liberate your own SPIRIT, your innovative core, and encourage it to take advantage of change: to predict, shape, define, and stimulate change in all facets of your life

To learn how to think, you must dislodge your brain from its fixed position, let go to make new connections, and be willing to look at your markets, products, services, strategies, policies, and procedures—again and again—so that you and your organization don't get stuck. To do this you'll need to be the thermostat, setting the temperature for change, rather than the barometer that measures it. And you'll need to get involved with changes on a daily basis in order to determine, govern, provoke, awaken, encourage, and frame the shift.

Organizations need people who have the spirit—the inner drive—to challenge tradition and leave the rut, the courage to push through their limits and unlearn habits that keep them entrenched in old patterns, and the humor to keep things positive. The Thunderbolt Thinking Model can help. It applies to all parts of your life and is a solid, proven way to welcome change, respond to signals, and produce effective outcomes. If you are stuck, using conventional resources won't give you or your organization a unique advantage. The Thunderbolt Thinking Model can.

How you answer the signal is more significant than how the signal reaches you.

Do You Need Thunderbolt Thinking?

One Sunday evening my husband and I were watching a Public Broadcasting System program on volcanoes. It was a fascinating documentary of two French scientists with a lifelong dedication to the study of volcanic activity.

During a particular scene in the Philippines, the ash from an erupting volcano had rapidly blanketed a nearby village, unexpectedly surprising the inhabitants. Because they were moving quickly to evacuate the tiny town, most of the livestock was left behind. In the aftermath a goat was trapped in the huge volcanic fallout. Twenty-four hours earlier this little guy had been roaming the cool mountainsides of the peaceful land. Now he was frozen, unable to budge, stuck in the solidified ash.

As we watched, I couldn't help but feel some empathy for the animal, struggling to be free and yet unable to move. Luckily the two scientists had the appropriate tools to literally chop away at the encrusted mass. Chunk by chunk they worked to release first the goat's front legs and then his back legs. Slowly the team was able to pull the animal out of the cementlike mass of ash. Once the barrier was removed, the liberated goat, although a bit wobbly, was able to courageously prance down the lane again.

Do you ever get stuck? Have you ever gotten locked into the "I've got the answer" syndrome? Or has "That's how we do it around here" rolled off your lips even before you realized what your employee or, worse yet, your child, was suggesting? It's happened to me. It happens to everyone. How about it? Are you stuck? Complete the "Are You Stuck?" Self-Assessment to see.

SELF-ASSESSMENT

"Are You Stuck?"

Think about it. How do you operate on a daily basis? What is your modus operandi—your usual way of working? What are your daily patterns? Review the scale below. After reading each question, rate your current mode of operation on a scale from 1 to 10. What is your usual response? Fill in the blanks, add up your points, and see how you feel about your score.

0	1	2	3	4	5	6	7	8	9	10

I'm Not at All Stuck   I'm Sometimes Stuck   I'm Really Stuck!

_____ I'm flexible and see things from several perspectives. I shift easily in my thought patterns. I value input from others and generally seek their suggestions.

_____ I'm usually prepared for change and never operate as if there's only one set of rules. I rarely step into a "That's how we do it around here" attitude. I often break with the past and blast through my usual routines.

_____ I consciously take time out to get refreshed and recharge my brain and body. Even in my hectic work environment, I generally laugh a lot—at myself and with others.

_____ I stay on top of change in my industry. I talk with clients, co-workers, and suppliers on a regular basis to get fresh ideas. Whether they are in the same location or halfway around the world, I manage to stay in touch.

_____ In the last year I've either planned or attended at least three training programs to enhance my skills. My staff either attended the same programs or went to similar ones.

_____ ÷ 5 = [_____] TOTAL SCORE

Think about the three most important reasons why you got the score you got. Write down your thoughts:

1. _____

2. _____

3. _____

Are You Stuck— Not Responding to the Signals?

Motorola, Inc., one of the world's leading producers of electronic equipment, systems, and components, continually hears the signals. To promote change, flexibility, and awareness among the rank and file, the company allowed its employees to completely redesign the factory floor of a new semiconductor plant in Chandler, Arizona, without being constrained by past practices and costly physical impediments.[1]

Then, to prevail in the pager business, Motorola called for a courageous revolution when the Japanese stormed the American electronic pager industry selling pagers at about half the price. Motorola realized that business as usual wouldn't be enough. They set out to develop the best off-the-shelf technology in the world. Through the action-oriented Bandit Project, they not only reduced production costs drastically, but also gained the flexibility to make each pager different to fit customers' specific needs. And, instead of taking a month or so to process orders, Motorola now transmits orders for customized pagers by computer to its plant at Boynton Beach, Florida. The pagers are manufactured, tested, and ready for delivery in less than two hours.[2]

Motorola has remained a flexible leader in wireless communications, not just a manufacturer of paging devices and mobile phones. They see themselves not as a producer of products or services, locked into markets defined by current customer demands, but instead as a set of core competencies responding to and proactive with new business potentials.[3]

Are You Stuck—Not Seeing the Power of Connecting the Pieces?

With a flexible focus—a willingness to concentrate activities while simultaneously being adjustable to change—you can strive for a clear vision and remain open to bridging the gap to new opportunities, new data, or a new situation.

Inferential Focus, a consulting firm, hones its insight skills masterfully and demonstrates the power of "connections" over and over. The firm gathers intelligence for clients, including Fortune 500 companies, money managers, and the White House. It does this by spotting what one member of its New York office called "anomalies in patterns" and by remaining aware in order to piece together facts that don't fit into a normal information mosaic. How does this work? Here is an example. A number of years ago, a member of the firm spotted four lines in the *Wall Street Journal* and made an inference that proved profitable to the firm's clients. The four lines said that Saudi Arabia was changing its shipping requirements for incoming goods, reducing by half the size of the containers and inspecting all, not just 80 percent, of the shipments. The consultant suspected fear of terrorism. The Saudis were known to respond to fear by stashing their oil money in a safe place—gold. Inferential Focus told its clients to buy gold. Six weeks later, the value of gold had doubled.[4]

Are You Stuck—Exhausted from Trying to Keep Up?

As the world grows smaller, opportunities expand. As a result, we need to develop the capability to react quickly to changing market conditions. The new innovations in communications such as cable TV, computer-based media, E-mail, and multimedia have shortened the communication exchange.

Speed has become an essential business virtue and no company exhibits quick, responsive performance like Caterpillar. In 1904, the name "Caterpillar" was coined for the Holt Manufacturing Company's first crawler (track-type) tractor. In 1925, the Holt and Best companies merged to form the Caterpillar Tractor Company. By the end of that year, the company had eighty-nine independent dealers worldwide who distinguished themselves by emphasizing parts-and-service support for machines in the field. Today, Caterpillar Inc. continues to be known for the reliability of its products and customer service, with Caterpillar Logistics Services, Inc., guaranteeing spare-parts delivery within forty-eight hours anywhere in the world.[5]

Today's powerful time dynamics have an effect not just on our brains, but on our fundamental organizational roles. In the past, these roles have created a stable environment; now they are continually being revamped by the clock. In a shrinking world, time has become a critical success factor. We have come to accept the importance of satisfying current customer needs, but what about our own needs? Can you give yourself the opportunity to drop out from operating responsibilities, to unchain yourself from the day-to-day tasks, and to take stock of where you are going and where you have been? Can you simply take the time to think—to move away from the chaotic, mind-wrenching muddle and reallocate space for a fresh view? To allocate time not only for yourself, but for your staff, too? Today, the limit to innovation in your home, in business, or in your community is not technology but a time-stuck mind-set.

Are You Stuck— Missing Global Opportunities?

The opening of global borders, free trade, mergers, and relocations call for daily reorganization, refocusing, and restructuring. This need to retrench has resulted in smaller groups that provide superior services through closely developed partnership alliances. The breakdown of these massive corporate structures has released a huge amount of stored energy—entrepreneurial energy. Millions of new jobs are created annually by midsize and small firms. How do these "little" firms do it? How do they fuse together the mass of energy that surrounds them? Basically, by not thinking straight. They give their teams the freedom to think over, under, and around a problem or issues. They sanction talk about possibilities as well as realities, using a small nucleus of people to release a vast amount of energy. They move out to the edges and capture the talent within their companies, and they respond to the world quickly. They remain unstuck.

From the beginning, II VI Incorporated, based in Saxonburg, Pennsylvania, has been determined to be the world's leader of light transmissive and reflective optics in the high-power laser industry. Through a committed and management-driven strategy, the company developed a world-focused, internal culture that stressed high performance standards for a quality product and an efficient worldwide distribution network. Here's how.

Facing growing global competition, II VI created work teams designed to continuously monitor evolving technological advances and subsequent product development opportunities. As laser technology and products evolved, Germany and Japan became the major buyers of optical components for the world market. II VI responded by negotiating strategic alliances with a key distributor and opening branch offices in each foreign market. Today, more than 50 percent of the company's $65 million annual revenues come from sales to foreign customers. Their early recognition of the realities of the global marketplace has positioned them as world-class manufacturers in a growing and dynamic industry.

"Reading, after a certain age, diverts the mind too much from its creative pursuits. Any man who reads too much and uses his own brain too little falls into lazy habits of thinking."

Are You Stuck— Suffering from Declining Returns?

It's time to rethink, to reassess your greatest resource and leverage brainpower as your sharpest competitive weapon. But "make no mistake," states Thomas A. Stewart in *Fortune,* "harnessing your intellectual capital is not easy. It will force you to think hard about what kind of outfit you run, . . . it requires a corporate culture that allows [brainpower] to flow freely, which means breaking down hierarchies and scrapping rules that stifle new ideas."[6]

Workers today are not bound entirely by traditional, hierarchical organizational structures. Now, new networks and matrices within organizations transfer the span of control from vertical, top-down funnels to horizontal bands. The strength in these new flexible structures is that power flows across the organization, feeding it and redistributing energies. Workers at Yamaha proved this.

Yamaha started out making traditional pianos. But its managers and engineers transformed the industry—first, by distinguishing the piano's function (the musical keyboard) from its traditional form such as uprights and baby grands, and second, by understanding how it could apply a new technology (digital sound encoding) to satisfy customers in new and unexpected ways. Yamaha's engineers used the new technology both to enhance the piano's existing functions—it could be kept in tune, put in a smaller space, and used with headphones—and to imbue it with entirely new functions, such as the ability to give a one-finger virtuoso the sound of a big band. In contrast, many of Yamaha's competitors remained stuck, not recognizing the threat the new technology posed to their business; they weren't flexible enough to separate the piano's function from its traditional product form and construction process.[7]

How will your work force's innovations affect the way you envision your organization's future direction? How will the growing gap between what your people want from their work and your organization's stated purpose change your strategic direction? What degree of awareness, insight, risk taking, flexibility, and courage will you need to move toward your future direction?

To effectually plan for tomorrow with the workers of today, you'll need unconventional methods. The most decisive question you'll have to ask is: "Who from inside and outside the organization can we use to fuse cooperative linkages and to thaw barriers that inhibit effective implementation of fresh ideas?"

Individuals behind your office doors, in your research labs, on your plant floors, and throughout your word-processing department are desperately sending a signal, an S.O.S.—a desire for a smashing, outrageous success! They want to be involved, to use all the talent they have, in ways that have not been tapped before. There's a new worker on this emerging horizon; don't miss the opportunity to reel in this fresh talent.

Bryan Beaulieu, while he was CEO of Skyline Displays, Inc., heard the S.O.S. and organized a project everyone would remember: building a community playground. At one annual sales meeting, instead of hitting the golf course in their spare time, employees and distributors donated engineering and carpentry skills, and area residents volunteered time and equipment to complete the project. "Whenever we had a bad day," commented Beaulieu, "we'd go down to the park, watch the kids playing and get revitalized."[8]

Drawing Pictures Liberates You and Jars You Loose

For many years, as I worked with our clients I began our thinking sessions by passing out plain white paper and colored, scented markers and then asking the participants to draw their brains. Obediently, most complied with a humorous self-portrait. Laughter often filled the room as their masterpieces were hung on the wall with care. And each time the same result occurred—a refreshing knowledge of who was behind the colored marker. This simple exercise forces awareness. It causes a shift. People think differently about themselves whether they want to or not.

D R A W · A · P I C T U R E

How Does Your Brain Look?

Are you aware of how you "see," how your brain looks? I think the power that lies within us is worth a good picture. So go ahead and draw your brain. There's no right or wrong, only your interpretation of the most extraordinary organ in your body, and there is no pain in doing this—honest.

If you are a bit uncomfortable with this exercise, that's natural. I have found that many of our participants are stuck when they are first asked to draw their brain. Research shows that in most adults, drawing skills have atrophied through lack of use, probably because they have been educated out of us. However, I believe there is a latent talent within us. Remember, there's no one way to draw a brain, and you are completely free to draw yours any way you want. You can do a very literal drawing or a symbolic representation. So go ahead and be wild. No one else is looking!

My Brain:

THOUGHT ATTACK!

Describe your brain with words that involve *all* five senses. For example: "If I could touch my brain right now, it would feel _____." "At this moment I imagine my brain to look _____." "If I could smell my brain, it would smell _____." Let yourself go and explore your brain in ways you may never have done before.

Words That Describe My Brain Are:

VISUAL WORDS	AUDITORY WORDS	KINESTHETIC WORDS (touch, taste, smell)
bright	*loud*	*flowery*
illuminated	*musical*	*soft*
skinny	*buzzing*	*luscious*

Three conclusions I can draw about my brain are:

1. _____

2. _____

3. _____

Harmonic Convergence

During one project, I worked with an all-male singing group investigating ideas and suggestions to increase motivation, energy, and commitment within their organization. Of course, the first thing we did was draw our brains. As each picture was posted on the wall, an uncanny phenomenon occurred: all the brains were drawn facing the same direction. Talk about harmony! After the members discussed the images and drew some conclusions about their specific group, they naturally fell into a conversation about commitment to the organization.

Although this exercise has given me the results I wanted—a shift in thinking—it never really occurred to me until recently why I used it. I "see" the world differently. I always have. I don't think in words; I think in pictures. Observing the reactions from group after group, I realized that I'm not alone. There are many people who think in pictures, many people who come alive when given a crayon, pencil, or marker. As a matter of fact, it's hard for me to even talk without a pencil and paper to stretch out my thoughts. My brain works that way.

NEED AN IDEA ON THIS?
See T•N•T 10, Draw-a-Brain.

Awareness: Laughing at Your Own "Seeing" Style Frees Your Frozen Thoughts

After drawing your brain, I'm sure you had a good laugh and may even "see" yourself differently. Seeing differently occurs not only with external vision, but inside, too. Thank heavens I learned early on to connect with this skill and recognize it as an advantage. Some label this "seeing differently" as dyslexia, reversal, or a learning disability. I label it *fun!* There's never a dull moment in my head. However, that doesn't downplay some of the challenges that I, or anyone like me who sees in pictures, have had fitting into our "word-based" institutions.

I love institutions. I come from a wonderful, large one—a thirteen-member family. But the rigidity of our formal institutions drives me crazy. Our educational system almost did me in. Because I've never been comfortable with words and equations, traditional, formal testing has remained a threat. As a matter of fact, it took three tries for me to accumulate a high enough score on my Scholastic Aptitude Test for entrance into a university. Further, plagued by my habit of reversing numbers and letters, I'm often frustrated by such simple tasks as entering the correct fax number to transmit a document. More than one document that I can recall has traveled to the wrong destination.

Actually, all these supposed strikeouts are hilarious. They continually give me an opportunity to laugh at myself and keep from taking life too seriously. And once I was accepted into college, I not only passed my courses but made the dean's list six of the eight semesters I was in school! I am far from alone. Story after story recounts the success of those who were doomed as failures early on but who took the dare, captured the spirit, and eventually turned a negative situation into a positive win.

Ray Charles was only six years old when glaucoma robbed him of his sight. He could have sunk into a life of despair, but he had a dream of becoming a musician. How did he triumph over such great odds? "The power of visualization," says Charles. "Regardless of how bad things got on the outside, I kept a clear picture in my head. . . . I saw myself as a recording star."[9]

How do you use your ability to "see" to trigger a difference? Do you leverage your vision? How do you see to foster effective thinking?

Using the Fringe: The Courage of Your Convictions Keeps You Unstuck

In grade school I stayed on the fringes, mostly trying to stay out of my teacher's direct eyesight. I hated to be called upon to read out loud; it was painful and embarrassing. The letters, words, and sentences continually jumped around on the page. Sometimes it took courage just to show up at school.

Distraught over this, I moved to the outer edge, away from any glimmer of the limelight that would force me to read in front of the

BRAIN DRAWINGS

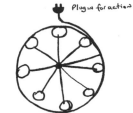

Jim Pealow
leader / explorer

William C. Byham
learner / teacher

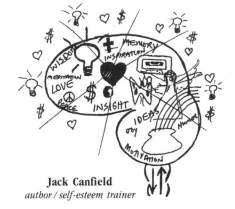

Jack Canfield
author / self-esteem trainer

P. Norman Roy
executive / problem solver

Nancy Lauterbach
business owner / juggler

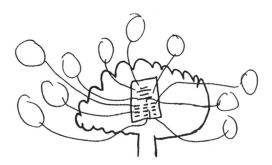

Stephen C. Carey
nonprofit executive / conductor

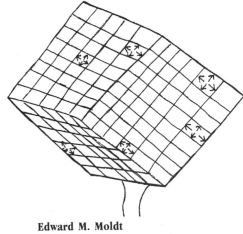

Edward M. Moldt
innovator / creator

BRAIN DRAWINGS

Good Thinking

personified + Shared

Mark Victor Hansen
speaker / writer

STORAGE   PROCESSING

IN
SIGHT
SOUND
SMELL
TASTE
TOUCH

THE RAINBOW OF
IDEAS OUT

OUT

R
O
Y
G
B
I
V. COLORS
NOT NECESSARILY
IN THE
CONVENTIONAL
ORDER

John W. Robinson
corporate manager / free spirit

I see my brain as
non-local, communicating
all over my body and
in touch with the
universe.

Ann McGee-Cooper
author / tap dancer

Ned Herrmann
whole-brain pioneer / artist

Rieva Lesonsky
editor / information junkie

Each person submitting a brain drawing
provided a caption describing his or her roles—
one more professional, the other more playful.

class. On the rim, I refined my skills. On the rim, I could see the whole picture—in fact, that's when I started thinking in pictures. I created my own environment to explore the pictures that popped into my head. I was safe. No one judged or criticized. I used my "seeing handicap" to energize my spirit and developed a different perspective: another way to approach a problem, another way to get the information across—without reading aloud! I drew pictures.

Historically, great ideas have emerged from the fringe. The most noted "fringe dwellers" include innovators like Albert Einstein and Thomas Edison. Or, in more recent times, Dr. Yoshiro NakaMats (inventor of the floppy disk and the digital watch), who holds twice as many patents as Thomas Edison. People on the fringe tend to be the strategic innovators who shape the future. Certainly, the computer world has been dramatically changed by such individuals as Steven Jobs, Michael Dell, and Bill Gates. The constant influx of their ideas from the outer edge refuted the current view of the world, unleashing a technological revolution that's become permanent.

Are you ready to tap in to the power of your convictions?

Staying Unstuck So You're Ready for the Dance

You won't stay the same; I won't stay the same. Our families, companies, associations, and institutions won't stay the same. Change has always been with us—enormous change, minor change, speeding change, slow change—creating its own dance of life. This dance of life has many partners, affecting each dancer in a unique manner. Do you have the luxury of waiting to be asked to dance? Can you remain in a holding pattern and wait till the music stops? Do you want to select your own dance partner? Or has the choice been made for you? The difference we face today is that in this global dance there is an intermingling of countless entities. The significant part you take in the dance is to understand the interrelationships and interconnected systems that affect all the parts of your life.

It's time to look to the outer edges, to pull in the talent that lies far from the limelight, to seek out a unique and different perspective, to sharpen your skills. It's time for you to blast through the barriers that hold you back and unleash your Thunderbolt spirit. It's time to pull your feet from the frozen ash and get unstuck, put on your dancing shoes, and dance.

The power of your convictions is the best tool you have to remain unstuck.

The Thunderbolt Thinking Model: What It Is and How It Works

The reason we are constantly faced with challenges is because they are driven by change. Change is everywhere. Since it's inevitable, organizations that define the marketplace do so by leveraging change. Leveraging change is a core component of innovation.

As a strategic innovator you need to be alert to potential change before it happens, aware of the opportunities it brings, and agile enough to step into action. Once you hone these skills, your ability to leverage change, turning it into a strategic advantage, will drive your organization's success. To really drive innovation, your role as a strategic innovator is to provide the leadership that will influence your peers, employees, co-workers, and friends to maximize those leverage opportunities. Once you recognize your powers of influence, you and your organization will reap three invaluable benefits:

1. *You will enhance your own personal passion.* By investing in your ability to lead and influence others, you will make a difference. Your contributions will have an impact on your life and those of the people you lead and will contribute to your personal success.

2. *You will capture and maximize your team's talents.* When you build on the ideas and contributions of team members, you give them a vested interest in the outcomes. If you enroll them in the process, allowing them to create value by providing them with growth opportunities, you will ensure employee loyalty by giving them a stake in the bigger picture.

3. *You will increase customer value.* In order to truly lead innovation, you need to listen to the customer's needs. By building customer feedback and expectations into your innovation process, you remain customer-focused and you maintain a competitive advantage.

As you step into the role of strategic innovator and develop your leadership skills, you will need the Thunderbolt Thinking Model.

The Model: A Flash of Insight

Since the mid eighties, I've worked with organizations to help them think more effectively. The flash of insight I had when I designed the original model was combining WHAT and HOW with the SPIRIT. Then the Thunder struck again, and I revised the model to incor-

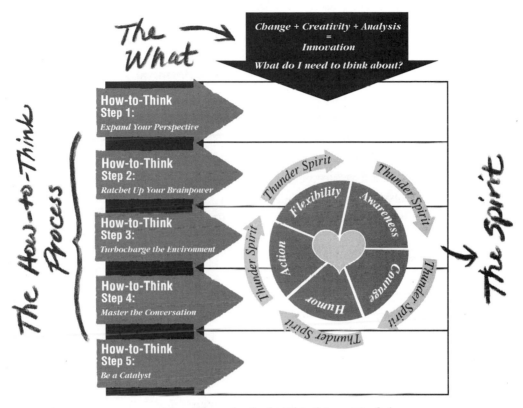

The Thunderbolt Thinking Model

porate a formula for innovation. What I wanted to do was craft a tool to help you and others think on purpose so you could blast through the rigid walls of traditional thinking, feel safe when you "stepped out of bounds," and cause enough of a shift so effective thinking would emerge from your home, workplace, or community. I wanted to create a resource that would help you to integrate innovation into day-to-day operations across your organization and sustain it on an ongoing basis.

In the model, three components blend together: WHAT you need to think about, HOW to think, and your SPIRIT, the heart of the model. It's a people-powered model that brings minds together and transforms them. The Thunderbolt Model reinforces the incredible potential of a group—the combined energy of their brains. The most powerful changes on this planet are caused by people. Everything comes back to people. Technological, economic, and political trends spring from a moving "people force." It is people who create and solve the problems; it is people who shape change. The Thunderbolt Model incorporates people into each of its three components by focusing on WHAT people need to think about, guiding HOW people think, and awakening each person's SPIRIT to drive the process.

This simple matrix, with the extra element of SPIRIT, makes the model a viable tool you can easily use so that you can meaningfully answer the signals and shift your thinking. Each part of the Thunderbolt Model has its own distinct function:

- *WHAT you need to think about* focuses you on your current need, issue, problem, or situation, directing you toward the content you should be considering.

- *How to think* guides you to think differently, to think on purpose, to be aware of the power you have to direct the thinking of yourself and of others.

- *SPIRIT, the heart of the model,* recharges your thinking and strengthens the WHAT and the HOW by blending five critical ingredients into the process to accelerate the group's thinking, producing outcomes that move from good to extraordinary.

As the core components of the Model, the WHAT, the HOW, and the SPIRIT are all driven by the Formula for Innovation. The formula reflects how innovation results when change is leveraged, explored with creative thinking, and then grounded with analysis. Through this combination of opportunity (change), creativity, and the analytical process of deciding "how this will actually work," an innovative product, service, strategy, procedure, operation, or model is born.

A Life-Based Model: The WHAT

The "WHAT you need to think about" component is the fill-in-the-blank part of the model. Issues at work might include exploring your company's visions for the next three years, creating non-traditional marketing strategies with a zero-based budget, trimming the budget while trying to do more with less, or enhancing your internal communication. At home, you might think about developing more streamlined ways to get everyone out the door on time each morning, establishing fair ground rules so everyone gets a chance to use the computer, identifying ways to discuss sex with your preteen, or creating a plan to select the best college for your child's education. And in your community, you might consider developing successful fund-raising strategies for the United Way, designing a recycling program that will motivate your neighbors to buy in, or coming up with ideas to attract support for a local child care center.

"The only rational way of educating is to be an example— if one can't help it, a warning example."

Getting Started:
The Shift from WHAT to HOW

The shift starts by getting away from the usual way of looking at your company's vision, the fund-raising event for the soccer team, or the traditional ways to celebrate your kid's ninth birthday; by taking things out of their normal context and creating a new pattern; by throwing away the concept of "My way is the only way!" It occurs when you consciously think, when you think on purpose, and when you take time to think about . . . how you think.

"Today we understand that success or failure doesn't come from just the people," recaps Walter Riley, young entrepreneur and founder of G.O.D. (Guaranteed Overnight Delivery), Inc., headquartered in Newark, New Jersey. "It comes from the process that you give your people to work with. It's a manager's job to constantly improve the process."[1]

This distinction between HOW (process) and WHAT (content) is not new. But many executives become trapped by thinking that "the product is the success" rather than recognizing the process. A premier product, however, evolves from a fine-tuned process: knowing your market, being a step ahead of your customers and anticipating their needs, experimenting, innovating, and taking risks. That is what creates and sells the product.

The basic principle is this: when you give your people a process for HOW to think, the answers to the specific WHAT (the issue, topic, problem) emerge. So if you want answers, stop spending time focusing directly on the problem, issue, or topic itself and start thinking about ways to enhance HOW you want your people to think about your service delivery system, your new phase of product development, or your next five years.

A Five-Step Format: Giving Direction to How You Think

The "HOW to think" component follows a five-step format that directs you to:

1. *Expand your perspective* by looking at alternatives

2. *Rachet up your brainpower* by tapping into your hidden resource

3. *Turbocharge the environment* by creating a stimulating thinking atmosphere

4. *Master the conversation* by identifying both parts of the conversation

5. *Be a catalyst* by moving to action with a system in place

 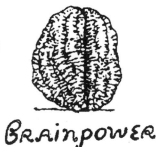 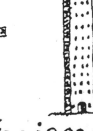

 PERSPECTIVE   BRAINPOWER   Environment

I've worked with all types of groups by helping them to think through various issues or problems. Curiously, the scenarios have all been the same: people told me WHAT they wanted to think about and then I'd go away and think about HOW we would do it. Project after project came together in a similar manner. It doesn't matter whether the WHAT was a company's vision for the next five years, marketing strategies for a local community hospital, a fund-raising event for a nonprofit association, a "reevaluate my life" session with a friend, a plan for helping a neighbor move, or a baby shower for a new mother of twins—my activities were generally consistent.

My first step was to focus like a laser beam on exactly WHAT we wanted to accomplish. Then I would usually retreat and seek ways to recharge my juices on HOW we would think, trying to focus on something different from the time before. I'd find myself designing an environment that would encourage contributions and diminish barriers, and creating ways to incorporate spontaneity by involving everyone's brainpower. Finally, I'd look for ways to blend in humor.

Over time, these ritualistic steps created the pattern I would use when I needed to focus on HOW to think. Most of the time, the HOW did not follow traditional rules or standards. My bizarre method of stepping out of bounds would again and again leverage the power of participants, stimulate creative ideas, and produce effective thinking within groups. A client referred to our sessions as "fast and furious."

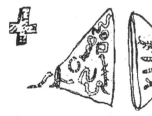

 Conversation

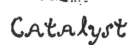 Catalyst

Success

Following are thumbnail sketches of each step. You'll find the big picture in Part Three of the book, where I'll go into more detail and give you additional explanations on how to use each step.

Step 1: Expand Your Perspective

❝**D**id you know that you have the potential for becoming a greater genius than Einstein? Just start *listening to your subconscious mind.* Throughout history, the greater discoveries have come not from meticulous consideration of facts and figures, but from 'irrational' flashes of insight.❞

—Richard Poe, *Success Magazine*[2]

Thumbnail sketch.   For Thunderbolt Thinking to occur at all, you must first be willing to broaden your outlook. We all tend to be creatures of habit, conditioned to think in the same way all the time. Refreshing yourself, expanding your thoughts, and letting go create a fertile ground for your flashes of insight to work for you. From this grows flexibility, awareness, and courage. Just as the goat needed the two scientists working with tools to free him from the frozen ash, you may need your own set of tools to deliberately pry your thoughts free from their traditional patterns.

Igniter.   Take time *now* to answer these trigger questions. (Do you want to move to action quickly? Go to Chapter Twelve for the big picture on Step 1.)

NEED AN IDEA ON THIS? See T•N•T 16, Idea Hatchery.

Think about your life at home, at work, and in the community. What is working well for you? What needs to be enhanced? What needs to be stopped? What areas of change do you need to think about?

Step 2: Ratchet Up Your Brainpower

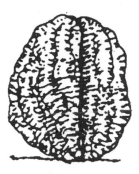

66**I**ntellectual capital [brains] is becoming corporate America's most valuable asset and can be its sharpest competitive weapon. The challenge is to find what you have—and use it. . . . The challenge is to capture, capitalize, and leverage this free-floating brainpower.99

—**Thomas A. Stewart,** *Fortune*[3]

Thumbnail sketch. Your second step is to assess who else you will be thinking with and then strategize on how to capitalize on your combined brainpower. Since brainpower is our most valuable resource, harnessing its collective power to satisfy future needs will set you and your organization apart. Racheting up raw brainpower means leveraging that brainpower. Proactively thinking of concrete ways to tap into the potential of your group, rather than just letting it happen, builds a steady stream of fresh, innovative, and inspired ideas into your organization. It is probably safe to say that you have a vast array of conceivable sources of brainpower. Going out to the fringes, to the untapped wells of ideas, creates a fabulous surge of energy.

Igniter. Take time *now* to answer these trigger questions. (Do you want to move to action quickly? Go to Chapter Thirteen for the big picture on Step 2.)

66*Everybody acts not only under external compulsion but also in accordance with inner necessity.*99

Just for the fun of it, list all the imaginable sources of brainpower available to include in your thinking group. Who is available inside your organization? Outside? From the past? From the future?

NEED AN IDEA ON THIS? See T•N•T 5, **Brain Stretch.**

Step 3: Turbocharge the Environment

❝If you want to encourage creativity and innovation in an organization, there are two basic ways to go about it. You can take a structural approach and focus on building an *environment* that fosters and encourages new ideas instead of squelching them. Or you can focus on the wellspring of ideas: You can try to teach people to think more creatively.❞

—**Jack Gordon and Ron Zemke,**
Training Magazine[4]

Thumbnail sketch. Your challenge is to create a thinking environment that fosters change, encourages innovative thinking, and produces meaningful outcomes. It doesn't matter whether it's a retreat, task force, think tank, committee, focus group, conference, dinner discussion, or den meeting—the thinking environment is a critical factor in determining outcomes. Seizing the opportunity to consciously enhance the quality of thinking places people in an atmosphere that stimulates and fosters a free flow of thought, rather than subjecting them to a confined, restrictive environment that shuts down the thought process. This environment can include everything from the color of the walls, the types and number of chairs, and the way the table is set up to the deliberate use of tools, which I call Toys for Thinking. Specifically tied to the subject at hand, these tools can range from a funny, toylike·hot-rod car to goofy and whimsical stuffed animals. The idea is to infuse the environment with items that encourage people to think differently about the issue, problem, or situation they face.

Igniter.   Take time *now* to answer this trigger question. (Do you want to move to action quickly? Go to Chapter Fourteen for the big picture on Step 3.)

**NEED AN IDEA
ON THIS?**
See T•N•T 2,
The Birth of
Bun-Huggers.

> *What is unique about the environment in your family room, your conference room, or your bank's community room that will add to effective thinking rather than inhibit it?*

Step 4: Master the Conversation

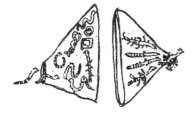

66**W**hen it comes to innovation, large, established corporations often find themselves at a disadvantage. Despite the lip service they pay to innovation and creativity as means to revitalize their stagnant bureaucracies and prepare for the future, they run into fundamental problems in maintaining programs that encourage new ways of thinking. 99

**—Jack Byrd and Julie M. Smith,
Training & Development Journal[5]**

Thumbnail sketch.   In order to set the direction for the thinking process, you need to understand the conversations people usually engage in during a group process. Any one-on-one or large-group meeting is really a series of conversations: your shared thoughts and ideas have a starting and end point. Awareness of the types of conversations occurring and skill in directing those conversations result in effective outcomes. The flow of ideas expands and contracts, involving both creative and analytical thinking. Generally, there is a "conversation of possibilities" followed by, but separate from, a "conversation of realities." Holding the conversation of possibilities first enhances the conversation of realities and strengthens your overall outcomes.

Igniter.   Take time *now* to answer this trigger question. (Do you want to move to action quickly? Go to Chapter Fifteen for the big picture on Step 4.)

NEED AN IDEA ON THIS?
See T•N•T 15, Hidden Communication.

> *Think about the* WHAT *(the specific situation you need to address). What kinds of possibilities do you need to explore?*

Step 5: Be a Catalyst

❝**Y**ou can't just take a stodgy organization, hire smart guys, and expect good things to happen.❞
—**Julio Rotemberg,** *Fortune*[6]

Thumbnail sketch.   The dream of most leaders is to break down thinking barriers, ease the group through the thinking process, and build bridges toward productive results. Your willingness to break the mold and become a catalyst opens the floodgates to a multitude of opportunities to fulfill this dream. As a catalyst, you essentially ignite the process. The catalyst is willing to step up to the bat and help to unstick group members, creating a safe, free climate that invites humor and encourages people to have fun. The catalyst liberates others' thinking to move them beyond their wildest expectations to a place where they can fully use their brainpower.

Igniter.   Take time *now* to answer this trigger question. (Do you want to move to action quickly? Go to Chapter Sixteen for the big picture on Step 5.)

What is the one thing you could do to stimulate change?

NEED AN IDEA ON THIS? See T•N•T 13, The Garbage Bag Dump.

The Thunderbolt Attitude: Your SPIRIT

All Thunderbolt Thinkers have SPIRIT. It's flexible and humorous, built on awareness and secure and courageous enough to move inspired and innovative ideas into action. In the Thunderbolt Model, SPIRIT is akin to attitude, the manner and style by which Thunderbolt Thinkers distinguish themselves. This SPIRIT emerges from a combination of five specific attitudes: flexibility, awareness, courage, humor, and action.

As the core, these attitudes create a power source; they are what makes the Thunderbolt Thinker tick. Since the Thunderbolt Model is people-powered, these attitudes keep the focus exactly where it needs to belong: on people. Without recognizing your attitudes, it is difficult to consciously and systematically change the direction of your thinking.

Finally, as the catalyst, your SPIRIT—the five attitudes—helps to define your thinking. As you begin to establish your how-to steps (how you are going to think about the project, problem, or issue), rely on your attitudes as a guide. Here's how.

Flexibility: Another Name for Change

Developing this attitude gives you the ability to see both ways, ensuring that you remain open to the signals and able to embrace the risks needed to challenge boilerplate solutions. A flexible focus allows you to shift constantly and still stay on track. This becomes a key factor in expanding your perspective. Here is a quick action step to help you develop a personalized flexible-focus prescription.

Start by assessing the three most essential points you need to focus on regarding a current project, problem, or issue. Then write down five different ways you could describe each point. Be as detailed and concrete as possible in your description. Put this into a written format and send it to everyone who is involved with the project, problem, or issue. Ask each person to create at least one more different scenario for each point you mentioned. When you sit down to think about the project, problem, or issue, first review all the various perspectives developed by each person. Then go for a solution.

NEED AN IDEA ON THIS? See T•N•T 12, Flexible Focus.

Awareness: Inside and Outside

This attitude awakens you from your stillness and prepares you for change. Being mindfully aware of each moment keeps you from operating as if there were only one set of rules. Awareness helps you recognize the power of others' thoughts and demands that you be open to their ideas; it lets you see the hidden brainpower right under your nose. Here is a suggestion for tuning into others.

On a three-by-five-inch card, list the people who you know will be involved in the project and jot down beside each name one or two descriptions that best characterize that person's most valuable trait. Slip the card into your pocket, purse, or notebook and carry it with you. During the time you are together, look for an opportunity to have each person demonstrate his or her most valuable trait. This not only will enhance your awareness of the talent that person has to offer, but will raise the group's overall sense of self-worth. Hint: During the time you're together, pull out the card as a trigger to yourself to remember each person's individual assets.

NEED AN IDEA ON THIS? See T•N•T 19, One Picture or One Thousand Words.

Courage: Risk and Vulnerability

This quality shores up our faith and makes it easier to take the leap and break with the past. Embracing courage daily ensures that you will continue to blast through your routines to break the mold and allow the catalyst within to emerge. This requires a fearless spirit of will, resilience, and resolution. Here's an exercise that can help.

On a sheet of paper, list the numbers from 1 to 10, starting with 1 at the top. Then relax, take a deep breath, and think about a specific project. What creates an uneasiness within you, stirs a twinge of fear, or causes you to break out in a cold sweat? Now write down a short phrase (but long enough for you to understand) for each of the things that will take courage for you in completing this project. Prioritize them on your paper, with 1 requiring the least amount of stretch and 10 requiring all the courage you can muster. Over the course of the project, commit to addressing each stretch by starting with the one that is least risky. As you proceed through the list, your successes will fortify you with enough courage to carry you through to the tenth stretch.

**NEED AN IDEA
ON THIS?
See T•N•T 21,
Spill the Beans.**

Humor: More Than the Frosting

Humor is one of our most underutilized gifts. Weaving humor into your tasks gives you a strategic tool to smash through the barriers of rigid thinking—yours, and your team's. Painting your environment with humor can be one of the most rewarding tasks you'll ever do. Build in humor this way.

Since humor is most often the result of a reversal in action, approach your project this way and go for the opposite. On a piece of paper, list the seven most terrible things about working on the project. Then flip your perspective and turn each of the seven points into something funny. During the time you are working on the project with your group, use the funny examples as a way to move the group through a slow period and a rough discussion.

**NEED AN IDEA
ON THIS?
See T•N•T 9,
Develop Your
Sense of Humor.**

Action: A "Can-Do" Attitude

Opportunities materialize in the power of the moment when you take action immediately. This attitude allows you to listen for the gems to surface in your conversations with others; it positions you to "hear" what others are saying so you can take action quickly. Here is a technique to encourage action.

Take a colored marker or a crayon and a three-by-five-inch card. Now, in a style all your own, make your best attempt to draw a can. If you need help, get a beer can, soup can, or can of green beans—any of these will do for a suitable model. Once you have completed this task, label the can this way: SUCCESS COMES IN CANS. Go ahead, put it right on the side of the can. Under the can, write your personalized action motto: "I can do this now because _____." Keep this card in a handy place (preferably someplace where you can see it) and refer to it if you get stuck doing your project.

NEED AN IDEA ON THIS? See T•N•T 17, Image Storming.

The Formula for Innovation (C + C + A = I)

Mountain climber Jim Collins made history as the first person to ascend an extremely difficult precipice in Colorado. For years other climbers had tried to conquer this challenge. They were unsuccessful because the cliff extended just beyond the reach of their arms. This climber realized that although his arms were too short to reach the tip of the cliff, his legs were not. He devised a way to hang upside down, using his legs and toes to hold on to the cliff. He was then able to reach the tip with his arms. He realigned the relationships involved in the process to come up with a new way of climbing, and this yielded an innovative solution.[7]

This story illustrates how the power of your thinking explodes from a combination of the creative and the analytical, the divergent and the convergent, the left brain and the right, the soft and the hard, the conversation of possibilities and the conversation of realities (discussed in Chapter Fifteen). The trick is to combine the two types of thinking without mixing them. You need to be aware that they are distinct and know the best time to use each.

A good analogy to justify the value of both types of thinking is that of a potter making a vase. If you've ever worked with clay, you know that it's a lot easier to shape, mold, and throw the clay if it's soft (brittle clay is hard to shape). By the same token, after the vase has been shaped, it has no practical value unless it has been put into a kiln and fired. Both the soft and hard stages are required, but at different times.

The Thunderbolt Model requires you to practice both types of thinking to be truly effective. Through practice you learn how to develop the thinking skills to deal with change and produce extraordinary and effective outcomes, such as:

- Concrete and specific recommendations that leverage your existing production systems, while reducing time and increasing quality

- New strategic rules of flexibility and responsiveness, and the guidelines to integrate these rules into clear business priorities

- Long-range business plans, fueled by innovative thoughts, that shift attention from what *should* be done to what *can* be done

As a strategic innovator, before you attempt to tackle your business challenges by combining creative and analytical thinking, you need to first establish clear definitions for each of these terms. Here are some basic definitions to use as a starting point:

Creativity: the realignment of two or more things or ideas into relationships that did not previously exist

Analysis: the critical, logical process of categorizing and selecting

Innovation: the process of zeroing in on effective ideas and finding ways to put new relationships that people have formed (through creativity) and selected (through analysis) into action

Although it would be nice to imagine an unobstructed road to innovation, this is rarely the case. People are often held back by barriers in their work environments that prevent the free flow of ideas. Three major barriers are common inside organizations:

1. *Lack of infrastructure.* Often, when employees generate new ideas that don't fit into an organization's overall business strategies or goals, they are accused of straying off-track. But with a system in place, these ideas can be captured, shared, and built upon, until an idea emerges that will be useful. Don't miss opportunities by forgetting to look at the big picture.

2. *Lack of time.* Limited time is a common barrier. But why not build in time to think? Instead of generating ideas only when a specific question has to be answered, build in time to think when there's no burning challenge that everyone feels pressured to solve.

3. *Fear of risk taking.* Getting people to take risks is a process that needs to be managed. Telling them what to do doesn't reduce their fear of taking a risk. Instead you need to invest in their success by encouraging them to take appropriate risks. In our office we call them "GOs," or Growth Opportunities. When you invest in others by giving them a chance to grow, you allow them to develop on a personal level, give them a reason to stay, and add value to your team.

To help your teams become more innovative, you must lead them past these barriers to the light at the end of the tunnel. Once you have defined the core ingredients, the following Formula for Innovation is a beacon that will help you to lead your team to new breakthroughs:

Change + Creativity + Analysis = Innovation

Knowing when to make the shift enriches your mastery.

Thunderbolt Innovators: Building an Innovative Workplace

The great poet Robert Frost once said, "The brain is a wonderful organ. It starts working the moment you get up and does not stop until the moment you get into the office." As funny as that sounds, sadly it can

THUNDERSTRUCK . . . .

often be the case. The problem: many work environments just don't stimulate our brains in a way that triggers us to make fresh connections, or see things in a new light. They don't encourage us to make the shift from WHAT we need to think about to HOW to think, and consequently we get stuck in the same old pattern of thinking, again and again.

It's been demonstrated time and again that environment does make a difference. People are influenced by subtleties in setting such as room temperature, wall color, or lighting. But even more importantly, people are influenced by the "attitude" that pervades their work environment. When an office is productive, open, and bursting with fresh ideas, you can practically smell innovation in the air. Similarly, if negative attitudes are dominant, they can permeate every facet of an environment.

Creating a workplace that builds and sustains innovation is not a matter of luck. As a strategic innovator, you need to provide the tools and the opportunities to change attitudes so that people let go of old mind-sets and learn how to think again. You need to create an environment where people feel comfortable welcoming change, and where innovation is encouraged regardless of success rate. It's a challenge that many organizations face. In fact, Arthur D. Little's Global Survey on Innovation found that although 84 percent of companies place a high strategic priority on innovation, fewer than 25 percent feel that they are effective innovators.[1] So what steps can you take to become an effective innovator capable of building a workplace that integrates and sustains innovation inside your organization?

Integrating Innovation in Three Stages

A couple of years ago, while preparing for a management retreat for a well-known Fortune 500 manufacturing company, I was interviewing some of the senior managers. When I asked one manager how he tried to create an environment that fostered inno-

68

vation, he replied, "Mostly I want to keep a low profile. I just try to get by each day without getting noticed." While it sounds surprising, it's actually a common scenario. Too often organizations don't enroll their people by giving them opportunities to add value and to contribute to the bigger picture. Without this, the employees become dissatisfied and will either shrink down, minimizing their potential, or leave the company, taking their talents elsewhere. So how do you protect your valuable human capital?

Traditionally, organizations have rewarded orderly, even rigid, thinking that delivers quick and quantifiable "right" answers. Less valued has been a flexible, exploratory thinking model that forces people to ask what-if questions and stretch beyond the "known." But by giving your people the opportunity to do this, you're saying, "Your ideas are important." In turn, if they feel they are making a contribution, they are more likely to feel valued and thus more willing to stay loyal.

So your challenge as a strategic innovator is to set up an environment that facilitates fresh thinking. To fully maximize each person's potential, an organization needs a leader who can:

- *Prepare* people to be more effective in their thinking

- Provide opportunities for people to *practice* their thinking skills

- Demonstrate innovative *performance* that leads to solid results

Preparation Stage

Being effective requires the ability to combine creative and analytical thinking in developing an idea, solving a problem, or responding to a challenge. It is important for you, as a strategic innovator, to encourage both types of thinking in your work group.

Unfortunately, in today's business world, people tend to leap into analytical thinking when they face a situation that requires innovation. Such a leap might make sense when people are working under incredible time and budgetary pressures, but it can be disastrous for the organization.

What might happen if, instead of relying on analytical thinking to confront the next challenge, the people in your organization took a leap of faith into the chaos that often results from creative thinking? The chances are that the fresh solutions will provide a stronger competitive position for your organization. Allowing chaos to exist before the analysis of ideas is a strategic innovator's first step in integrating effective thinking into an organization.

But people in your organization cannot just be thrown into chaos. As a strategic innovator, you need to use your power to influence them and prepare them to take the leap.

Practice Stage

All people are creative. However, this natural ability is often stifled by the time people reach the workplace. To reenergize and nurture creativity, you need to lead with a commitment to practice it.

Practicing creativity every day strengthens and enhances thinking, in much the same way that physical exercise increases strength and endurance. The more people practice, the more "connections" they make—and the more innovative their results, actions, and outcomes become. So it's critical for people to have opportunities to practice being creative.

As a strategic innovator, you can provide people with these practice opportunities.

Performance Stage

In a fast-paced work environment, people may resist the idea of "practicing" anything or "wasting" time on creative thinking. You, as a strategic innovator, can't change these attitudes by decree, but you can promote a change in behavior. Often, when people see that changing their behavior leads to positive results, they naturally shift their attitudes.

The biggest barrier to shifting attitudes and changing behavior is fear. A world that rewards analytical, either-or thinking conditions people to drive for perfection. Fear of losing a customer or a promotion or a job drives people toward perfection at work.

A more effective approach to work—and a key component of being effective—is a drive toward excellence. Rather than stemming from fear, the drive toward excellence emerges from a person's courage, flexibility, humor, awareness, and commitment to action. To encourage this spirit, you need to lead with a flexible focus, which means that you can bend without breaking and are willing to change to make a difference—not only to your organization but also to yourself.

As a strategic innovator, your power to influence will be enhanced when you lead with a flexible focus and build it in those you lead.

The Lucky 13: Strategies for Building an Innovative Workplace

The Lucky 13 is a proven set of strategies that strategic innovators can use as they foster, nurture, and build an innovative workplace. They are strategies that have been used by senior executives, managers, and work team leaders like you to maximize their leadership skills and get the most out of their teams. Using the thirteen strategies in each of the three stages is a surefire way to create an innovative workplace and to lead your team to get results by helping them to think innovatively.

Preparation Stage: The Theory Behind Being Effective

1. *Define* innovation to take out the mystery. The mandate to innovate can intimidate people, but you can eliminate or reduce fear if you give people information and prepare them for what they can expect. Define for them what you are looking for—the expected outcomes—in as much detail and with as many examples as possible.

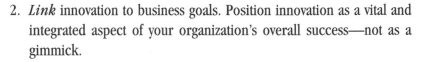

2. *Link* innovation to business goals. Position innovation as a vital and integrated aspect of your organization's overall success—not as a gimmick.

3. *Define* challenges specifically. Rather than attempting to create an "innovative" team or department, focus on the challenges that require innovative solutions; become innovative by *doing*.

Practice Stage:
Becoming More Innovative Through Practice

4. *Discover* how individuals think they are most creative. Ask them for their input. Some people might think they are best at generating possible solutions to a problem; others might feel most creative at developing effective ways to implement solutions. Taking the time to uncover each person's strengths will benefit your team and organization.

5. *Embrace* play. Play relaxes people, opens their minds to new possibilities, and helps them make connections that improve the quality of their thinking. With adults, however, play can be unfamiliar, especially in the workplace. Give your work group opportunities to master their play skills.

6. *Take* deliberate, observable steps to enhance creativity. Just as adults need to master their play skills, they also need to practice being creative. The more people enhance their thinking, the stronger their instincts and skills will be. Provide tools and diverse models for thinking.

7. *Allow* incubation. Allow adequate time for ideas to develop and mature. Innovative organizations recognize that ideas need to gestate in the subconscious, where the mind nurtures them. This process takes time and requires that people be given ample support. The payoff to the organization is that people develop and produce truly powerful results.

Performance Stage:
Leadership That Leads to Innovation

8. *Set* an example. You can manage innovation effectively only when you enhance your own creative skills and behavior.

9. *Maximize* opportunities to learn. Help people gain the courage to act by serving as a buffer and finding ways to absorb risk. Stress the importance of learning from mistakes and follow through by looking for those learning opportunities.

10. *Set* a tone through your attitude. In addition to modeling innovation, show people that you support their attempts to innovate. Give half-baked ideas a chance, support learning from mistakes, and recognize innovation when it happens.

11. *Encourage* active communication. Innovation requires communication. Sharing thoughts multiplies the opportunities for unique and powerful ideas. Communication also creates an environment of mutual support among co-workers. Set up hot lines for groups and individuals that are specifically designed for sharing ideas.

12. *Facilitate* action. The barriers to taking action are often difficult to scale. Set up a system that allows you and your work group to take immediate action on converting creative ideas into specific innovative changes. Clarify logistic issues, such as approval channels, and build in rewards for *doing*.

13. *Take* personal responsibility: Make a commitment to develop a climate for innovation in your organization. Be there and help it happen.

Are You Building an Innovative Workplace?

Leaders who are strategic innovators foster, nurture, and build innovative workplaces not by chance, but by implementing proven strategies and by maximizing their power to influence. To what extent are you implementing the Lucky 13 strategies to ensure that you capitalize on your work force's brainpower? Staying competitive today requires you to leverage your organization's most unique advantage— its people!

Circle a number on each continuum to give your response.

PREPARATION STAGE: THE THEORY BEHIND EFFECTIVE THINKING

1. We have *defined* innovation to take out the mystery. As a team, we have defined what innovation really means inside our organization. We've developed a clear, concise definition of innovation based on our organizational culture and internal/ external parameters.

1	2	3	4	5
Not at all	Minimally	Somewhat	Mostly	Consistently and effectively

2. We have *linked* innovation to our business goals. As a strategic innovator, I have positioned innovation as an integrated aspect of our organization's overall success—not as a gimmick. We have created an Innovation Model that ties our business strategies into the day-to-day innovative process.

1	2	3	4	5
Not at all	Minimally	Somewhat	Mostly	Consistently and effectively

3. We have *defined* challenges specifically. As a team, we have targeted important challenges that require innovative solutions. We have prioritized these areas and I have allocated resources to ensure that the implementation starts at the top and penetrates throughout the organization.

1	2	3	4	5
Not at all	Minimally	Somewhat	Mostly	Consistently and effectively

PRACTICE STAGE: BECOMING MORE INNOVATIVE THROUGH PRACTICE

4. We have *discovered* how individuals think they are most creative. As a team we have assessed how each of us is creative and how this strength benefits our team and our organization.

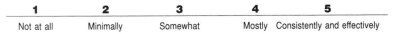

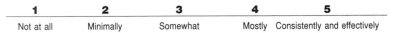

1	2	3	4	5
Not at all	Minimally	Somewhat	Mostly	Consistently and effectively

5. We have *embraced* play. As a strategic innovator, I have integrated play into group interactions as an alternative means of relaxing people and shifting thinking. I have directed thinking exercises using toys to help people think through various situations. I have positioned play as a productive exercise and have encouraged people to expand their thinking by developing play skills.

1	2	3	4	5
Not at all	Minimally	Somewhat	Mostly	Consistently and effectively

6. We have *taken* deliberate, observable steps to enhance creativity. As a strategic innovator, I have introduced models for thinking, tools that foster innovation, and techniques and training to enhance our team's ability to build thinking skills. I have also put together a plan of action to effectively build these skills that outlines day-to-day how-to actions as well as longer-range actions.

1	2	3	4	5
Not at all	Minimally	Somewhat	Mostly	Consistently and effectively

7. We have *allowed* incubation. As a team we have allowed adequate time for ideas to develop and mature. We have collected ideas, let them gestate, and then revisited them as a group. In our second round we worked the ideas through, maximizing the perspective gained during the incubation period.

1	2	3	4	5
Not at all	Minimally	Somewhat	Mostly	Consistently and effectively

PERFORMANCE STAGE: LEADERSHIP THAT LEADS TO INNOVATION

8. I have *set* an example. I have taken responsibility to enhance my own creative skills and behavior by integrating specific actions into my overall development plan. Components of this plan may include how-to actions for ways I can model innovation, ways to set a tone through my behavior and attitude, and strategies to show people that I support their attempts to innovate.

1	2	3	4	5
Not at all	Minimally	Somewhat	Mostly	Consistently and effectively

9. I have *maximized* opportunities to learn. As a strategic innovator, I consider it important to learn from mistakes and have created supportive ways of handling initiatives that have failed. I've put into place systems and procedures for following through on mistakes by looking for learning opportunities.

1	2	3	4	5
Not at all	Minimally	Somewhat	Mostly	Consistently and effectively

10. I have *set* a tone through my attitude. As a strategic innovator, I understand the importance of purveying an "innovation attitude." I have consciously made an effort to encourage innovation by learning from mistakes, giving all ideas air time, supporting others in their attempts to innovate, and recognizing innovation when it happens.

1	2	3	4	5
Not at all	Minimally	Somewhat	Mostly	Consistently and effectively

11. I have *encouraged* active communication. As a strategic innovator, I have created an environment of mutual support among co-workers. I've facilitated discussion across the organization by helping to set up effective lines of communication not only in our own team, but also among other departments and divisions.

1	2	3	4	5
Not at all	Minimally	Somewhat	Mostly	Consistently and effectively

12. I have *facilitated* action. As a strategic innovator, I have set up systems for our teams to take action on converting creative ideas into specific innovative changes. I've facilitated discussions to establish a clear, step-by-step flow process that outlines how an idea moves from concept to analysis to solution and that includes monitoring to determine that results are achieved.

1	2	3	4	5
Not at all	Minimally	Somewhat	Mostly	Consistently and effectively

13. I have *taken* personal responsibility. As a strategic innovator and team, we have made a commitment to develop a climate for innovation inside our organization. I have personally made myself available to coach my team through the process and have introduced appropriate tools to help innovative ideas happen.

1	2	3	4	5
Not at all	Minimally	Somewhat	Mostly	Consistently and effectively

The power is in the moment.

PART TWO

The Thunderbolt Spirit

Spirit: The Stuff That Makes Thunderbolt Thinkers

Flexibility. Awareness. Courage. Humor. Action. These are the dots, and Thunderbolt Thinkers have a unique way of connecting the dots together every day. Thunderbolt Thinkers purposefully look for the patterns and seek out the pictures that lie before them. They have the lid off their boxes and their noses are high in the air, trying to smell out the next solution, solve the current problem, or generate a new idea.

The future is shaped by present events—events driven by people who are willing to stretch their imagination's borders and peer into the universe of possibilities. Thunderbolt Thinkers are the chief architects who draw those futures in their workplaces, homes, and communities.

"Don't Let Your Spirit Be Stolen"

"Try not to become a man of success but rather try to become a man of value."

These words of advice from a seasoned physician who spent twenty years among Southwest Native American tribes still echo in my ears. During my afternoon visit to Dr. Carl Hammerschlag's Phoenix office, his message was one of choice: "We have given up our power and have subordinated our spirit; we have allowed science to give reason and minimize what we feel." He continued to emphasize the urgent need to rekindle, rediscover, and reclaim our choice about our SPIRIT within. We talked about the risk—the shift, almost a leap of faith, required to trust your inner self. "Don't wait for change to come to you, because then you get pushed into it," he went on to say. "Come to it, not to just seek it, but to welcome it."

Dr. Hammerschlag described the awakened human spirit as an internal force that, once it is presented with change, deals with it and confronts it without shrinking away. "By facing it is how we participate in change," he said. "These experiences create our stories, the life experiences that we tell and hear." He stressed the need to break down the ordinary "so we don't get hard," fixed in one way, unable to move with the flow of life. Toward the end of my visit, I asked him, as I do with almost everyone I meet, to draw his brain. What a beautiful and vivid visual emerged. His flow of life was depicted through his heart-mind, "the heart that the mind never knows," he revealed. "I thought my head was very big, but now I know I don't know. I take in life through my heart and realize that feelings are as important as knowing."

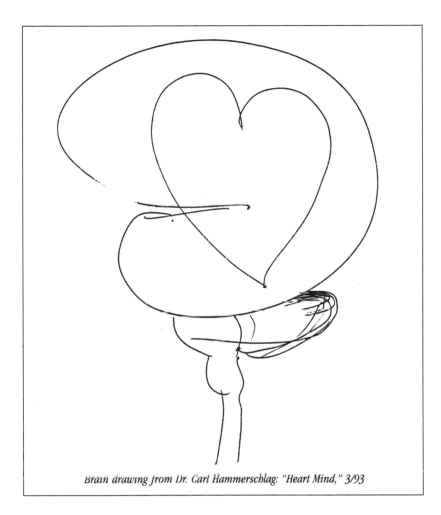

Brain drawing from Dr. Carl Hammerschlag: "Heart Mind," 3/93

As a Yale-trained psychiatrist, Dr. Hammerschlag helps us to feel our SPIRIT within and to see the gap between what we know and what we understand. In his second book, *The Theft of the Spirit*,[1] Dr. Hammerschlag does just that.

Make a Difference, Cause a Riot

Find an attitude. The Forum Corporation studied a group of high-performing executives to determine the key factors related to their success. The report showed that it was their attitude, not their intelligence or skill, that made the difference.[2] The attitude that pervades an organization's culture can enhance or distract from its overall success. An unimaginative, unreceptive attitude destroys opportunity; aligning individual and organizational attitudes can produce powerhouse results.

"Our life is what our thoughts make it," said the Roman emperor and philosopher, Marcus Aurelius. Napoleon Hill, author of *Think and Grow Rich,*[3] among others, enlightened us with the idea that success begins in the mind. More profoundly, whatever you believe is true for you. Today, we need an attitude, an outrageous attitude, that disregards common truths, causes an internal riot, and forces a difference.

The Thunderbolt Model's power source is this attitude, this SPIRIT that comes forth from your passion and commitment. The intensity of your passion and commitment will energize not only you, but your whole group, toward action. What you do with this SPIRIT depends on the communication you have with yourself and with others. However, the most important meeting you'll ever attend is the one you attend with yourself. Your internal dialogue—the free-flowing exchange of your thoughts—sets the tone for all your external discussions. Be aware of your self-talk and of whom you are creating with the messages you send.

Share your SPIRIT; share your passion. Often the real driver behind flexibility, awareness, courage, humor, or action is the intensity we feel for a project, idea, or program—the passion. The important point here is to let others know. Your passion, the fire in your belly, can propel more projects forward than all the money in the budget. Your passion can take a mishmash of thoughts and cook up a wonderful blend of stewing ideas. Your passion tied to your commitment can send a strong, vital, and visionary message to those who are locked behind your office doors and who long for a magical brew to set them free.

In his book *Emotional Intelligence,* author Daniel Goleman talks about the importance of harnessing your spirit and recognizing the inner passion that drives your success. In the face of all the technological changes that often seem to direct the business world, he suggests that "a new competitive reality is putting emotional intelligence at a premium in the workplace and in the marketplace."[4] Harnessing your spirit by leveraging these five qualities in all the ways you work will result in more productive interactions, more job satisfaction, and more effective leadership skills.

So step into the power of your passion and commitment and look for ways to reveal your true Thunderbolt SPIRIT. Over the next couple of weeks try these ideas.

Build Excitement into a Meeting

Make a conscious commitment to create an interaction that will make a difference. Even if the next time you get together is the regular Monday staff meeting, build excitement. For example, hold it in your staff's most disliked working area. Generate ideas for making the space more workable. Break the patterns of past meetings by setting up situations that will lead the participants in new directions. Have the attendees decide at the beginning of the meeting what the results of the meeting must be so everyone will feel that it has been a success.

**NEED AN IDEA
ON THIS?
See T•N•T 28,
Reel to Real.**

Achieve a Goal

Decide to achieve the goal on your new project no matter how much you need to stretch. Think through ways to move out of the rut; use your passion to inspire you. Give yourself permission to be silly, which is a lot different than being stupid. Define what additional helpful resources you need and don't get hooked into focusing on why you can't get them. Instead, decide how you might, in fact, be able to attract those resources, their equivalents, or their benefits. If you find yourself saying, "I don't know what to do next," ask yourself the question, "If I did know what to do next, what would it be?" Once you've finished developing your resource list and identifying first-step strategies, follow through. Take the next step with passion to obtain the resource.

**NEED AN IDEA
ON THIS?
See T•N•T 22,
Theme and
Tools for
Thinking.**

SELF-ASSESSMENT

The Thunderbolt Spirit

Review the list below. Which attitude influences you the most and keeps you from getting stuck? Prioritize each of them from 1 to 5 (with 1 having the highest influence and 5 having the lowest influence).

_____ *Flexibility:* Willingness to challenge assumptions

_____ *Awareness:* Openness to change at any moment

_____ *Courage:* Passion and commitment to take risks

_____ *Humor:* Taking your work seriously, but not yourself

_____ *Action:* Doing it, even when you don't know exactly what to do

Cultivate an Action Attitude

Become a user of information, not just a giver and taker. Continually ask, "How can I use what I've just heard, read, seen? What immediate action is appropriate right now?" Remember that with each action you initiate, you are opening the opportunity for the following action. Taking an action creates an automatic reaction forming a series of links leading to your success. It is critical to recognize that in real ways we lose the opportunity for future actions by not taking action now. This does not imply that we must make a decision immediately just to be able to say that we did; instead, we should ask ourselves, "With the information I have, what can I do right now to move forward in an intelligent way?"

**NEED AN IDEA
ON THIS?
See T•N•T 23,
Thought Walk.**

Develop Meaningful Communication

Communicate both verbally and in writing to each member who will attend your next meeting to let them all know that their contributions count. Think of ways to do this that might be new and different; for example, you might have the agenda delivered before the meeting by a town crier. If, at the conclusion of a meeting, another meeting is being planned, consider appointing as chairperson an attendee with special expertise in the topic of the next meeting. Then commit to working with that individual until he or she feels comfortable and prepared. A new and insightful set of perspectives may emerge.

NEED AN IDEA ON THIS?
See T•N•T 4,
Brain Jolts.

Expose Yourself

I mean this figuratively, of course. Often leaders do not share their passion and commitment with the group for fear of becoming too dominant or too vulnerable. Forget that. Don't miss the opportunity to show your support for your group's purpose. If you do it with sincerity, you will find that others respond. A consequence can be that the entire group will come together in new ways with a shared passion and commitment. Actually talk about the group's passion for the project, then discuss the passion that the group is capable of creating within the rest of the organization. Serve "purple passion punch" at a luncheon to "fill" the group with passion.

NEED AN IDEA ON THIS?
See T•N•T 21,
Spill the Beans.

Thunderbolt Thinkers are the chief architects drawing the future pictures of your organization.

Flexibility:
Another Name for Change

THE NATURE-OF-LIGHT PARADOX:
❝Depending on how we look at it, light can appear sometimes as electromagnetic waves, sometimes as particles.❞[1]

S ince my chemotherapy treatment in 1984, I've been rebuilding my body. My approach at first was intense exercise and a strenuous workout program. But I wasn't making the progress that I needed. Luckily, I was referred to a homeopathic doctor in Toronto who introduced me to the power of stretching. Stretching relaxed my tense muscles, allowing my body to become limber and resilient. Open and ready for change, my blood infused with oxygen, I saw a new life flowing into my chemical-ravaged body.

The results were terrific. Energy seems to surge through me now and my general well-being is elevated to a super level. I still exercise, but the added flexibility from stretching heightens and enhances all my workouts.

The Lesson Learned: Flexibility

E asily influenced. Soft. Pliable. Supple. Stretchable. Impressionable. In most corporate settings these adjectives would be judged unacceptable, especially when used to label the CEO, president, executive vice president, director, or senior manager. Yet in order for you to let go and make the shift, you must use these very words; they can send an extremely powerful message and set the tone for change throughout your entire corporate culture.

As I found in my personal learning, strong organizations, as well as strong bodies, result when the energy is there, when the ideas on how to solve your production problems or meet a tight customer turnaround flow from your people's brains. This emphasis on flexibility does not mean that you should be limp, loose, flimsy, or slack, but that you should garner an appreciation of flexibility and remain open to different ideas and suggestions as they come your way—that you value the difference.

In the final analysis, it's your attitude that creates the hotbed that will allow flexibility to grow and mature within your organization. Richard Bach, in *Biplane,* reminded me of this same lesson: "I learn that the repairing or rebuilding of an airplane, or of a man, doesn't depend upon the condition of the original. It depends upon the attitude with which the job is taken. The magic phrase, 'Is THAT all that's wrong!' and an attitude to match, and the real job of rebuilding is finished." [2]

Flexible Focus: Zigzag Lightning in the Brain

Being able to bend without breaking and being able to adjust to change without terror is a trait desired by most, but demonstrated by few. Winston Churchill was often described as a man with a highly versatile mentality. On any given weekend, Churchill might work on a speech for Parliament, paint a picture, walk in the garden with his grandchild, plan a military campaign, write on the history of Western civilization, engage in spirited conversation, contemplate a major political strategy, and carefully plan a detailed sequential operational plan. [3]

Dr. Howard Gruber, while he was a psychologist at the University of Geneva, called such a hodgepodge of interests a "network of enterprises." He suggested that by shifting from project to project, people can bring elements and perspectives from one area to help with another. This also means that if you've hit the stage of frustration in one project, you can put it on a mental back burner while you turn to another. [4]

Zigzagging back and forth between highly diverse activities enhances your flexibility. I call it a flexible focus. A flexible focus transforms our homes, workplaces, and communities by turning our stumbling blocks into stepping-stones, and by creating experimental venues within our organizations that foster and allow tentative responses, trial and error, and momentary craziness. Each activity requires a particular mix of thinking, but when they are put together over a period of time, each separate outcome benefits from the energy applied to the others.

The Thunderbolt Model
Encourages Flexibility

With the desired outcome of effective thinking, the Thunderbolt Model focuses on ways to achieve that result. Incorporating flexibility provides an avenue, a way to break with rules that bind us and confine us within certain parameters. Flexibility taps our energy and our reserve of enthusiasm. It loosens the ideas stuck in our mind's "Chinese finger lock," minimizing the struggle of both sides of the brain to win and easing the tightness of the lock to allow the ideas to freely move forward.

The Thunderbolt Model relies on flexibility to help expand our perspective. As an essential attitude, flexibility adds to the medley a welcome dimension that is often missing in business environments. Try instilling greater flexibility in your organization by checking off the areas that would provide an opportunity to try a different mode of operation:

- ❑ Work hours of all employees
- ❑ The dress code
- ❑ How the pay periods are decided
- ❑ The benefits program
- ❑ Ownership in the organization
- ❑ Job titles for specific functions
- ❑ Production schedules
- ❑ Open parking availability for all employees
- ❑ A special one-time assignment for an employee
- ❑ Special recognition awards
- ❑ An award to an individual whose bright idea didn't work
- ❑ An award to a customer's employee who brings in an important idea

Thunderbolt Thinkers
Do a Stretch a Day

Headlines everywhere warn: "Organizations now succeed or fail depending on how well they can adapt to change, anticipate change, and create positive change." The bottom line is that change has always been a factor, but today its impact is occurring at lightning speed. It is true that some of us adjust more easily than others. For instance, take the late Sam Walton, founder of Wal-Mart Stores, Inc. "Change was his middle name," recalled Sam Walton's close friend and business associate, George Billingsley. "He was a terror to travel with. You never knew where you were going next." Sam Walton was esteemed for his ability to change. Flexibility was often cited as his most endearing trait.[5]

NEED AN IDEA ON THIS? See T·N·T 1, The Art of Brain Flossing.

Leaders who are flexible and willing to change the playing field are the ones who are going to cause the riots and make the difference. Developing your flexibility is a must. You need to reach out and take the risks that threaten your boilerplate solutions; you need to put on some silly glasses and open your eyes to see a future of possibilities. Joseph Schunpeter, an economist, said that we need to create the "gale of creative destruction" that will catapult us in the direction of new, daring, and bold ideas.[6]

For Thunderbolt Thinkers, a morning stretch maintains flexibility. Think about how these tips could help you maintain a flexible attitude:

There is no logical way to the discovery of . . . elemental laws. There is only the way of intuition, which is helped by a feeling for the order lying behind the appearance.

- Physically change your frame of reference. Try standing all day to do your work, even when you are in your office or on the phone.

- Emotionally shift gears. Allow both facts and feelings into your thought process without forfeiting your ability to think clearly.

- Dare to be positive. Stop imagining all the reasons why something won't work and start being flexible: ask the questions that *will* make it work.

- Focus on what you've identified as your current priorities and then concentrate on what specific steps you can take to create positive results.

- When you recognize a problem, challenge yourself to define an answer.

- Call a friend. Let the friend know that you're not looking for a solution, but that you just wished to talk through a current problem.

- Dare to be different. Sometimes the most ludicrous ideas work out to be wonders!

- Create your own "network of enterprises." Start several unrelated projects all at once. Let go of your anxieties and take the next step on each project as it occurs to you.

- Change responsibilities with someone for one day, at home or at work. It's amazing how one day's change from the normal routine can influence your perspective, broadening it a little or a lot!

Shift constantly.

Awareness:
Inside and Outside

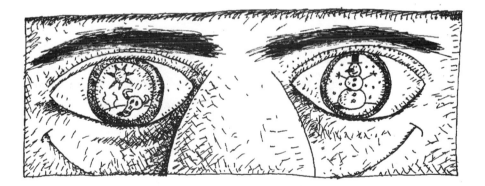

THE MANAGING PARADOX:
66Managers who can hold opposites in
their vision simultaneously can win the
kingdom.99[1]

C lose your eyes and imagine a warm summer evening in late August. You're sitting on your back porch, relaxing as the day draws to a close. The still evening lulls you into a calm state. You gaze lazily across the yard into the darkness. The air's closeness engulfs you. As the hour passes you slip into a dreamlike state and your mind wanders. It's a soothing late-August night; Mother Nature settles down quietly. Your mind becomes silent, too.

Suddenly, the blackness, split by flashes of light, presents unpredictable patterns that illuminate your world in a new way. You can almost feel the static electricity being released, the pent-up energy crackling free. The sky is being awakened from its stillness by connecting flashes of brilliance.

You focus on the lightning that abruptly flashes on and off. With the humid day and the tranquil night, the environmental conditions were right. It's almost as if the empty black sky was set as an appropriate stage for this marvelously erratic lightning that dashes its jagged messages across the night. The quiet sky was ready for change, ready to flip its perspectives and try something new.

"Imagination is more important than knowledge."

Mindlessness: Can You Relate?

D o I mean that your mind should be emptied and quiet? Yes. And, aware as well. The August night was empty, but open to change at any given moment. Likewise, Thunderbolt Thinkers need to prepare their brains and organizations for change. They need to create environments that not only invite change, but actively support and encourage it.

In our lives, we often act as though there is only one set of rules. Operating with only one set of rules is not only dangerous; it also inhibits change. We become trapped in an inflexible world where everything belongs in specific boxes. We commit ourselves to a classic mind-set because "we always do it this way" and we can only see predetermined outcomes. We've become mindless and don't even know it.

Mindlessness smothers talent. Almost as if we were mechanical beings, we blindly follow our habits, unwittingly carry out senseless orders, thoughtlessly act on information—all with potentially grave consequences for ourselves and others. Ellen J. Langer, in *Mindfulness*,[2] explains that mindless behavior can occur because of repetition, premature commitment, belief in limited resources, and the notion of linear time. Further, she warns that mindless states can become the status quo, instantly, in almost any profession. W. Edwards Deming, the well-known international consultant who was credited with being the father of the quality movement, became a self-proclaimed enemy of the status quo.

As skills and proficiency develop, individuals move to a mindless state of just completing tasks. In the novice's mind, there are a multitude of options, while in the expert's mind, there are few. Mindlessly, organizations apply yesterday's tried-and-true solutions to today's business problems. According to Langer, "This single-minded approach leaves both you and your organization dangerously vulnerable."[3]

NEED AN IDEA ON THIS?
See T·N·T 7, Breaking Through Conditioned Responses.

Awareness: A Lifetime Partner for Success

It doesn't matter who you are. Even the most accomplished person needs a reminder. Awareness, continuously refined during your entire life, reduces your margin of error, limbers up your state of mind, and offers you a chance to make a real choice by sharpening your ability to feel the subtle vibrations of the changing signals. We often get trapped into thinking that it is intelligence that produces the "big idea." *Not so.* Frequently, brilliant ideas, innovation, and phenomenal creations are the product of an aware person rather than a highly intelligent one. The aware person is capable of creating new categories, receiving new information, and seeing new distinctions. He or she understands that the potential perspectives will never be exhausted. The aware person is not preoccupied by the outcome, but

NEED AN IDEA ON THIS?
See T·N·T 3, Brain Fantasy.

instead focuses on the moment and allows the process to take its course. In the end, it's not the project that really matters, but the learning. Not the result, but its meaning. Not the outside, but what happens within.

The Thunderbolt Model Comes Alive with Awareness

The rapid impact of change today demands that Thunderbolt Thinkers take advantage of the opportunities presented by change and not be mindlessly frustrated by it. Managers must live with the knowledge that there's more than one right answer or solution and that there are no wrong answers, just suggestions that don't fit at the moment. Awareness awakens that reality. Focusing on the "people power" within any organization, awareness breathes in a new sensibility that others may have a lot to offer. This opens the door of possibilities even wider.

While this is simple to say, it's harder to swallow. To help you, the Thunderbolt Model purposely challenges you to look at your people's potential, to become aware of this potent brainpower resource, to strategically ratchet up the brainpower at your place and look for ways to capture that talent. Remember these simple tips to encourage more awareness of the brainpower available to you:

- Staying alert and cognizant can pay off one hundred times over.

- Being consciously competent produces more effective results than unconscious expertise.

- Perception is in the eye of the beholder. Make sure your eyes are open.

- Gaining consciousness is more than only opening your eyes—you need to open your mind too.

- Be open and expect ideas to come to you from unexpected sources and at unexpected times.

- Know that flashes of insight can often be triggered by the simplest input, whether it is visual, auditory, or kinesthetic.

Thunderbolt Thinkers Awaken Their Internal Environment

Bodhicitte, a Buddhist concept, means "Awaken your state of mind." Derived from the words *bodhi*, meaning "awake," and *citta*, meaning "heart," *bodhicitte* or awakened heart suggests that we be mindful of our state. When we continuously examine and connect with our state of mind and actively engage our brains, we tune in to the ever-shifting environment that affects us. As leaders in our organizations, we need to operate with mindful awareness.

Managing from a mindful awareness and perspective, you'll give consent to: guesswork among your staff, alternate routes for completing tasks done by those who report to you, and a continuous flow of unique questions from the new people in your organization. Understanding that "mindfulness is the attunement to today's demands to avoid tomorrow's difficulties" prepares you to make the shift.[4]

Most of us are comfortable with our routines, but there's a downside to that sense of security. It is almost a trap. Our expectations of how things are "supposed to be" limits us and replaces what, in fact, we do see. This can dramatically affect your organization. In a rapidly changing world, the skill of "fine-tuned seeing" commands us not to miss the trends, shifts, or opportunities or coast through life on automatic pilot, living by mechanically preset conditions that control our every action.

Thunderbolt Thinkers are aware, tuned in, and open and charged up for change. Here's how you can do this:

- Check daily (hourly, if needed) to see if you are on automatic pilot. If so, tune into the moment and become consciously aware of the task you are performing. Ask yourself, "What did I just complete over the

"Man like every other animal is by nature indolent. If nothing spurs him on, then he will hardly think, and will behave from habit like an automaton."

last half-hour?" You should be able to recount each of your most significant steps. If not, you are on automatic pilot.

- Without going out into the hallway or into your reception area, make a list of the ten smallest items in that area, then go and look for yourself. If you don't have at least eight of the ten correct, you are on automatic pilot.

- Think back over the last two weeks and count the number of different routes you took to work. If you have not gone at least five different ways, you are on automatic pilot.

- Try to remember what you had for dinner over the last week or, if you watch television at home, try to remember what programs you watched last night—in order! If you can't remember in either case, you are definitely on automatic pilot!

- Can you sleep on the opposite side of your bed? Have you ever tried? If you answer no to either question, you are on automatic pilot.

- Do you believe that all meetings start late and therefore will run past their scheduled ending time? If you answer yes, you are on automatic pilot.

Deautomation clicks off your autopilot. Each day, spend at least one minute in the morning and one minute at night looking into the mirror. Very deliberately, reach up and touch your forehead, click off your automatic pilot, and then go on about your activities. Do this for at least thirty days. This exercise is guaranteed to break down potentially limiting stereotypes, rigid categories, and the tendency to cling to your own point of view.

Stay aware, in tune, open, and charged up for change.

9

Courage:
Risk and Vulnerability

THE COURAGE PARADOX:

❝It is a seeming contradiction that *we must be fully committed, but we must also be aware at the same time that we might possibly be wrong.*❞[1]

In their book, *If It Ain't Broke . . . Break It!* Robert J. Kriegel and Louis Patler state: "The future—unpredictable and uncertain—is coming toward us like enormous waves of change. . . . The future belongs to those who decide to ride; to those who have the courage to paddle out where the big ones are breaking; to those who welcome the unexpected."[2]

Even when you plan the change, courage becomes a must. Why? Because you need to be committed to making the change without really knowing what will result. "Planning is damn scary if you do it right, because what you're really talking about is change," said one executive in a computer company. "It's much easier to say, 'Next year's going to be better,' and leave it at that."[3]

Inventing the future requires the ability to leave the past and continually replace your old habits with new ones. It takes conviction to argue with the status quo, and faith to believe in the possibility of what is to come next. Riding the current demands nerve. You are exposed because you are never really too sure if the undertow will pull you down.

"The ideals which have lighted my way, and time after time have given me new courage to face life cheerfully, have been Kindness, Beauty, and Truth."

Courage to Break Your Habits

Courage comes from the French word *coeur,* or "heart," and courage lies at the heart of the Thunderbolt Model, so let's call what we need Thunderbolt Courage. The courage to change means pushing through your limits and unlearning habits that keep you frozen in old patterns. This letting go of comfortable and safe relationships in your consciousness releases a dynamic and ·exuberant flow of energy from your subconscious mind.

With each new situation, you need courage to let go of the old familiar patterns. But saying yes and letting go creates inner tension. In *Writing the Natural Way,* Dr. Gabriele Lusser Rico refers to the Latin *base, tensio,* meaning "stretched." She describes this inner tension as an "extension, a stretching out, a reaching for ways to join images, connect new patterns, reconcile opposites."[4] This tension fueled by using the both-and perspective rather than an either-or view sets up a paradoxical state that seems contradictory. Yet paradoxes compel us to transform our thinking patterns in order to resolve them. The mental agility, built by courage, that we exercise to solve paradoxes nourishes our brains and encourages fresh, invigorating solutions.

**NEED AN IDEA
ON THIS?**
See T·N·T 21,
Spill the Beans.

The Thunderbolt Model Relies on Courage

"Everyone can see what's in the light. They can imitate it, they can underscore it, they can modify it, they can reshape it. But the real heroes delve in the darkness of the unknown," says Benny Golson, jazz musician and composer.[5] It takes courage to use the Thunderbolt Model, to break through the wall of fear and criticism that threatens to stop you.

The power of the Thunderbolt Model is that through blending the five attitudes, you bring forth a SPIRIT that tames the wild monster of fear. Of all the attitudes, courage most notably demands that you step out in front, that you trust your inner resources and go with the flow. When you think of it, stepping out in front is really stepping out in front of the fear dragon within; it's holding up a mirror and facing your inner anxiety. That's courage. The steps outlined in the Thunderbolt Model present nontraditional strategies to help groups think more effectively. And because these tips and techniques are not your everyday methods, courage is essential for making the model a success. Therefore, to be successful with the Thunderbolt Model, you need to be willing to try new methods and to have a certain degree of faith and security that allows you to use courage, along with humor and flexibility, to let go and make the leap.

Thunderbolt Thinkers Create Their Own Badge of Courage

We could be stuck forever, locked in by habitual thinking styles, if we refuse to change. Further, since the way we group information determines how we later use it, the ability to transform our thinking is imperative for developing new ideas and solutions. Don't miss the opportunity while reading this book to be aware of your own courage. Recognize your power. Recognize that the everyday barriers blocking your organizations can be broken when you step forward and exhibit courage. Recognize that courage and faith always bridge the gap of fear and doubt. Give yourself a badge, a license to do it. No one else will. Courage takes transformation. Here are some ways to transform yourself:

- Do something totally opposite from what everyone would expect you to do.

- Feel good about yourself when someone laughs at you.

- Do it again, even though you failed the first time, when you know it's the right thing to do.

- Say "I don't know" out loud when you really don't know.

- Admit that you are wrong when you know you are; people appreciate honesty.

- When you come to the end of your rope, let go.

- Pat yourself on the back when you know you've done a good job and appreciate others when they have done the same.

Fear eats away at your spirit. Feel the fear and then go for the possibilities.

10

Humor:
More Than the Frosting

THE HOT-COLD PARADOX:

Question: What food is hot and cold at the same time?   *Answer:* Baked Alaska.[1]

Growing up with six sisters, three brothers, two parents, one grandmother, two dogs, and an array of cats offered a few humorous moments. However, life at 54 Overbrook Road was pretty normal. We lived in the typical Middle American family style of the forties, fifties, and sixties (we span three decades) with the "standard" family growing pains.

What I took away from those early years was the value of using humor, a strong learning I got from my mom and dad. I can see now how strongly my mother's viewpoint affected me. She was always able to see the humor in the worst situation and would lovingly remind us that we all had the same option when we were in the throes of a major crisis. Her words echo in my ears today: "When you can't see the humor in a situation, then it's really serious."

Practical Joking

A well-conceived practical joke is the highest form of comedy. The kind of good-natured prank seen on "Candid Camera" is funny to everyone. Rarely did an April Fools' Day pass in our house without the salt and sugar containers being switched, or the water shut off, or the kitchen clock turned ahead one hour. My dad became a model for me. His tricks, then, were a mild irritant (who likes all that salt on their Rice Krispies?), but now are a symbol of the small joys life can offer with such a tiny effort. Today, my husband, friends, clients, and family benefit from my well-honed skill at humor. As a matter of fact, I've come to learn that other Thunderbolt Thinkers give the same value to humor. They welcome it and unabashedly flaunt it.

You don't need to wait for April Fools' Day to engage in some fun. Why not offer a special birthday wish to a colleague by filling his or her office with inflated balloons or putting a rubber fish in the watercooler. People who work well together also play well together, and vice versa. Strong teams can be built through a variety of methods. Remember the movie *Brian's Song*? An article in *The Laugh Connection Newsletter* describes the team's practical joke: "When Gale Sayers joined the team, they told him the coach was hard of hearing in one ear. The scene that ensued was hilarious, with the football star moving from side to side behind the coach as he was talking to him."[2]

So, Seriously, What Is Humor?

“Before God we are all equally wise—equally foolish.”

According to writer Arthur Koestler, humor is "a fundamentally creative act"—that is, the collision of the rational with the unexpected, producing totally new ideas or insights or illuminating old ideas to make them fresh and powerful again.[3] It can be seen in these sayings: "All the world loves a lover—except those waiting to use the telephone," or "If at first you don't succeed, give up; failure may be your thing," or "The shortest distance between two points is usually under construction."[4]

In our structured and staid environments, humor offers the relief of breaking away from predictable, set patterns. In *The Light Touch*, Malcolm Kushner shows the power of humor this way: "The world of commerce is a shifting maze of human interactions. And humor provides a powerful tool for navigating the maze—a tool that you can learn to use successfully."[5] Humor adds a second dimension or the "other view" to our perception. As a matter of fact, it arises directly from our perception; it allows our mind to flip and look at something in a completely new way. Humor is absolutely essential for effective thinking. It is the basis of creativity and we cannot be effective without creativity.[6]

Humor helps you break away from a tired mind-set and end up with a wholly logical insight that is also fresh and astonishing. Remember that you can convert the fun you are having into powerful outcomes. Recently, I worked with the presidents-elect of an international association. They were generating ideas for fund-raising events for the year to come. While we were playing with toy cars and having a very silly conversation, the idea of hosting a family sports car rally emerged and developed into a very concrete and down-to-earth possibility.

The Thunderbolt Model Develops Strategic Humor

As a critical ingredient of the Thunderbolt Model, humor smashes through the barrier of rigid thinking and permits participants to think in new directions. "Never be afraid of humor when you're searching for creativity. It is often the fastest way to open the floodgates to new ideas," states David Thornburg, a California-based management consultant.[7] It gets people's attention, puts them at ease, can increase retention, and enhances rapport. Think of the people you work with—isn't it pretty hard not to like someone when you are all laughing together?

Throughout the Thunderbolt Model, I strategically encourage humor to raise its funny head. In my opinion, your meetings (or think tanks) will be flat and lifeless if humor is not an integral force. As you think, laugh, because this laughter will invigorate your thinking, adding the real frosting to the cake. I suggest that you go one step further and actually develop ways to use humor strategically; be proactive and use humor on purpose. To get your ideas flowing, use one of these ways to build humor into your environment.

Get Serious About Humor

There's a saying, "Get serious—we have work to do." Actually, this is exactly what I want you to do. I want you to get serious about humor, to see the value of this God-given gift, and to legitimize humor within your organization.

NEED AN IDEA ON THIS? See T•N•T 29, Sing-a-Song.

We don't see the power of humor. Even though it is such an enjoyable gift, we discount its power; we tend to see it as trivial and overlook how fundamental and vital it is to our thinking process. Silicon Valley computer executive Ronald Braniff feels that "managers who use humor in their presentations with employees come across as more approachable, and people are more likely to open up with them." He continues, "If you manage a lot of people, it's easier to maintain morale and enthusiasm by showing you have a good sense of humor."[8]

With fifteen facial muscles at work, you have countless ways to make yourself smile and laugh. Your cardiovascular system works, too, pumping up your heart rate, blood pressure, and circulation. Simultaneously, all this physical activity activates your brain and increases your alpha waves, the relaxed, resting, meditating, wakeful waves. All the while, according to scientific research, natural chemicals produced while you are laughing flow into your system, reducing your stress and anxiety.

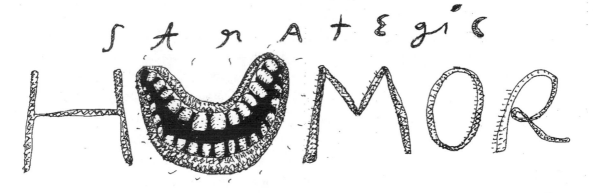

Studies in nursing homes demonstrate that elderly patients complain less about pain when a regular diet of comedies is prescribed. As a matter of fact, some doctors even recommend laughter as a great cure for constipation.[9] Certainly, many organizations suffer from a constipation of ideas and could benefit from a good laugh! Humor now plays a critical role in various therapy programs. Because of the growing evidence that laughter strengthens the immune system during the recovery period, it has become one of the primary tools in alcohol and drug rehabilitation programs.

Fun proved to be a key factor in Mattel Toy Corporation's turnaround from a loss of $113 million in 1987 to record earnings of $91 million in 1990. The second day on the job, John Amerman, the new CEO at the time, announced that he was letting in some fresh air and that the operative word was *fun*. When Amerman entered the corporate scene, morale was low and Mattel was suffering a huge loss from a series of toys that bombed. Among many nontraditional events, he and two senior executives dubbed themselves the "Toy Boys" in a Las Vegas–style review at their annual corporate meeting.[10]

Here are some suggestions for funneling humor's power toward your "serious work":

- Laugh at least fifteen times a day, whether you want to or not, while trying to isolate which muscles in your face are moving. A mirror is quite helpful in this exercise.

- Develop your own custom brand of laughing pills (jelly beans, nuts, hard candy, . . .) and distribute this "new product" to all your key management staff along with directions: "Take two to relieve your constipation of ideas." This is a great idea to use prior to a strategic meeting where fresh, innovative ideas and solutions are essential.

- Create an on-site "Laugh-In Therapy" program. Open it to anyone in the organization who seems to be in serious danger of never laughing on the job. Record all the symptoms and generate ideas to solve this epidemic. Appoint the most serious person on the staff to head it. Ask for weekly reports outlining the ideas suggested to solve the "serious" nonlaughing epidemic.

- Use a wall in a highly visible, high-traffic area and present a gallery of humorous cartoons. Use cartoons produced by professionals, but ask your staff for donations, too.

- Ask small children to tell you the latest funny story they've heard.

66We should take care not to make the intellect our god; it has, of course, powerful muscles, but no personality. 99

Develop an Awareness of Humor

Several years after I started my business, I attended a one-day seminar at Pennsylvania State University; C. W. Metcalf was the presenter. C. W. Metcalf & Co., based in Fort Collins, Colorado, delivers workshops to corporations that demonstrate the power and benefits of humor. This probably was one of the most valuable workshops I've ever attended.

Even though I grew up accepting humor, I wasn't convinced that the business community felt the same way. I had gotten the message that "business was serious work." There was no time for fun, let alone switching the salt and sugar. The more experience I had with companies, the more I saw what Metcalf calls "terminal seriousness: the fear of appearing foolish." As a humor consultant, he talked about this fear and other common attitudes within business. Although I was new to the business world, I knew that this fear was crippling. In many organizations, stress accounts for some pretty scary facts: 75 percent of all sick days in the North American workplace are due to stress-related illnesses, $150 billion is spent by companies to deal with stress related illnesses, and almost 90 percent of businesspeople regularly feel stress.

In one article, C. W. Metcalf recounts the prevailing view within companies: "Let's tighten up, put our nose to the grindstone, and beat the SOB's." He goes on to say, "But when you bear down, you get brittle, and when you are brittle, you break." [11]

Here are alternative thoughts for breaking out instead of breaking (or cracking) up:

- When you fail at something, laugh first, then see the opportunity; look for the nontraditional idea in the failure.

- Try singing. When a tense situation occurs, sing out your frustrations, worry, or anger. A friend of mine told me that at a Rotary Club meeting she attended, the meeting did not begin until after the group had sung a song together. It impressed her because she felt that it had been intentionally orchestrated to give these serious businesspeople a quick break from seriousness—a chance to be silly in a safe environment.

- Form laugh patrols: have people on call who can help you through a tough period by using their laughter and humor.

- Reach for your favorite toy. It's magical what a small rubber ball, a golden-colored wand, or a tiny race car can do to relieve pressure and open up a new way to view the situation.

- Rely on your energy joke book. Collect funny sayings, pictures, or jokes and compile them in a handy notebook; when you need a laugh, reach for your book.

- When you feel yourself getting tight, ask yourself: What is the worst thing that can happen? What is the probability of this happening? How would I handle it?

- Create phrases to use as antidotes to tense clichés. For instance, instead of saying, "When the going gets tough, the tough get going," say, "When the going gets tough, it's time to find a better way."

Think from a Humorous Perspective

Thunderbolt Thinkers look for opportunities to use humor, even though they know that every time they open their mouths they're at risk of being boring, obnoxious, or irrelevant. They realize that their role is not to be a clown, but to be a good communicator. Humor can become a powerful management tool to create rapport, break through barriers, or communicate a message—directly and effectively. Each time I enter the office of one of my clients, the "corporate portrait" of the four partners wearing children's Mickey Mouse sunglasses brings to mind their willingness to laugh together, at each other, and, more importantly, at themselves. Here are ideas to create a transition to humor:

- When presenting information, look for ways to add a graphic such as a funny picture or a drawing to illustrate your point.

- Leave fill-in-the-blank sections on your reports; ask for volunteers to complete your thoughts.

- Think in opposites: present from the back of the room, start the meeting from the end of the agenda, or give a series of answers and ask what the questions are.

NEED AN IDEA ON THIS? See T•N•T 8, Corporate Portraits.

Practice Playing Again

Imagine a meeting where the president poses as the Wizard of Oz. That's what Jim DiPiero, president of Pittsburgh's General Systems Services, did to build ownership in his staff. As the Great and Powerful Wizard, Jim gave each person a "share" in the company and an outrageous title. By giving each character what he or she lacked, Jim focused his staff on what they needed to help determine the direction of the company. "The levity helped everyone to loosen up and had an uplifting effect on the meeting," Jim recalls. "It takes a bit of risk to try some of these things, but I'm a firm believer in the creative process. It's a way to make the job more fun, and it helps to enhance our day-to-day performance."

On a different occasion, a bank was experiencing low morale among the tellers because of constant complaints about a few horrendous customers, so they created a Worst Customer of the Week Award. Each Friday the employee with the best horror story won the award (a bottle of champagne). Both morale and customer satisfaction improved. Tellers seeking to win *actively* solicited the worst customers and the customers got more attention.[12]

Martin Gonzales, manufacturing program manager for Hewlett-Packard Company, plays with masks. He uses them to win over people to his point of view and has fun doing it. During a budget meeting attended by several fellow managers, the goal was to decide on allocation of resources for the coming year. Since each manager was trying to get as much as possible, Gonzales jokingly put on a "pig snout" and won the votes needed.[13]

NEED AN IDEA ON THIS?
See T•N•T 14,
Head Bowling.

Hey, I Like This Kid Stuff!

The sad thing is that many people are stuck in the adult state. They've lost the ability and vulnerability to let go and live in the moment. Many stuffy adults don't know how to play. Even worse, some don't even recognize humor when it hits them in the face. More than anything, humor is an attitude that surfaces from your particular outlook on life. From my early youth until my adult years, my parents always taught me the value of maintaining a good sense of humor. Before my father passed away, I remember one April Fool's Day when I had the occasion to stay with them in Pittsburgh. And you'd think I would have learned. But as I flew to the window, trying to assess how much damage the garbage truck had done when it hit my rental car— as reported by my father—the thought of a joke never crossed my mind. In fact, the car was in one piece, sitting firmly in the driveway. And as I turned from the window and smiled, the three of us stood there with the warm feeling of the family lore in our hearts.

Thunderbolt Thinkers laugh at themselves and enjoy play as useful for creating ground-breaking ideas. Here are some ways to "play" while you work:

- Call a daily recess; take time out to laugh. Read a book of jokes for a few minutes or call a dial-a-joke number.

- Make conversation with a co-worker about something that interests you other than business. Go over the results of a recent sports event.

- Allow time for unstructured nothingness. Go for a walk through your community, parking lot, or park after lunch.

- Rediscover that five-year-old child. Be silly. Put on an old pair of shoes and stomp in the puddles after the next rain shower.

- Take time just to doodle; see what happens. Start with a clear sheet of paper and doodle continuously for ten minutes. Use a lot of colors.

- Stop time: take off your watch and turn the clock around. Go all weekend without wearing your watch. Go all *week* without wearing your watch. You'll be surprised at the way your internal clock works.

- Experiment! Try doing something different. Go to an ethnic restaurant that you've never visited before. Go to a movie on Thursday afternoon.

- If your company will allow it, dress casually one day each week. If they don't, change the rules!

- Turn on music. Tune in a station that you normally don't listen to, perhaps classical, and relax.

- Dance to your next meeting, appointment, presentation. Make a move like an athlete who has just scored a goal or belted a home run.

- Keep a "report card" and rate yourself on how well you play each day. Note it in your appointment calendar and review the results next Saturday morning.

Mastering play skills should be your number-one goal.

Action:
A Can-Do Attitude

THE FOREST PARADOX:
❝A forest would not exist unless each tree had started out as a seed, but a sack of seeds does not make a forest. *Making* an idea work is every bit as important as having the idea in the first place.❞[1]

"The most beautiful thing we can experience is the mysterious. It is the source of all true art and science. "

"Deliberation is the work of many. Action, of one alone," maintained Charles de Gaulle. Sam Walton also stressed flexibility and action over deliberation.[2]

The thought of deliberation and action reminds me of a child's spring toys, the ones that come in various animal shapes. Remember how they work? If you have kids, you probably played with this type of toy last weekend. Frogs are my favorite. The frog, perched on the end of a spring, is attached to a suction-cup base. You slightly moisten the base, set it on a flat surface, then gently push the frog down until the spring compresses totally under the small suction base. The frog sits, ready and waiting, poised to jump into action the minute the compressed strength of the spring exceeds the pull of the vacuum.

Can't you just see Sam Walton poised for action? When vision is not backed up with action, a tremendous sense of alienation occurs. Action must follow or disappointment destroys the dream. Just look at your kid's face when the frog flops over instead of shooting straight into the air, doing a double flip, and landing in your coffee cup.

The Benefits of Leaping into Action

Some people I know freeze in their steps. Trapped by fear, they can't or won't take a step forward. I can relate to this because it has happened to me. The value of moving into action is that it keeps us on our toes, even if we don't know what move we will make. Like the cowardly lion in *The Wizard of Oz,* we need to understand that as we leap into action, our courage springs forth. Action creates momentum. It is only one step in a series of events; part of the cycle, not the final act of a win-lose drama. Action is what makes the process worth it and the result real. Don't waste the energy around you because the airways or hallways aren't cleared for swift action to take place.

NEED AN IDEA ON THIS? See T•N•T 17, Image Storming.

The Thunderbolt Model
Moves You to Action

Action holds the Thunderbolt Model together. When you transform your ideas into action, you elevate the process and the results. Combining your flexibility, awareness, and humor with courage provides results that are useful to you and to others.

The Thunderbolt Model funnels your activity into deliberate actions and then streamlines these actions into targeted steps that successfully implement them. To focus on action, ask yourself how you would answer the following questions:

- Think of a current project you are responsible for managing. What bureaucratic obstacles could be removed to facilitate quick action? What bold steps could you take in this direction that may be inspiring to others?

- How do you reward those who take immediate action, even if the outcomes aren't exactly as planned? Remember that there are no bad ideas or wrong answers; some ideas or answers simply do not fit the current situation. It is important to encourage everyone.

- What statements or tactics are common barriers to swift action in your organization? Negative phrases and other forms of inertia usually have long-established and familiar patterns in each company. Your role as a leader, no matter what level you hold in the organization, is to counter these conditions with action and wisdom.

Thunderbolt Thinkers Transform
the "Nothing Ever Happens" Mood

Moving into action means creating a can-do attitude with precise and specific action steps well outlined. This constructive attitude allows you to move forward without any debilitating effects. A can-do attitude starts *now* with you in control, so you don't lose focus. Develop your own "do-it" action attitude, and guard against leaving the sack of seeds on your office floor, by using the following six do-it guidelines.

Do It Now: The Power Is in the Moment

Don't forget this rule. This book concentrates and focuses you on moments of learning, encouraging immediate action. At times you may feel like the frog springing into the unknown abyss, but take heart and enjoy the free-sailing feeling you get in the leap. Take the risk; own the power behind the vulnerability. You can always bounce back. List some immediate actions you can do today. For example:

1. Recap all the key learnings from the last time your team met and fax them to everyone.

2. Pick up the phone, call a colleague, and discuss a relevant point that can move the project ahead.

3. Seek additional fresh input from someone who is not a member of the project.

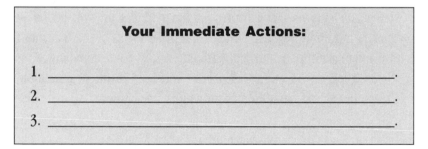

Your Immediate Actions:

1. _____.
2. _____.
3. _____.

Do It with Quality

Unfortunately, the word *quality* has been overworked, losing its true meaning. What's important is that you institute an action plan and put everyone inside and outside the company to work to accomplish a quality transformation. Who else can you involve in your project to lead you toward a quality outcome? Think about these suggestions and then build your own list:

1. Talk with your maintenance people and review the essential aspects of the project that deal with quality. Suspend consideration of quality from an economic point of view and deepen your understanding of the mechanical and logistical aspects. Be open to the input of others who come with different insights.

2. Ask your customers for their ideas about the way quality relates to your project. Go beyond contacting only the individual who makes the purchasing decisions and get input from the actual end users of the product. Talk to their engineers and find out if their accounting departments have any input for you.

3. Bring in three ten-year-olds and ask them to draw a picture of quality as it relates to your project. Remember that visual input is powerful. A young person might very well trigger a key idea that leads to a breakthrough solution.

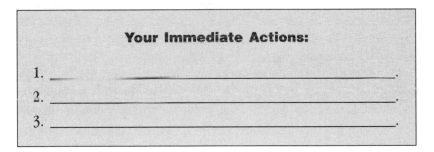

Your Immediate Actions:

1. _____ .
2. _____ .
3. _____ .

Do It Quickly

Time is the kingpin in our global marketplace. Among the major retailers who demonstrated this through their distribution systems are The Limited, Inc., and United Colors of Benetton. Wal-Mart Stores, Inc., converts information into action virtually immediately, a phenomenal accomplishment for a company that has sales in excess of $1 billion a year. Wal-Mart managers seek information input Monday through Thursday, then meet and debrief the ideas on Friday and Saturday. On the following Monday morning, they roll out the decisions and have the action plan in place.[3]

List three ways you can take time out of your decision process within your organization. Here are some ideas to get started:

1. Push down all decisions to the lowest level possible.

2. Broaden the scope of authorization on the project.

3. Limit the number of essential criteria required to make the decision.

4. Slow down in order to get ready to move quickly. Take time out to think; at least once a day stop for thirty minutes to reflect and think.

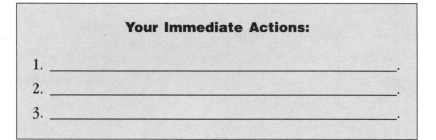

Your Immediate Actions:

1. _____ .

2. _____ .

3. _____ .

Do It and Have Fun

Master this question: How can I do this and have fun while accomplishing my goal? Break all the rules and create a fun experience no matter how difficult the task. Here are some ways to have fun while completing this project:

1. To stress the seriousness and importance of your project, issue a black-tie invitation requiring formal attire at the initial meeting.

2. Conduct a survey to assess who on the team has the most outrageous pet. Then adopt that pet as the project mascot. Code-name the project accordingly (Project Parrot, Project Ferret . . .).

3. Hold each meeting in a different location, such as the park, a gym, an empty warehouse, the washroom, the cafeteria . . .

```
┌─────────────────────────────────────────────────────────┐
│                                                           │
│                Your Immediate Actions:                    │
│                                                           │
│   1. _____ .   │
│                                                           │
│   2. _____ .   │
│                                                           │
│   3. _____ .   │
│                                                           │
└─────────────────────────────────────────────────────────┘
```

Do It with a Social Conscience

Today we see several socially conscious companies in the big leagues. The Body Shop's founder and co-chair Anita Roddick recalls, "It is hard to know which of our campaigns have been the most successful . . . but in terms of empowering and motivating the staff, instilling in them a belief that they are the most powerful people on the planet, Stop The Burning, our campaign to save the rainforest, probably had the most impact." The idea behind the effort was to motivate public opinion to try to stop the annual burning of the rainforest in Brazil.[4] Roddick sums up doing business with a social conscience this way: "Business is, after all, just another form of human enterprise, so why should we expect less from it, in terms of social ethics, than we do from ourselves and our neighbors?"[5]

Think of ways to infuse a "social conscience" into your project or organization, such as the following:

1. Professional Convention and Management Association's Network for the Needy sponsors efforts to help those less fortunate. A "sneaker drive" was held at their annual meeting in Dallas. Members were asked to bring a pair of sneakers or "sensible shoes" in good condition or pick up a new pair to share with a homeless person. A collection bin was located in the registration area. More than one hundred pairs of shoes were donated.

2. The Unocal Corporation, an El Segundo–based oil company, completed an innovative program in which the company and other busi-

"Something deeply hidden had to be behind things."

nesses spent more than $6 million over four months to buy 8,376 registered cars and trucks manufactured before 1971, regardless of their condition. The owners were given a $700 check and a bus pass if they needed one. Their purpose? To create political goodwill and reduce pollution in Southern California. "Unocal is very much to be praised for putting the thing into action," said Larry Arnn, president of the Claremont Institute, a Southern California research center that supports the idea of cars-for-cash programs. "It's treated sometimes as P.R. but it's not. It makes an impact."[6]

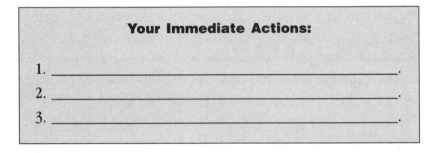

Your Immediate Actions:

1. _____.

2. _____.

3. _____.

Do It and Keep It Simple

"Hierarchy doesn't matter," recalled General Electric Company's CEO, Jack Welch, as he recounted a visit to Wal-Mart. "They get so many people in the room and they all understand how to deal with each other without structure. Everyone there has a passion for an idea and everyone's idea counts."[7] Keeping it streamlined and straightforward lays the groundwork for an action attitude.

In addition to these ideas, think of other ways to apply the KISS (keep it simple, stupid) principle:

1. Using a laptop computer, take summary notes during the meeting that capture key decisions and action steps. Print and distribute them at the end of the meeting.

2. Limit meetings to three or fewer major agenda topics.

3. Create the next agenda at the conclusion of the current meeting.

Your Immediate Actions:

1. _____.
2. _____.
3. _____.

Move into action—quickly!

PART THREE

The Five "How-To"
Thinking Steps

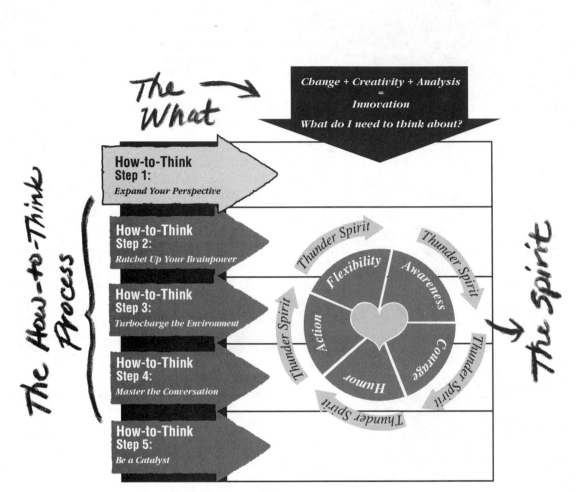

The Thunderbolt Thinking Model

Step One: Expand Your Perspective

The first how-to step in the Thunderbolt Model asks you to break away from your normal way of looking at a situation. As a strategic innovator, you need to consciously and deliberately prepare yourself to welcome change from the inside out. Two ways for this to occur are by launching yourself into the unknown and by challenging assumptions through asking questions.

How can you stretch to get powerful results that will turn your next committee meeting, retreat, task force, or family discussion into a think tank?

- Launch yourself from a stuck state.

- Challenge assumptions: ask the dumb questions.

- Maintain a flexible focus: develop the art of questioning.

- Strengthen your front-end thinking: prepare.

- Back it up with questions: follow up.

Launch Yourself from a Stuck State

As you prepare for your next meeting, be aware of the existing barriers that block you. Close your eyes and relax, and ask yourself what you want to shake up. Allow a bit of momentary craziness to occur while you launch yourself into the unknown. Look for the challenge and welcome it. Get inspired, be dramatic, and think outrageously.

How can you let yourself go? Sharpen your sensory awareness. Develop a rich fantasy life. Have some fun! Risk being foolish as you plan for your next meeting. If, for instance, you want to create a powerful meeting, then first connect with your own internal powerhouse.

THIRTY POUNDS OF

T•N•T

TIPS AND TECHNIQUES
to Put Thunderbolt Thinking into Action

Sometimes we need an extra power surge to move us into action. The T•N•Ts (tips and techniques) were created for just these moments. Easy to follow, they have been used by Fortune 500 companies and small entrepreneurial firms alike to craft breakthrough solutions for their toughest problems. These proven ideas can help you to transform your insights and options into powerful business results.

Let the T•N•Ts work for you, not against you! Adapt them to fit your specific need or situation. The last thing you want is to get stuck because a T•N•T isn't a perfect match for your problem. Change it. Adjust it. Flex it. Have fun with it.

The T•N•Ts are tools that will help you transform your thinking and that of your group. They are listed here by number. In addition, at the end of this section, I have provided four matrices that cross-reference the T•N•Ts with various issues, problems, or desired outcomes.

T·N·T
1

The Art of Brain Flossing

What is this? This technique helps you clear away noise, junk, and mental barriers so you can hear your inner voice and access fresh ideas. Flossing is a short, focused period of time in which you sit, relax, and freshen your thinking.

Why is it important? By mastering the Art of Brain Flossing you get rid of all the extra junk that builds up as accumulated tensions and inner conflict. This better equips you to see insights when change comes your way. When you take time on a regular basis to stop and relax, you'll see breakthrough ideas on a more consistent basis.

How do I do it? If you can't take two hours, set aside ten to fifteen minutes each morning to relax and unclutter your mind. Brain Flossing is an activity that refreshes your thinking when you need to focus on a particular challenge. It's a fun way to open a meeting and motivate participants to generate fresh ideas. You may also want to introduce it into your team's daily routine as an activity to rejuvenate their thinking regularly. You can use the official "Thunderbolt Brain Floss" or a piece of string. Wrap the floss around your index fingers and hold it up behind your head; then wrap it over your ears and pull it back and forth around the back of your head. When you're done, don't throw the floss away; instead just place it around your neck. You may need to use it again later if you get stuck on something else.

What are some ways to use this? In the beginning, when his company was changing quickly and doubling in sales every six months, Neal Patterson, president of Cerner Corp. in Kansas City, Missouri, realized that as a strategic innovator he needed to slow down so that he could capitalize on the opportunities coming his way. He said, "Whoa, I need to slow down and preserve some time to think," so he scheduled weekly two-hour, early-morning sessions to "talk to himself." He discovered that when his mind was clear his concentration and creativity improved, and he was able to make better business decisions.

The Birth of Bun-Huggers

What is this? This technique shows you the power of doing a warm-up, an exercise that charges up the group's thinking by doing something fun, ridiculous, or relaxing *before* heading into "serious" work. It is guaranteed to turbocharge your meeting environment.

Why is it important? You want to signal to your participants that you're not interested in yesterday's solutions; instead, you want them to stretch out, challenge their thinking, and create new and fresh options.

How do I do it? To stretch your group, present them with a challenge: redesigning panty hose for the male consumer. Use panty hose samples (pick them up from a lingerie shop), and pass the "old product" out to the group, so they can actually feel and see them. Then present your group with a series of questions to facilitate development of the "new product," such as:

- "Who is our target market?"
- "What do panty hose for men look like?"
- "How do we package panty hose for men?"
- "What is our product's name?"

Ask the participants to generate as many concrete ideas as possible for each question. Then ask them to draw a prototype of the new product and its packaging. Review the ideas and look for the "Aha!"—a multimillion-dollar idea such as "bun-huggers" sold to retired athletes, who have poor circulation and sagging muscle control. A great market and great fun!

What are some ways to use this? This is a marvelous way to increase the insight of your team and kick off a marketing planning session or a new product development think tank. It pushes the members of the group to significantly stretch themselves to the limit and develop innovative ideas for new names or prototypes of the product and package. This technique is good to use when the energy is low or there is a lack of new ideas.

T·N·T 3

Brain Fantasy

What is this? This technique guides you in using fantasy to encourage the group to relax and think of solutions for problems, to generate ideas, or to ratchet up the brainpower in the room.

Why is it important? Fantasy associations allow you to quickly tap into the deep recesses of the brain (the idea source) so that latent ideas can surface. In addition to increasing participation, it also increases awareness, energy, creativity, and fun.

How do I do it? Use Toys for Thinking such as magic wands, pixie dust, stars, crystal balls, and miniature magic carpets to create a fantasy atmosphere. Forget your "real" topic or purpose for the meeting for the moment. Then have the members of the group close their eyes and lead them through a guided fantasy with a verbal narration by you. Take them into fantasyland and then pose a

series of questions to elicit their fantasy thoughts. Give the group time to relax and move into a fantasy state, then ask for their responses to the questions. Write down the ideas and post them for everyone to see. Now come back

to your real topic. Have the group start to sort through the ideas and look for the gems that could apply to your real topic. You'll be surprised to see how many ideas do correlate to the purpose of the meeting.

What are some ways to use this? Here's an example of a magic carpet ride that leads a group toward smoother internal communication: "Close your eyes and gently climb onto your magic carpets. Let yourselves go as I easily lift you off the ground and you travel toward the soft clouds. You are surrounded by fluffy, cottony air, and gentle voices fill the air. You are free and the sounds are crystal clear as they ring through your brain. You instantly understand the messages and respond joyfully to the calls from fellow carpet riders. How does it feel among the clouds? What are you saying? What do you like?" Gently, ask each person to respond to the questions with closed eyes. Capture and post such ideas as "It feels great to be free," "Up here I move smoothly," "Wow, the view is great," and "The softness on my face is comforting." After each participant has provided input, slowly bring the group back to earth. Sort through the ideas and look for the fantasy thoughts that could be turned into solid actions. From "How does it feel among the clouds?" move to "What do we need to do to feel great about this project?" or "How can we make this project run smoothly?" or "If our customers buy this product, how will they feel?"

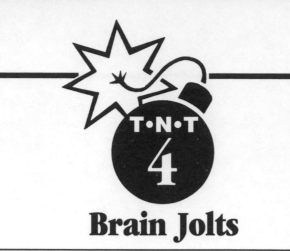

Brain Jolts

What is this? This technique uses analogies and metaphors to force insights into a problem by analyzing a completely different situation and then going back to the problem at hand.

Why is it important? It shifts and expands your attention and focuses you on details that you would otherwise ignore. Working with the metaphor that governance is a vehicle for solving problems, think-tank participants in the ASAE Foundation of the American Society of Association Executives drew pictures of various types of transportation that, in their opinion, reflected the concept of governance. Some of their examples were a sailboat, a roller coaster, and a school bus. The next step was to see what the types of vehicles had in common and to examine their attributes. The outcome? The group determined that accountability, representation, leadership, and consensus decision making were the four most basic attributes of governance.

How do I do it? One of the most fruitful ways to feed our imagination is to play with creative analogies. A classic example solved a problem with potato chip breakage. According to industry legend, the creative process went something like this: Forget about potato chips and think about nature. What in nature reminds you of potato chips? How about leaves? Dry leaves crumble when you press them together, just like potato chips. But wet leaves pack together tightly without crumbling. Suppose you formed moist potato slices into a uniform shape before they dried. They could then be stacked and packed tightly. The result, as you may have guessed, was Pringles.

What are some ways to use this? You can use this almost anywhere; let your imagination go. This is a good way to ensure that the group remains flexible and allow them to communicate in a different way. Metaphors help groups move from traditional linear problem solving to image building, enabling members to draw relationships along the way, then come to a final conclusion.

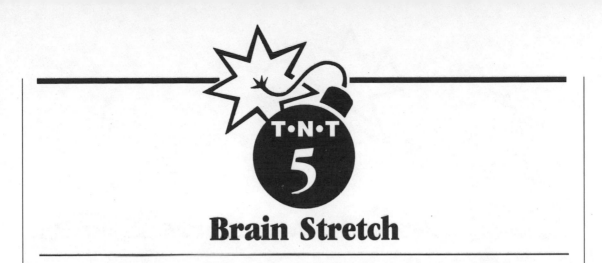

Brain Stretch

What is this? This is a different way to start off your meeting that quickly Involves each participant in a fun manner. It also provides a stress-releasing toy (Play-Doh) for the participants to play with during the meeting.

Why Is It important? It sets up an environment to help stretch, reshape, and remodel your group's thinking process. It demonstrates how easily and painlessly we can "remold" our shape in order to develop fresh ideas. This is a wonderful remedy for stuckness.

How do I do it? Using plastic Easter eggs filled with Play-Doh, create a debate over which came first, the chicken or the egg. Establish quickly that the egg came first. Ask the participants to crack open their eggs and stretch and pull the "gob" (Play-Doh). Assure them that by the end of your time together, they will have a "chicken." Explain the parallel: that you would like them to "crack open their minds," stretching and pulling their brains (thoughts, ideas, suggestions) in various directions, allowing new ideas (chickens) to emerge.

What are some ways to use this? This is a great way to kick off a morning breakfast meeting. Use it as you begin to create a new service or product, develop a plan, or solve a business problem. You can personalize the eggs with your company's name, get an eggcup for each egg, and encourage the participants to take the egg and eggcup back to their own offices and crack open the egg when they feel stuck.

Brain Transformers

What is this? This is a way to change perspectives by putting yourself and your group on the other side of the situation or problem.

Why is it important? An outside perspective can suggest a multitude of solutions you wouldn't otherwise encounter. Likewise, a different perspective can stimulate controversy and raise "sticky" questions that can lead to a flurry of possibilities.

How do I do it? First, ask the group to decide whose perspective they will take on. Instead of being managers today, have them be first-week employees, or ask them to try feeling like patients in a waiting room, as opposed to being part of the office administration, or tell them to imagine themselves as attendees at your annual conference, instead of in their normal role as staff preparing the conference. Then ask questions that are guaranteed to flip everyone's perspective: "What do we do that really gets our buyers angry?" "Why does our product or service have to be this way?" "Instead of cutting costs, how could we spend *all* the budget by the end of the month?" List all the responses, then flip the perspective and generate ideas to turn the negative ideas into positive solutions. Look at the principle behind the negative responses and develop the idea to create an appropriate possibility. Capture all the unique ideas that emerge from your group and turn them into solid actions.

What are some ways to use this? This is an excellent technique when you are really stuck on a problem, issue, or situation. Instead of tackling it straight on, go for the opposite. Plan out all the reasons why the product could fail, you could lose the deal, the fund raiser could bomb, or the volunteers could get mad and leave. Then flip your perspective and build solid strategies to ensure success with your situation. Here's an example.

Kidnapping anyone, let alone Ted Kennedy, is a fairly outlandish thought, but that was the idea that surfaced during a session several years ago. After we all had a good laugh, we stepped back and asked, "What's the principle behind this?" As the group discussed the idea, the main thrust became to create a big media splash. So we worked with the idea of "creating a media splash" and developed an appropriate media program.

The results: two weeks after kickoff, the organization got recognition on the front page of the *Wall Street Journal*.

T•N•T 7

Breaking Through Conditioned Responses

What is this? This technique is a good way to demonstrate just how stuck in our conditioned responses we are and how easily we slip into old patterns.

Why is it important? It helps you to recondition your group's brains so you can move more quickly to action and then to viable solutions, through becoming aware of conditioned responses.

How do I do it? Make a list of well-known commercials that your group can quickly identify, leaving the tagline out (given in parentheses here), such as:

- "How do you spell relief? (R-O-L-A-I-D-S)."
- "Good to the last (drop)."
- "Winston tastes good, like (a cigarette should)."

Then start off your meeting by asking the members to replace one of these commercials' taglines with a new ending. (As you recite its beginning, do not read the tagline.) *This will be almost impossible for the group to do.* Their conditioning will have them completing the tagline before you even get to it, even though some of the commercials haven't been used in twenty years.

What are some ways to use this? Think about all the conditioned responses people are locked into when they attend meetings (the same people sit in the same chairs, the same coffee cups are always used, the agenda always starts out the same way).
Instead:

- Serve coffee in china cups, not Styrofoam.
- Flip a coin to see whose issue is presented first.
- Request that all reports be handwritten and less than one page long.

Ask yourself whether any of these ideas would serve as a breakthrough to alter people's usual responses and create a "new ending" to your meeting?

T·N·T
8
Corporate Portraits

What is this? This technique shows you how to capture outrageous and fun moments. I first read about photo funnies from C. W. Metcalf, a humorist who believes in laughing it up, not cracking up.

Why is it important? Examples and reminders that show how easy it is to laugh at ourselves and with others provide a quick and easy way to capture the magic that lies hidden within our corporations. You can use your corporate portraits to reignite the energy and excitement of the meeting.

How do I do it? Invest in an instant camera or bring your regular camera to the meeting. Then, as ideas pop up, pop out the camera and capture the moment. Make sure to get pictures of specific work groups. Even go as far as having them pose for a group shot. Encourage them to act silly, snap the picture, and distribute a copy to each team member as a reminder of how they laughed together. This is particularly useful with an overbearing boss.

My husband and I did this several years ago during our summer vacation. Growing up on a farm, Dunc had never gone into one of those four-for-a-dollar, arcade photo huts, so we did. Our four pictures are wild and silly; the two I have in my wallet really lift my spirits and make me laugh on hectic days. They also serve as a real energy boost on extended business trips.

What are some ways to use this? Make sure to snap shots of people acting wild and crazy—it's a great reminder of what fun the team can have, especially later when you're in a tense meeting negotiating the annual budget. My most memorable set of pictures is from our parish council meeting. There, sitting ever so proudly around the church hall table, are

Photo Funnies

the pastor, housekeeper, and management staff, all wearing children's party favor glasses!

Develop Your Sense of Humor

What is this? This technique gives you ideas that encourage you to proactively develop your humor skills and use them every day.

Why is it important? *Remember*, take your work seriously, but not yourself. Encourage team development. Most people can be more productive and more useful team players when they are loose and stress-free. A well-developed sense of humor keeps you flexible.

How do I do it? Start creating your own humor library. A must: *Claw Your Way to the Top* by Dave Barry. "Visit" this library every day and especially before each meeting. Try surrounding yourself with people who make you laugh— enjoy at least ten laughs a day. Take a situation to extremes: Create some laughs at your next meeting by saying, "Why, George, if we fully expand our company's sales force any more, we'll rule the

world." Try imagining people naked as a way of reducing tension and intimidation. A recent ad in *USA Today* showed Luciano Benetton, CEO of United Colors of Benetton, standing there with nothing except the ad's copy to cover him. Imagine your toughest customer completely nude. How hard could the sale be?

What are some ways to use this? Always be able to laugh at yourself (your company, your department, etc.); it will release the pressure and produce faster results. On a personal note, I developed a real sense of humor about some of the side effects from my cancer treatment. For example, my sweat glands dried up as a result of the radiation. Now I laugh and tease my clients, telling them that no amount

of pressure is going to make me sweat. They'll just have to work with me without putting on the pressure!

Draw-a-Brain

What is this? Drawing your brain jolts you and causes you to look at yourself differently. Many of us are not aware of our brains. Most people have never drawn a picture of their brains, so 99 percent of the time this will be a first.

Why is it important? We need to ratchet up our brainpower to fully leverage our potential. When members of a group draw their brains, they may never see themselves in the same way again. The drawings help to increase their level of awareness, of themselves and others.

How do I do it? As you open your next board meeting, staff retreat, or employee update session, have the participants introduce themselves in a new way. Pass out blank white paper and colored markers or crayons. Then ask the members of the group to draw pictures of their brains on the blank paper (if you want, you can tie this in to the specific reason for the meeting—for example, "Draw your quarterly review brain"). Ask each person to write down several words that describe his or her brain. Post the pictures on the wall and have the group talk about what is similar about the brains and what's different. Post these responses on the wall too. Next, have each person tell the group one thing about his or her brain that no one else knows and post these responses as well. Finally, have the group come to a conclusion about their collective brains, such as "Our brains are open, funny, and flexible" or "Our group is made up of brains that are serious, logical, and always busy." Bridge back to the topic of the meeting by emphasizing that this group has the collective brainpower to address the issue under discussion in a very powerful way.

What are some ways to use this? Use this instead of ordinary introductions to start off a meeting. Or, to demonstrate the impact of participants' brainpower, break them into small groups. Ask each group to draw their brains, discuss one thing about their brains in the small group, and craft a unique way to introduce their small group to the others. It's great fun and a quick way to understand the group dynamics.

T·N·T 11

The F.I.S.H.™

What is this? This technique gives you a way to control inappropriate, negative input. The F.I.S.H.™ ensures that you and the group hold to the 90/10 rule—90 percent of the time you are focusing on positive thought patterns, creating a positive experience.

Why is it important? The principle behind the F.I.S.H.™ is to tell individuals, in a noncritical way, "right now we want to be positive and *all* ideas are okay." It allows every idea to be voiced, regardless of how ridiculous or stupid it is. This is extremely valuable in the effective thinking process. The F.I.S.H.™ works tremendously well in groups where the "boss" is present, because it is truly okay to flip the fish to the boss. Remember, the F.I.S.H.™ eats *Fatally Inappropriate, Slimy Hits.*

How do I do it? First, establish ground rules outlining when you will generate ideas and when you'll be evaluating them. Be sure to cover this thoroughly at the beginning of the meeting; post the rules if that will help. Kick off the meeting by having the group identify and write down "negative" phrases that stop the free flow of ideas cold. Post them in a prominent place where they'll remind everyone *not* to use them. We lay a red plastic fish innocently on the table. Then, if a negative or demeaning reaction surfaces, we instantly pass (or sometimes throw) the fish to the offending party. This sends the message that we're in a positive mode and that negative or critical input is not desired. Given the nonthreatening nature of the fish, the "zap" is usually well received. The fish becomes a symbol of and a barometer for the expansive thinking mode.

What are some ways to use this? This technique is good to use at *any* meeting, especially if there is a mix of participants from various levels of your organization. In one case, flipping the fish to the boss was a major breakthrough for a management team. We were caught in the traditional "boss speaks, all listen" mode and ideas for the five-year strategic plan were not flowing. During the first hour, most of the suggestions were given by the president and all the management team members would agree with him. Nothing new was emerging from the group. It was only after one of the managers kiddingly tossed the fish to the president, who had criticized the manager's idea, that the logjam was broken. After that, the fish enjoyed the company of many of these managers, the group loosened up, and more people started to participate.

T·N·T 12

Flexible Focus

What is this? Flexible focus is a technique to purposefully and deliberately change your perspective.

Why is it important? When you are mindful and aware, the "answers" that are right under your nose become easily attainable and bring forth your courage, allowing you to quickly take action with new ideas.

How do I do it? Either have each participant bring a pair of outrageous glasses or start collecting some of your own for the group. At strategic times during your meeting, ask the group to don the glasses and look at the situation with a new perspective. Ask the following trigger questions:

- How does the situation look from your new perspective?
- What else do you see?
- With your eyes on new sights, what is on the horizon of change?

What are some ways to use this? This technique is particularly applicable to "visioning" sessions, when you are trying to create a strategic vision for the company that distills your message to its most important essence. It can also be used when the same people (especially if they are the experts) have been working on a task or problem for a long time (more than three months). Have them refocus on their purpose and on their desired results. Ask them to be willing to "look" again at what they are doing.

The Garbage Bag Dump

What is this? This technique is a safe way to clear the air and let go of the past so that fresh ideas can surface to move the project, group, or company forward.

Why is it important? Hanging on to old complaints or grievances only blocks the individual and stifles the group. The idea of writing down a complaint and then tossing it away frees individuals from the past and helps to build strong teams.

How do I do it? Pass out three-by-five-inch cards. Ask everyone to write down things that they are upset about, that bother them, or that irritate them. Get them to do their own internal "garbage" review and search back for any hidden agendas that still bother them. Let them know that this is for their eyes only. Then, using a large kitchen garbage bag, collect all the "old stuff." Have the participants tear up their cards and toss them into the bag. Then tie the bag into a knot and toss it away, or, to be more dramatic, burn the cards right there in the room!

What are some ways to use this? This technique is helpful to use if the group has been hostile about the project or about some aspect of working together. Please note: It is best to use an independent facilitator (not yourself) to monitor this activity, so there can be a bias-free perspective on the situation.

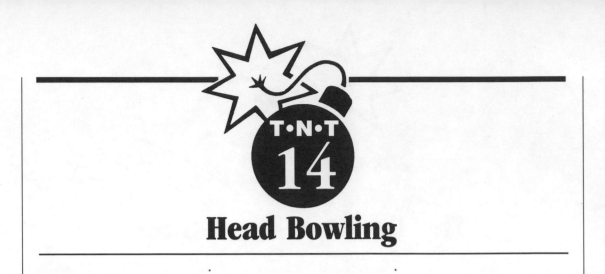

T·N·T 14

Head Bowling

What is this? This technique was first introduced at the annual meeting of one of the Big Six accounting firms. Head bowling offers you a marvelous twist on a well-established corporate phenomenon—head rolling.

Why is it important? Created by Maura Farrell, one of our staff members, head bowling is a great way to say that "those who criticize will pay," but it's done in a light and humorous manner. It's a nice way to build team spirit among your group.

How do I do it? During your session, keep score of who "dings" the group most often. At the end of the session, roll a Nerf-type ball toward that person and name him or her the winner of the head bowling contest (we use a soft, Nerf-style pumpkin head with an ugly face; it's great for getting your point across).

What are some ways to use this? Have a head bowling ban-quet on a quarterly basis and recognize all the winners. Keep the atmosphere fun, light, and positive. Stress that any idea is potentially good and may only need to have life blown into it rather than being condemned as a strikeout. Ask all the "winners" to come to the banquet with ten out-rageous ideas that could be the foundation of new ideas for the organization.

T•N•T 15

Hidden Communication

What is this? This technique shows how listening and questioning skills affect the communication process and the eventual outcomes—especially in mastering the conversation.

Why is it important? Organizations must pull together collective brainpower in order to remain viable and competitive. The best way to do that is to break down existing barriers that might hinder effective communication.

How do I do it? Before the meeting, get small, multicolored, triangular shapes of plastic or construction paper, sheets of cardboard, and reclosable plastic bags. For each pair of participants, create two sets of identical shapes (matching colors and numbers) and place each set into a plastic bag. During the meeting, work in pairs and explain that two people will work together by communicating verbally to complete a task. Ask one person to create a design using the triangles but to keep it hidden behind the cardboard.

Then have the other person try to create the same design by listening to his or her partner's description of the shape and directions on how to construct it. Let the listeners know that they can ask questions to get details and to resolve any confusion. Give the groups three minutes to complete the exercise, then debrief them to see what worked, what didn't, and why. Show examples of effective ways the pairs communicated and draw conclusions about communication styles and how they might affect the group's mission, goals, objectives, or tasks.

What are some ways to use this? This exercise is great for building teams and showing the power of listening, and for groups who think they communicate effectively with each other. Because it shows the various styles and needs of the group, it also serves as a super learning tool.

Idea Hatchery

What is this? This technique gives you an easy and fun way to program the right and left sides of your brain to ensure that both sides work effectively together to produce meaningful solutions for your tough problems.

Why is it important? Our subconscious is working continuously, so the idea behind this technique is to direct that work by giving the brain specific input. By directing our thoughts, we enhance our awareness and facilitate action quickly.

How do I do it? At the top of the first page of a pocket-sized notebook, write, "In what ways might I . . . ?" (fill in your own situation, a problem, or an issue you need to deal with). Then write down some key issues regarding that situation. Head the second page with an unrelated word or idea—the first one that pops into your mind. Tuck the notebook away and let your unconscious

"incubate" the problem. As additional thoughts spontaneously appear throughout the day, enter them on the situation page. At the same time jot down any unrelated thoughts on the second page. Next, pick the two most intriguing entries and combine them to create new, synergistic ideas to head the next day's pages. Keep doing this for a week or so, then review your entries. The solutions will be right there! Anne Talvacchio, one of our staff members, used the Idea Hatchery to develop an effective organizational planning system for herself. She started with the problem of "getting better organized" and played with food and color words. Pop! The idea emerged: a color-coded system.

What are some ways to use this? I've developed some of Albert Einstein's quotes into "Einstein's

Thought Book" and handed it out at the beginning of a session along with directions for setting up the Idea Hatchery. I've found that this is a great way to encourage after-hours thinking on the WHAT you are addressing during the meeting. Each time you come together as a group, check to see what ideas have "hatched."

T·N·T 17

Image Storming

What is this? This technique helps you to rev up the group's energy when an individual has trouble articulating an idea.

Why is it important? Remember, the Thunderbolt Model is people-powered, working from the combined energies of the entire group. Image storming gives you a way to draw on the group's collective brains. This exercise stresses taking immediate action and soliciting the help of others—a great team-building activity.

How do I do it? When someone is stuck, immediately have that person draw *any* image that comes to mind. Remember to encourage drawings that include images that are *seen, heard, tasted, touched,* and *smelled.* Have others in the group help to articulate the thought by drawing their ideas, too. Remind everyone to keep their minds open and allow the images to surface. Come back later to add words to the drawings, then link the thoughts, ideas, and graphic representations together to see what strong threads appear.

What are some ways to use this? When the Cancer Guidance Institute in Pittsburgh, Pennsylvania, was trying to develop a new theme for their telephone hot line service, one of the board members had an idea but couldn't articulate it. Quickly, the board members each drew their own interpretation of what they imagined. After posting the drawings and mixing the words into several combinations, Pop!—the idea emerged of a singing logo and a jingle based on the song "Happy Days Are Here Again"! This was very significant for the board because they wanted to send a message via the hot line that a positive future could be realized by cancer patients.

**T·N·T
18**

A Name Tag Is a Name Tag
Is a Name Tag

What is this? This technique uses the ordinary name tag in an out-of-the-ordinary way to get participants to describe their expectations, buy-in, vision, and so forth as they relate to the meeting or project.

Why is it important? This creates immediate, active participation in a way that makes everyone feel involved. It also gives people an opportunity to introduce themselves from a different perspective.

How do I do it? Instead of using the name tag just for names, have participants include some information that relates uniquely to the meeting, such as a word they would use to describe the organization's current status or how they plan to give life to the project. Ask them to complete the tag and wear it.

Then, at the appropriate time during the meeting, debrief the group and discuss each person's tag.

What are some ways to use this? I've used name tags in many different ways. Unique name tags can be made from pre-printed two-by-three-inch

Post-it Notes. The sayings can usually be adapted to fit your meeting and add fun to the opening. Or just make your own. Some phrases that I've used and name tags that have worked include: "Planning, Projects, and _____" (for a long-range planning session); "I plan to help this project lift off by _____" (good for any type of major project—you can add balloon stickers to the name tag); or "Today I feel _____ about _____" (for a team-building project or when you are deep into a long-term project).

T I P S   A N D   T E C H N I Q U E S

T·N·T 19

One Picture or One Thousand Words

What is this? This technique emphasizes the power of drawings and symbols as communication formats.

Why is it important? Since we absorb information through visual input about 85 percent of the time, people will gain a better sense of the project and communication will be faster and more effective with a picture than with a phrase or sentence on the topic. Drawing also helps to develop awareness and humor skills.

How do I do it? Give your group the following task: "Within one minute I would like you to write a story about your dream vacation. Be as detailed as possible and include as many aspects of the vacation as you can." Now say to them: "Within one minute I would like you to draw a picture of your dream vacation. Be as detailed as possible and include as many aspects of the vacation as you can." Once they finish both tasks, ask for volunteers to read their story and show their picture. Have the group determine: Which one gave a clearer image of the volunteer's dream—the story or the picture? Which was more complete and detailed?

Which was easier to do? Which restricted their thought process the least? Move to the WHAT (the problem, topic, or issue) that you are discussing and have the group draw a picture of it.

What are some ways to use this? Use this when you need to get all the facets or details of a project or situation out quickly. It's great to understand various people's perceptions of the current situation. At 3M Canada, a staff artist sits in on an executive "visioning" session and sketches images of where the company wants to go. You can use an artist, graphic recorder, or simply the individuals attending the meeting to create your masterpiece. The important thing is to use images to build understanding and shared meaning.

T·N·T 20

Regressive Introductions

What is this? This technique shows how introductions can uncover the hidden talents of your group by taking the members back to their childhood days.

Why is it important? When people open up, walls start to break down. Really showing who we are to others helps to create team unity and sparks discussions of a new nature.

How do I do it? Ask the participants to think back to when they were five years old. Then ask them to draw a picture of themselves at that age. Do a round-robin and ask each person to introduce himself or herself as a five-year-old.

What are some ways to use this? This works especially well with in-house groups such as teams that have been together over an extended period of time. It loosens up the teams, allowing them to develop a new kind of intimacy with each other so that they can interact more effectively as team members. Finally, it offers an opportunity for the groups to coalesce in new ways.

Spill the Beans

What is this? This technique offers a relaxed way to get all the hidden agendas onto the table.

Why is it important? Hidden agendas are often based on assumptions that are just that—assumptions. Opening up the discussion and getting the items on the table encourages understanding and clarification.

How do I do it? Buy everyone who will attend the meeting a small can of baked beans. Give each person his or her own can. Then do a round-robin and ask who would like to "spill their beans" about some part of the project and discuss their thoughts. Repeat this with all the participants.

What are some ways to use this? This is appropriate to use if the project appears to be stalled for reasons you are not sure of. Please note: It works best when you have an independent, unbiased facilitator to handle the discussion.

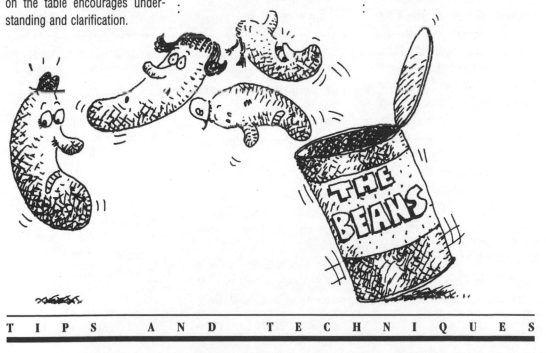

Theme and Tools for Thinking

What is this? This technique shows you how to develop a theme that reflects your meeting's purpose.

Why is it important? Creating an environment where people feel comfortable and energized about making suggestions and discussing ideas increases the chances of a successful outcome.

How do I do it? Before the meeting, write out your purpose: Why are you meeting? Think about the group and the organization itself. Look for threads that link the topics together, such as "vision" for long-range planning, sports teams for team building, or a holiday motif for meetings held on a calendar basis. Once you have found the link, blend the theme into the entire process, then look for toys that can help the participants think more effectively. Here are some examples:

- *"A Future View":* This theme for strategy sessions focuses on mission, vision, or long-range goals. Potential Toys for Thinking: Try funny sunglasses, as the participants develop long-range goals, or put spaceship stickers on name tags and have participants describe the organization's trip into the future in five words. At the break, serve futuristic foods like freeze-dried ice cream.

- *"Key Strategies for Success":* This theme is appropriate when you are solving a problem, developing a communication program, or examining a quality issue. Potential Toys for Thinking: Use large plastic baby keys as a trigger or cue. Ask participants to generate key ideas. Pass out "golden" keys when you hit a Thunderbolt idea.

- *"Cross-Pollination":* This is a great theme when you are working with a team that's been together for a long time. Potential Toys for Thinking: Use jars of honey, pictures of bees, and bags of pollen. Pass out the bee pollen when you want the group to focus on cross-pollinating their ideas.

What are some ways to use this? Regardless of whether your meeting is a one-hour get-together or a three-day retreat, themes and toys can be a stimulator to move people to action. Invest the time in developing both, and you'll receive payoffs from your efforts. Themes and toys also help to carry the momentum forward after the event is over.

T·N·T
23
Thought Walk

What is this? This technique revitalizes the group's energy by using walking as an excellent aerobic brain energizer.

Why is it important? Walking is a natural mood elevator with no side effects. It relieves stress and lowers blood pressure. Walking produces an immediate sense of relaxation and freedom that allows you to move into action.

How do I do it? About midway through your meeting ask your participants to stand and merely walk around the room several times. If the room is small, try using outside halls (if this is not too disruptive) or even going outside. Ask the participants to walk quietly, allowing all the input from the meeting to settle in their brains. To ensure a relaxed atmosphere, play some music in the background (different kinds may be appropriate for the various moods of the meeting—soft for a serious problem topic, more lively for idea generation). When the participants return to their seats, proceed with the meeting.

What are some ways to use this? This technique works when the agenda is heavy with decision-making items, or when the topics to be discussed have a tendency to cause a lot of hot air or steam to occur, or when the group is just plain stuck in coming up with a solution.

Thunderbolt Show and Tell

What is this? This technique invites the participants to create their own atmosphere, theme, or environment.

Why is it important? This create-your-own environment technique allows participants to glimpse their co-workers' "other" side. The principle here is to smash gridlock thinking. If you always see people the same way, you'll always expect the same thing from them. If you change your perception, anything is possible.

How do I do it? Ask the members to bring a favorite "toy" that they keep in their office or home. Things that have shown up at our show-and-tell sessions include photo funnies—outrageous pictures of co-workers in hilarious circumstances—an executive's golden Slinky, a plaque with an inspirational saying, a small, soft teddy bear, and pixie dust. Give the participants air time to describe how their toys help them think more effectively. Capture the ideas. Then draw two or three key conclusions about the way your group thinks best. Maybe you'll even want to adopt a few toys as mascots!

What are some ways to use this? This technique is great for team-building meetings such as sales meetings. It helps to break down competitive walls and encourages a more cooperative environment.

Total Immersion: Using Sense

What is this? This technique encourages you and your group to use all five senses to sort through a problem or generate ideas.

Why is it important? Total immersion increases your awareness of a situation and enhances your productivity by using various ways of processing information. Each of us has a developed preference for perceiving the world through one of our senses:

- *Visually:* Through the eyes
- *Aurally:* Through the ears
- *Kinesthetically:* Through touch, taste, or smell

Recently, Nissan Motor Co. Ltd. showed a great ad that illustrated how they incorporate all five senses to reach their potential customers. The headline was, "A shade, a smell, a sound, a feeling . . . a voice in the back of your mind." The copy in the ad went on to ask: "What does quality feel like? Look like? Sound like? What should the steering wheel feel like? What should the car look like? What should its interior smell like?"

How do I do it? Next time you are under pressure (solving a staff conflict, adjusting the year-end budget, or preparing for a major sales call), try total immersion into your five senses and formulate questions that force your participants to think from the perspectives of all their five senses. Ask the group how the situation feels, smells, tastes . . . Ask questions like the following:

- What does our budget feel like?
- How does our competition smell?
- How do our customers sound?
- What does our service feel like?
- How does the conflict sound?
- What do low profits smell like?
- How does our sales staff sound?

- What does it taste like to attend our annual conference?

What are some ways to use this? Here is an example of using a five-sensing question: "What does our budget feel like?" Response: "Our budget feels like wet burlap. . . . It has no appeal and it seems as if we can't do anything with it." But what if we imagine that it feels like foam rubber? It bounces back and can comfortably support more than we thought!

T•N•T 26

The Shape of Things to Come

What is this? This technique is a good way to determine areas where your team needs to build more flexibility into the workplace to accommodate change.

Why is it important? Since change is a constant, leaders and work forces need to remain flexible in today's business environment. But sometimes it's hard to pinpoint areas where flexibility needs improving. By tackling the issue from a new perspective, people often see things in a fresh light.

How do I do it? Do this activity while standing. Ask the members of your team to place a chunk of Play-Doh in the palm of their hand, extend their arm, and squeeze the Play-Doh as hard as possible. Tell them to focus on the transformation undergone by the Play-Doh and concentrate on how the Play-Doh feels. Pause for a few moments and get some initial reactions from the group. Then ask them to do it again, but this time ask them to imagine that the Play-Doh is the work force and their hand is the pressure of change. Have them think about how flexible the work force needs to be to immediately adapt to instantaneous change. Conduct a round-robin debriefing and ask each individual to give a short description of how the Play-Doh felt, offering an example of where he or she sees a need for more flexibility in the workplace. From there, focus on the dynamics of your specific "change" situation.

What are some ways to use this? At Honeywell, George Dramowicz, director of quality assurance, led a planning session where he used this technique with a group of engineers. They used the Play-Doh to create forms showing the way they saw themselves as change agents inside their organization. Using this exercise, they gathered key insights about how they perceived their roles. Some of the shapes that were created included a giant ear, symbolizing one participant's listening skills, and a hammer, showing another person's willingness to be a barrier-blaster.

Eggs-straordinaire

What is this? This technique uses plastic eggs as idea incubators. As the eggs are rotated, new people build on the ideas that are already incubating inside. With fresh input and sufficient incubation, the ideas will hatch into viable solutions.

Why is it important? Often, ideas are quickly judged and discounted. They aren't given enough time to "cook," and consequently people never really start thinking about how they might work. Using the eggs reinforces the idea that incubation is a natural part of the life cycle. Just as chicks need time to grow and develop before they hatch, so do good ideas.

How do I do it? Using a set of plastic eggs, fill each egg with a question you would like your team to work on. Place the eggs in a basket on the table and have each work group randomly select an egg. Allot fifteen minutes for them to work on the idea. When the time is up have them fold up their ideas and put them into each egg. Then rotate the eggs and repeat the process. (If there are too many ideas, capture them on flip charts and rotate the groups around the charts.) After all the eggs have been rotated, have each group read out the ideas for each challenge. Use this as an opportunity to solicit further input from the group as a whole and decide on final actions.

What are some ways to use this? We used this at an annual business strategy kickoff meeting for AT&T's national General Markets Distribution Group. It was a fast-paced, interactive team-building exercise for the senior leadership team incorporating General Markets Distribution's vision and business strategies. Once the group had had time to expand their thinking and develop new ideas, they reviewed the information that had been generated and prioritized the ideas. In a few short hours, this large national team created several concrete strategies to take back to the workplace.

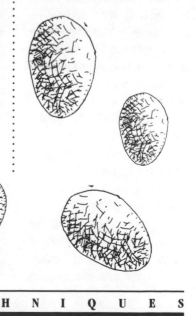

Reel to Real

What is this? This technique uses movie themes, motifs, and characters as a backdrop for your project: colors, props, room decor, music, and costumes all conform to the theme, creating an environment that relaxes and engages team members.

Why is it important? By immersing your team in a thinking experience that engages them and expands their perspective, you inspire real insights. Adopting a theme that everyone can relate to and integrating it across the board also builds buy-in among team members.

How do I do it? As you plan how you're going to work through your latest challenge, think of a movie that sparks your imagination. The subject matter doesn't have to relate directly to your challenge, but you may find that underlying themes, elements of design, or the actions of the characters fit with what you are trying

to do. You may want to use clips to create a presentation, use names as headers in your report,

or start a discussion based on the behaviors demonstrated by the characters. Remember to make concrete connections between people's conclusions about the film and how they relate to your project.

What are some ways to use this? During one project for the Council of Logistics Management, we created a thinking experience called "The Wizard of Aha's" based on *The Wizard of Oz*. The session focused on team building, and we used clips from the film to identify the core values demonstrated by the characters. This spawned a discussion that led to a set of supporting behaviors and, ultimately, to a solid communication plan. "We all identified with the characters in *The Wizard of Oz*," said executive vice president George Gecowets. "The observations will help us focus on the motives and feelings of colleagues in the office."

T·N·T 29

Sing-a-Song

What is this? This technique is a fun way to tune up presentations and meetings to create an experience that engages team members and your audience.

Why is it Important? Involving people in a way that breaks with their expectations catches their attention. In this state, they are more receptive to information, are more interested in learning, and have more fun.

How do I do it? Take time to think about a presentation you need to make in the next two weeks. Now think about a song. It could be one that directly relates to your presentation, your favorite song, or even the song you sing in the shower. If you're working with a team, choose your song together. Then think about a dynamic way to incorporate the song into your presentation. You may decide to write your own words, play the music in the background, or maybe even use the chorus as an opener. As you prepare for your presentation, build in time to rehearse so that everybody feels comfortable about performing.

What are some ways to use this? At US WEST Communications, Inc., market manager Michelle Mink took part in a forum to present ideas, find out what other groups were working on, and discuss opportunities to use and expand the ideas. For her presentation, "Free Installation Proclamation" (FIP), Michelle wrote a song entitled "Frosty the FIP Man," printed out lyrics for everyone, and had them all sing along with her (to the tune of "Frosty the Snowman") right before her presentation.

The results? Michelle says, "Everybody sang. I was surprised. Everyone lightened up a little bit." Michelle credits the lighter atmosphere in the room with achieving a freer exchange of information during and after her presentation. "It got their attention, got their blood flowing," she says.

T·N·T 30

The Flash Cap

What is this? This technique is an idea-sparking tool that calls on each member of a team, or each participant at a meeting, to offer her or his ideas and share input. The Flash Cap can be used as an "energizer" to get the flow of ideas started.

Why is it important? The Flash Cap is a fun symbol to alert and remind everyone in the group that each person's input is important. Sometimes participants feel freer when they can wear the hat. Being a little outrageous loosens the tensions and reduces the risk of an "off-the-wall" idea, so people are more comfortable speaking their minds. By encouraging them to do this, the Flash Cap allows ideas to surface that might otherwise have been left unsaid.

How do I do it? Select a flamboyant hat that is distinct and catches people's eye. The hat may be humorous or superheroish, and it should definitely have a certain outrageous flair. Introduce the concept of the Flash Cap to your team during a meeting, and casually integrate it by setting the example yourself. Then encourage your group by passing the hat around and inviting each person to share his or her flashes.

What are some ways to use this? We use a hat with red and yellow Thunderbolts "thunderbolting" out from either side. Our hat has become such a fixture in our sessions that people often check to make sure we've brought it, and everyone wants a chance to wear it. It's amazing to watch the transformation take place as people who are normally reserved put the hat on and immediately feel more relaxed. The hat is often a source of humor at our meetings, and it has also been the impetus for many a great idea.

RECHARGE YOUR THINKING
Try These T•N•Ts if You Want to Increase Your Insights and Options

T•N•T	Expand Your Perspective	Ratchet Up Your Brainpower	Turbocharge the Environment	Master the Conversation	Be a Catalyst
1. The Art of Brain Flossing		X			
2. The Birth of Bun-Huggers	X		X		
3. Brain Fantasy	X	X			
4. Brain Jolts	X	X			
5. Brain Stretch		X	X		
6. Brain Transformers	X				
7. Breaking Through Conditioned Responses	X				
8. Corporate Portraits			X		X
9. Develop Your Sense of Humor			X		X
10. Draw-a-Brain		X	X		
11. The F.I.S.H.™			X	X	X
12. Flexible Focus	X			X	X
13. The Garbage Bag Dump		X		X	X
14. Head Bowling			X	X	
15. Hidden Communication		X		X	
16. Idea Hatchery	X	X			
17. Image Storming		X	X		
18. A Name Tag Is a Name Tag Is a Name Tag	X			X	X
19. One Picture or One Thousand Words	X	X	X	X	
20. Regressive Introductions	X	X			
21. Spill the Beans		X		X	X
22. Theme and Tools for Thinking	X		X		
23. Thought Walk			X		X
24. Thunderbolt Show and Tell	X	X		X	
25. Total Immersion: Using Sense	X		X	X	
26. The Shape of Things to Come	X			X	
27. Eggs-straordinaire		X		X	
28. Reel to Real	X		X		
29. Sing-a-Song	X		X		
30. The Flash Cap			X	X	X

THE THUNDERBOLT SPIRIT
Try These T•N•Ts if You Need an Energy Boost to Get Your Spirit Moving

T•N•T	Flexibility	Awareness	Courage	Humor	Action
1. The Art of Brain Flossing		X			
2. The Birth of Bun-Huggers	X			X	
3. Brain Fantasy		X			
4. Brain Jolts	X	X			
5. Brain Stretch	X			X	
6. Brain Transformers	X	X			
7. Breaking Through Conditioned Responses		X			
8. Corporate Portraits			X	X	
9. Develop Your Sense of Humor			X	X	
10. Draw-a-Brain		X		X	
11. The F.I.S.H.™	X		X	X	X
12. Flexible Focus	X				X
13. The Garbage Bag Dump			X		X
14. Head Bowling			X	X	X
15. Hidden Communication		X			X
16. Idea Hatchery	X	X			X
17. Image Storming	X				X
18. A Name Tag Is a Name Tag Is a Name Tag	X				
19. One Picture or One Thousand Words		X		X	X
20. Regressive Introductions		X			
21. Spill the Beans		X	X	X	X
22. Theme and Tools for Thinking	X				
23. Thought Walk		X			X
24. Thunderbolt Show and Tell	X			X	X
25. Total Immersion: Using Sense		X		X	
26. The Shape of Things to Come	X	X			
27. Eggs-straordinaire		X			
28. Reel to Real	X		X	X	X
29. Sing-a-Song	X		X		X
30. The Flash Cap			X	X	X

MATRIX 3 THE WARNING SIGNALS
Try These T•N•Ts if Your People Are Not Picking Up These Warning Signals

T•N•T	Stuck in Stuckness	Lack of Insight	No Time to Think	Lack of Global Perspective	Undervalued Human Capital
1. The Art of Brain Flossing		X	X		
2. The Birth of Bun-Huggers		X			
3. Brain Fantasy	X				X
4. Brain Jolts		X			
5. Brain Stretch	X				
6. Brain Transformers	X			X	
7. Breaking Through Conditioned Responses	X				
8. Corporate Portraits					X
9. Develop Your Sense of Humor		X			X
10. Draw-a-Brain					X
11. The F.I.S.H.™	X				X
12. Flexible Focus		X		X	X
13. The Garbage Bag Dump	X				X
14. Head Bowling					X
15. Hidden Communication		X			X
16. Idea Hatchery		X	X	X	
17. Image Storming	X	X	X	X	X
18. A Name Tag Is a Name Tag Is a Name Tag		X			X
19. One Picture or One Thousand Words			X	X	
20. Regressive Introductions		X			X
21. Spill the Beans			X		X
22. Theme and Tools for Thinking	X	X		X	
23. Thought Walk		X	X		
24. Thunderbolt Show and Tell					X
25. Total Immersion: Using Sense	X	X			
26. The Shape of Things to Come	X			X	
27. Eggs-straordinaire		X			X
28. Reel to Real		X			
29. Sing-a-Song		X			
30. The Flash Cap		X		X	X

Try These T•N•Ts if You Are Stuck with One of These Deadly Seven

T•N•T	Lack of Participation	Overbearing Boss	No New, Fresh Ideas	Low-Energy, Lifeless Environment	Weak Team Spirit	Myopic Vision, Preconceived Answers	Poor Preparation and Follow-Up
1. The Art of Brain Flossing			X			X	
2. The Birth of Bun-Huggers			X	X		X	
3. Brain Fantasy	X		X			X	
4. Brain Jolts			X			X	
5. Brain Stretch	X			X		X	
6. Brain Transformers			X			X	
7. Breaking Through Conditioned Responses			X			X	
8. Corporate Portraits	X	X		X	X		
9. Develop Your Sense of Humor		X			X		
10. Draw-a-Brain	X				X		
11. The F.I.S.H.™		X	X	X	X	X	
12. Flexible Focus			X			X	
13. The Garbage Bag Dump		X			X		
14. Head Bowling			X				
15. Hidden Communication	X				X		
16. Idea Hatchery			X			X	X
17. Image Storming	X		X	X	X		
18. A Name Tag Is a Name Tag Is a Name Tag	X		X	X	X		
19. One Picture or One Thousand Words			X	X			
20. Regressive Introductions	X				X		
21. Spill the Beans		X			X		
22. Theme and Tools for Thinking			X	X			X
23. Thought Walk			X				
24. Thunderbolt Show and Tell							X
25. Total Immersion: Using Sense	X		X	X			
26. The Shape of Things to Come	X					X	
27. Eggs-straordinaire	X		X			X	
28. Reel to Real				X	X		
29. Sing-a-Song	X			X	X		
30. The Flash Cap	X	X	X				

Launching yourself takes guts. Not because it's hard, but because it's different. To break out and do things unconventionally requires you to muster up your SPIRIT to propel you forward. To let yourself go, try expanding your perspective by blending in flexibility, courage, awareness, humor, and action.

Change Your Frequency Dial

Open up new avenues of information for yourself. If we always rely on the same source, we tend to get stale and think the same way. When this occurs, there's little chance for new ideas to spring forth. Before your next meeting:

- *Read something outside your immediate area of specialty.* Go out to the fringes. Try an out-of-town newspaper, your kids' school newspaper, or a fiction novel. Look for interesting, off-the-wall reading to broaden your perspective.

- *Role-play; be someone else.* How would Humphrey Bogart act while leading your next meeting? Rhett Butler? Queen Elizabeth? If you were a Russian economist, a teenager, or a computer designer, what kind of information would you be paying attention to?

- *Take a few minutes and examine one of your products or services.* Now change the original intent. Think about what it isn't. Come up with ideas to sell this new use at your meeting.

- *Think on purpose, but think in opposites.* While planning your next meeting, write out your agenda using your opposite hand. This allows your left hand (right side of your brain) to control your thoughts. If you're a left-hander, see what happens when the right hand (left side of your brain) takes over and what results you get. Add one more twist by planning to start the meeting in the middle of the agenda. Or place objects side by side that would not normally go together: cat food and caviar, paint and pudding, pushpins and slippers. What do you see? What new products could you create from the two items?

What new service could be offered by blending the concepts behind each of the two items? What new game could be created? The list of questions is endless. Help expand the perspective of the people at your meeting by starting the meeting with this exercise.

Capture Your Thoughts in a Notebook, Journal, or Sketchbook

John Briggs tells us that "writing something down when you're thinking about it, even if you don't review what you've written again, is a way of giving weight to the thought process."[1] What I have found is that committing my thoughts to paper keeps my ideas flowing.

Models for you to consider include Charles Darwin, who kept voluminous notebooks in which he carefully recorded the movement of his thought processes on the issue of evolution. For Virginia Woolf, a diary was one ongoing project in her network of enterprises. She wrote in it daily after tea. Beethoven wrote in his sketchbooks obsessively. He told a friend, "I always carry about a notebook like this, and if an idea comes to me I make a note of it at once. I even get up in the night when something occurs to me, for otherwise I might forget the idea."[2]

My dad was the model I can best relate to. Ever since I could remember, he carried a small three-by-five-inch spiral-bound notebook in his breast pocket. At even the slightest hint of an idea, he'd pop the notebook out so he could capture the thought, write down the action needed, or record an important date.

There are limitless ways to capture your thoughts. The principle behind this exercise is for you to capture your life. Use your recorded thoughts as a base to generate new ideas, rethink old ones, and welcomingly expand your perspective from where it was yesterday. Here are more ways to "write it down":

- Turn your scrap time into a scrapbook. Everyone has bits and pieces of time throughout the day. Seize those moments and take time to jot down your thoughts.

- Start a morning journal. If your days are too hectic, write down the first thing that comes to mind when you wake up each morning.

- Create your own mile-high recorder. My journal gets attention while I'm traveling. The fun part is that I start the entry off noting the city I'm in or where I'm going!

**NEED AN IDEA
ON THIS?
See T·N·T 16,
Idea Hatchery.**

Sharpen Your Sensory Awareness

Faith Popcorn calls it "brailling the culture"; I call it "getting in-sensed." The idea is the same: to keep the senses alive; to reach out and add sensory value to as many parts of yourself, your organization, or your project as possible; and to do it on a regular basis. Among the most famous creators of our time was Albert Einstein. It is reported that "his thought processes when working on a problem were accompanied by muscular contractions and visual images and that he could sense when he was on the right track by a tingling at the end of his fingers."[3]

The whole idea behind the Thunderbolt Model is to diminish barriers that mentally wear you down and to create a voyage of discovery that perpetuates mental alertness. Anita Roddick explains: "So we're toying with adding textures and sounds to the visuals: getting slit bamboo, pipes, rubber suction cups, anything that makes a sound. So as you walk down this corridor, you can actually make sounds—press something and it whizzes or pops. It's a totally silly idea, which would be wonderful for six-year-olds. But I want to experiment with it to see how you can make going to work just a little bit more exciting."[4] The enhanced sensory awareness that results from adding texture and sounds to the visuals takes the boredom out of the environment and infuses it with the essence of adventure.

Think of music and its dramatic effect on us. I once arrived at a client's for a meeting early on Saturday morning to do staff training. However, I was the one who was "trained" when one of the partners opened the meeting with a rap routine! Mike McDowell, of McCrory and McDowell, a Pittsburgh-based accounting firm, used a funky rap tune

Five-Sensing a Scientific Equation

Albert Einstein indicated many times that his most powerful theoretical problems did not yield readily to logical thinking about equations. He is reported to have said, in searching for a way to describe how he did approach such challenges, that it was more like feeling the equations in his muscles. First, he felt a sort of muscular excitation or tension that told him he was on to something. Then came mental images, such as the famous one of a little boy riding a beam of light, that foreshadowed the abstractions of the Special Theory of Relativity. Finally, the follow-through: $E = mc^2$. "Feeling it in my muscles" is probably a metaphor. But such metaphors continue to serve scientists, and the rest of us, well.

in a presentation about how they set themselves apart from other regional accounting firms. Mike's dramatic approach to kicking off the meeting not only illustrated his point (literally); it also inspired the staff and set an energetic tone for the whole day.

Most of us get stuck in our ruts much more than we realize. As you work through this book, be aware of your own ruts and be willing to let go. Who knows? You may like the change! Here are a few more ideas to expand your perspective:

- Start paying attention to your own creative moments, and capture (write down) your flashes of insight. This is a very beneficial habit to develop. Accumulate your flashes over a period of time. You may well be amazed at the volume you generate, and some analysis may show you patterns you did not previously recognize. New combinations of creative thoughts will spawn still more creative thoughts.

- Sit back and think of your next "task." Rather than concentrating on the results or what the outcome will be, think about *how* you will go about accomplishing the task. It takes action to achieve results. Actions result from answering "how" questions. So turn all your questions into "hows." Instead of asking if something can get done, ask how you can get it done.

NEED AN IDEA ON THIS?
See T•N•T 25, **Total Immersion: Using Sense.**

Challenge Assumptions: Ask the Dumb Questions

To survive in an uncertain world, we have no choice: we must question. We must constantly disregard what is, seeking instead what could be and questioning any and all assumptions. Just think of how different our lives would be if the following people hadn't asked the "dumb questions":

- Bill Bowerman (inventor of Nike shoes): What happens if I pour rubber into my waffle iron?

- Fred Smith (founder of Federal Express): Why can't there be reliable overnight mail service?

- Walt Disney: Why can't there be a better place to take your children, where you can have fun together?

Questions force you to expand your perspective and invite you to walk at the edge of chaos. Questions are a natural fertilizer, feeding the mind with new ideas.[5] With every provocation comes a chance for change, growth, and improvement. Sun Tzu, in *The Art of War,* reveals that "opportunities multiply as they are seized."[6] Grab those breaks. Jump through those rare windows of adventure.

Benjamin Franklin was a questioner extraordinaire. With no formal scientific training, he questioned views on electricity that people had believed for centuries and replaced them with new concepts that shook the scientific world. He questioned why books should not be available to everyone and founded the first public library. He questioned everything in his hometown, from fire prevention to hospital care to education, and founded such organizations as a fire company, a city hospital, and a college, which became the University of Pennsylvania. As a philosopher, Franklin also had a rare insight into the psychology of questions. He knew that questions changed the conversation from a one-way harangue to a lively back-and-forth exchange of ideas. He knew that questions demanded two-way participation, brought people closer together, and warmed up a meeting.[7]

Maintain a Flexible Focus: Develop the Art of Questioning

Remaining flexible allows for individual interpretation. Flexible questions encourage us to think over, under, and around our assumptions. When flexibility is combined with enough focus, it keeps us headed in the right direction toward our dream, vision, or mission.

Questioning is an art. You may ask: why question? Good for you! You're already on the right track! The purpose of questioning is to help you think uncommonly about common problems. Also, asking the right questions helps you find, formulate, and focus your ideas. Questions make you think in fresh ways, which is vital to seeing new opportunities and solutions.

The art of questioning develops strategic insights. Powerful questions result in powerful answers. Strategic insight means knowing what questions to ask. Two specific types of questions that yield valuable information are *have* and *want* questions. *Have* questions ask the

The important thing is not to stop questioning.

organization what it likes about what already exists, while *want* questions ask what areas are lacking within the organization.

Have questions might include:

- Do we have the right economic perspective for looking at our company's future growth and development in the service industry?

- What market niche do we currently have as our strongest segment?

- Does our personnel system have everything it should for our company to do excellent selection and promotion?

- Do we have the appropriate equipment to meet the demands of worldwide distribution?

- Do we have the right focus with our research and development efforts?

- Do we have an adequate computer system to keep our organization at the optimum level for the effective use of all information?

Want questions might include:

- What products or services will we want to offer our changing markets?

- How will we want to respond to the changing needs of our customers?

- What new markets do we want to serve with existing or new products or services?

- How do we want to train our current employees to meet our industry's advances over the next three years?

- How do we want to be perceived in the communities where we operate?

- How do we want to deal with environmental issues facing our organization and the suppliers we work with?

Try to avoid *why* questions. They tend to create havoc when they are improperly wielded. "Why?" is often seen as an attack question designed to root out the causes of problems. Therefore, it tends to put people on the defensive, which obstructs the discussion.[8]

As your skill in asking insightful questions develops, you'll be able to drive toward a breakthrough more quickly. Simultaneously, a well-developed questioning process will enhance your ability to see business opportunities sooner. Encouraging a questioning mentality, not only among management but throughout the entire organization, floods the atmosphere with possibilities. The art of asking questions requires this questioning mentality. Here are a few triggers to inspire you:

- What do you want your organization to be over the next few years? Think beyond sales and growth and market shares. Decide how you want to be viewed by your customers, your employees, and your community. What do you value most in terms of a long-term perspective for your company and its products and services? How can these values be nurtured and enhanced?

- How many of your key people would answer with the same response when they were asked about the organization's mission? How was your vision conceived and developed? How thoroughly has it been articulated to employees, customers, suppliers, and the public at large?

- How does your staff support your corporate strategies? How well do you communicate your company's strategies in terms of both your words and your actions? Are you consistent in your messages or might there be some mixed signals going out?

- Is your organization's performance reviewed both strategically and operationally? Again, the consistency between what you intend to do (strategy) and what you actually do (operations) is vitally important in terms of achieving your intended results (goals). Are there mechanisms or policies in place that block your progress?

- How do you want to enhance your internal communication? Perhaps you could involve a cross section of employees in developing a creative and effective ongoing process.

- How have you reduced waste of your resources—time, dollars, and people? Have you documented your results or are your opinions

NEED AN IDEA ON THIS? See T•N•T 6, Brain Transformers.

mostly intuitive? Again, actively involving employees in defining and executing effective programs in this area will yield outstanding results.

Strengthen Your Front-End Thinking: Prepare

Mark McCormack, author of *The 110% $olution,* says, "Prepare for everything."[9] Start your preparation off with questions you ask of yourself. The real power of the Thunderbolt Model lies in premeeting thinking and postmeeting follow-through. Essential preparation includes answering these front-end questions:

- *Purposes:* What's yours? Is it focused? Is it attainable in the time allocated? Have you targeted it toward the participants?

- *Topics:* What main points do you want to cover? Are they specific and detailed enough to get the results you want? Do you have too many?

- *Issues:* What are the central issues? What answers do you need to move forward? Have you invited people with the skills and information to help answer questions? Are you prepared to allocate resources to act on the answers generated?

- *Outcomes:* What outcome do you want? What does it look like? Who needs to read it? When do you need it? How will you use it?

While planning for your next meeting, don't get stuck on any one step. Use the Action Ladder to capture ideas that will enhance your skills and your meeting outcomes. A sample Action Ladder is shown here. Remember, it's easier to solve problems and generate ideas when we see the whole picture. The Action Ladder can catapult you toward success. As you think about each question, jot down your thoughts.

After you have expanded your thinking and collected all your thoughts regarding the upcoming meeting, use the Thunderbolt Planning To-Do Chart to assist you in funneling your thoughts into clear, succinct action steps that will help you prepare. You'll notice that the guide has five columns. Think through all five areas and make sure you allocate time up front to prepare. This will ensure a successful outcome to your meeting.

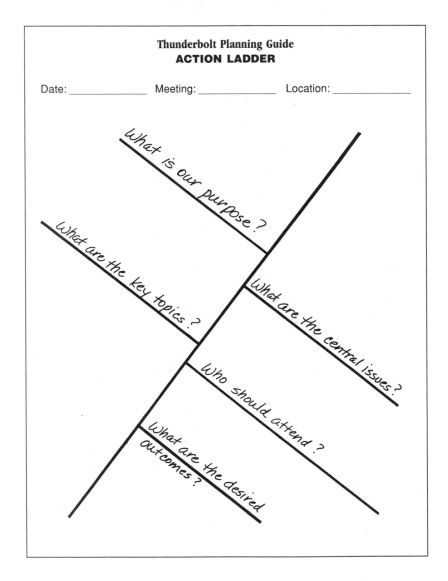

Thunderbolt Planning Guide
ACTION LADDER

Date: _____   Meeting: _____   Location: _____

What is our purpose?

What are the key topics?

What are the central issues?

Who should attend?

What are the desired outcomes?

Thunderbolt Planning Guide
TO-DO CHART

Date: ——————————————— Purpose: ———————————————

Meeting: ——————————————— Location: ———————————————

THINGS THAT NEED TO BE DONE	DATE	WHO	RESOURCES NEEDED	COMMENTS

Once you have your main ideas thought through and you've completed any to-do's in preparing for the meeting, you can design a working agenda for yourself. I suggest that you use an agenda that breaks down each section into a specific time allotment. This becomes a good working document for you and will help you monitor the flow of the meeting. A sample agenda is provided on the following page.

It is important that you, as meeting leader, are prepared minute by minute; however, it is not essential that your participants have this much detail. Therefore, you can be creative in how you craft the agenda you send out to your participants. To help expand their perspective on attending your meeting, why not send a pictograph agenda. See the sample and design one that fits your own needs. Remember, it's important for your participants to be prepared, but you can make it fun, exciting, and inviting for them.

SAMPLE THUNDERBOLT AGENDA

"Finding the Key Accounts"

Time in Minutes	What/Why	Points to Emphasize	Materials and Activities
5–7	Purpose: Why the group is together.	We're here to generate ideas to obtain key accounts for our organization.	
10–30	Introductions: The time depends on the number of people. A good way to get buy-in from everyone.	Everyone is a locksmith—with the key to open the door to key accounts.	Give people their own keys and ask them to explain what unique skill they have to bring in key accounts.
10–15	Background review: Depends on the amount of material to be covered. Define terms.	Highlight the past history of the organization; focus on sales and marketing: "What is a key account?"	Bring in as much visual information as possible—charts, graphs, brochures, etc.
7–10	Warm-up: Make sure to build in an exercise to loosen up your group.	Ask the group to recycle panty hose so they could sell them to men—and do it profitably.	Sample panty hose. Prepare a list of market-focused questions, e.g., What do the product and package look like?
30–45	Idea generation: Encourage the group to explore all possibilities. Plan ahead to have a series of stimulating questions ready for the group.	Where are all the opportunities to seek out new relationships? Who could be great referral sources to key accounts? What are all the outrageous ways we could attract new accounts?	Have questions posted on cards or flip-chart sheets. Post all the ideas as they are generated.
10–15	Break: Never go longer than 90 minutes without a break.	Play soft music that relaxes the group.	Use a tape recorder and audiotapes.
30–45	Focus and analyze: Sort through the ideas and discuss the principle behind each. Define the criteria for selection.	If we were going to really do this, what would it mean to our business? What in this idea would really make an impact on our business? How does this idea meet our criteria?	Post the criteria somewhere so everyone can see them.
20–30	Select the ideas: Review all ideas and select the most appropriate.	Of all the ideas we generated, which ones best meet our needs and fit into our specific criteria?	Post all the selected ideas.
15–20	Plan the next step: Overview and outline the key next steps so the ideas get put into action.	Our action plan will consist of the following: tasks, who will do it, what is the expected outcome, and the resources needed.	Post the action plan so everyone can see it.
5–10	Summary: Recap the entire time together and thank the attendees!	Review the purpose and get buy-in as to whether or not you met the stated goal. Recap all input points and actions needed.	Refer to the action plan.

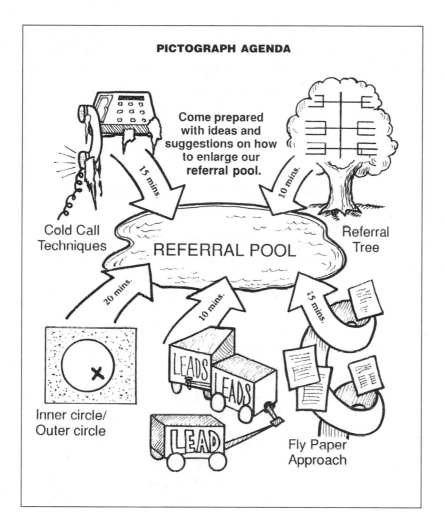

PICTOGRAPH AGENDA

Come prepared with ideas and suggestions on how to enlarge our referral pool.

15 mins.

10 mins.

Cold Call Techniques

REFERRAL POOL

Referral Tree

20 mins.

10 mins.

15 mins.

Inner circle/ Outer circle

LEADS

LEADS

LEAD

Fly Paper Approach

Back It Up with Questions: Follow Up

Once each quarter, several executives of Staples Inc., a $120 million discount office-supply chain based in Framingham, Massachusetts, meet with employees at each of the company's thirty-four stores. Employees get a chance to ask questions and raise any other issues of concern. A month later Staples distributes to all its employees a booklet featuring answers to the most-asked questions at each meeting, as well as additional company news and information. "The meetings make people feel that management is interested in them and in the best ways to do things," said a vice president of marketing. The booklet ensures that everyone at all of the company's branches gets to share in each employee's wisdom.[10]

Develop and use a tracking and monitoring system. In order to achieve truly effective results, build in an ongoing review or questioning process. Plan ahead to establish a tracking and monitoring system that includes:

- *Tracking mechanisms:* Tangible ways to assess how you're progressing, such as monthly reports, sales quotas, or performance reviews

- *Methods of communication:* A plan to "spread the word" and to keep people updated, such as announcing the outcomes in a one-page memo to everyone in the company, adding a few paragraphs in your internal newsletter, or including update messages on your voice-mail, computer, or fax options

- *Ways to deal with inhibitors or barriers to completing the plan:* Allocation of resources to put out daily fires so that the action plan can be completed, such as ad hoc task forces targeted to problems, support lines of communication, temporary help to get through crunch periods, or procedures for sticking to your plan of action

- *A review cycle:* Actual times and dates for review and follow-up— weekly, monthly, and yearly

Don't let those ideas get cold! In order for you to move into action quickly, you must be prepared to capture the outcomes in some sort of format. You can use one of the following: a summary report, pictograph minutes, traditional minutes, or a next-step action list. Whatever you choose, just make sure that the participants receive the information *at least* within two weeks of the meeting date.

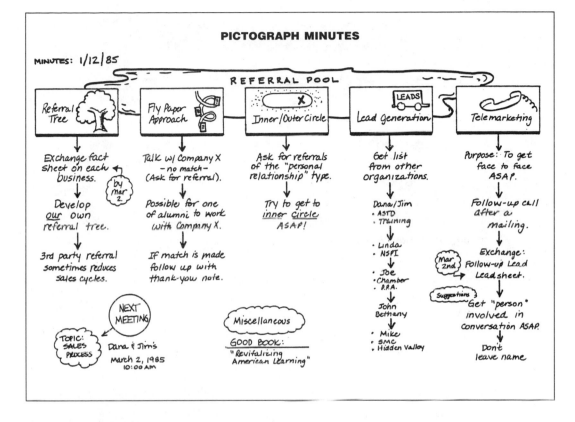

Instead of using traditional minutes, why not try a pictograph format. See the sample and design a format that will fit your meeting.

Through solid thinking, the blending of flexible and focused questions, and a tracking and monitoring system, the Thunderbolt Model produces the following results:

- Agreed-upon ideas that offer you a competitive edge

- A unified "team" that buys into the outcome of the meeting

- An action plan for the next step, including prioritized tasks, resources needed, start and completion dates, and expected outcomes

✔ CHECKLIST

LAUNCHING INTO THE UNKNOWN

Check off the items that you need to do in order to expand your perspective:

_____ I'll launch myself into the uncertain future by starting a journal to record my present-day activities. I'll review the journal at least once a week and look for the challenges and surprises!

_____ I'll let myself go by being outrageous; as the Russians say, *"Pshychelogeecheskaya ataca,"* or "Have a thought attack." I'll let my thoughts cook into ideas and not throw them away too quickly. I'll put them in my journal and keep them for weeks, months, or years.

_____ I'll sharpen my sensory awareness and get my whole self involved, particularly all my five senses. I'll dare to ask: "How does it taste when I walk into the boardroom?" or "What's the smell of our last meeting report?" I'll create a list of these types of questions to sharpen my sensory awareness—and potentially to ask my staff to increase their awareness too.

_____ I'll develop a rich fantasy life and *do this while I am awake.* I'll dream about my next meeting in Technicolor, be crazy, create bold, vivid images. I'll draw the visuals in my journal. I'll doodle in my journal at least three times a week.

_____ I'll value play by having fun, laughing at myself, and even risking being foolish while planning my next meeting. To have some fun, I'll show my journal entries to someone else. I'll do a ten-minute tune-up each day by reading one chapter of Gary Larson's book, *The Far Side Gallery.*[11]

Need a T•N•T power boost to get your spirit moving? See Matrix 2.

Always question your thinking at the beginning, middle, and end.

Step 1 Fast Summary

For Thunderbolt Thinking, remember:

1 The idea is never to get stuck. Start by expanding your perspective.

2 Momentary craziness often offers an opportunity to create options that may never otherwise have surfaced. Encourage trial and error, allow tentative responses, and depart from tradition.

3 Powerful questions elicit powerful answers. Keep a flexible focus and ask the naive questions; ask them before, during, and after you think. Avoid endless-loop *why* questions.

4 Think of meetings as more than just people in a room. Instead, position meetings as think-tank or change laboratories with you as the "mad" scientist. Experiment. *Be willing to go beyond the norm to get extraordinary results.*

5 Since you spend so much time in meetings, it is important to make the time and dollars spent worthwhile by:

- Being aware of the barriers that block your meetings and the group's thinking

- Thinking through the key elements that will affect your time together: your perspective, the brains present, the environment, and the conversations

For Thunderbolt Thinking, ask yourself:

1 What thinking traps do I want to leave behind?

2 What are all the ways I can turn thinking *barriers* into *bridges?*

3 How can I use meetings as think-tank or change laboratories within my organization?

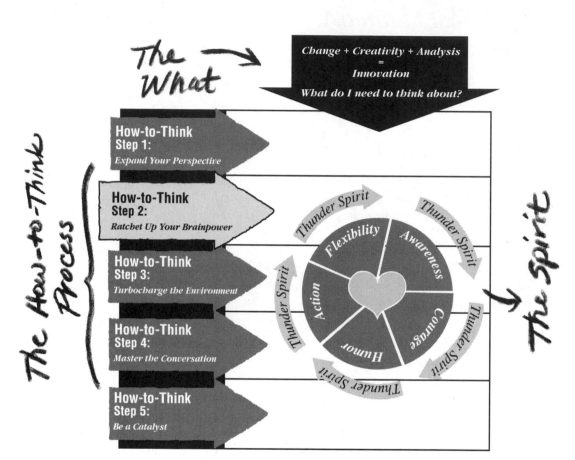

The Thunderbolt Thinking Model

Step Two:
Ratchet Up Your Brainpower

The second
how-to step broadens your
perspective by directing you
toward methods that leverage the brainpower of those
you work with, by tapping
into a pool of talent that can
fuel today's projects to meet
tomorrow's challenges.

How can you best leverage brainpower to turn your next staff meeting, focus group, training session, or church council meeting into a think tank?

- Capture brainpower: your greatest resource.

- Maximize your brainpower: pull together both sides of your brain.

- Use a B.A.T. to hit those home runs.

- Blend the brainpower: create a super-plus team.

- Create a personal brain trust.

- Feed your brain: food for thought.

Capture Brainpower: Your Greatest Resource

"Only a life lived for others is a life worthwhile."

Change involves training. To help facilitate change in your meetings, you'll need to retrain your group's brains. Accessing your greatest resources means stretching your group to think beyond the norm and leverage their brainpower. I've found no better way to help move people to capture the essence of their brainpower than to ask them to draw their brains. Powerful drawings can quickly mobilize a group. The drawings create a unique community expression of how the group views itself. And since there's no right or wrong way to do this, so far, to my knowledge, having people draw their brains hasn't caused any pain.

In fact, brain drawing has led to insights that might have otherwise been left uncovered, since it often triggers people to make connections that they might not have "seen" without the visual aid of the drawing itself. Connie Schoeller, an executive in the banking industry, uses it as an awareness-building technique to enhance performance among her teams. Once, when one of her customer service representatives' sales figures lagged behind those of others in the branch, she asked the team to draw their brains on easel-sized paper. When they reviewed the drawings, team members saw how they viewed themselves. The most noticeable differences were the brains' sizes: some were as small as dimes, others as large as pumpkins. When the customer service representative saw her drawing next to the others, she recognized that she'd been focused on her own "inability" to succeed, which kept her from listening to her customers. She began to shift her perspective. As a result, Connie said, "in the last six months, she has often been the sales leader."

You may be asking, "Why should I draw my brain?" Maybe you are even asking, "What does the brain have to do with managing at all?" According to the late Ned Herrmann, a former GE manager and a leading brain researcher and management consultant, "The brain and our learning about brain dominance have everything to do with managing, because the brain and learning management pose some fundamental questions in critical areas." In his book, *The Creative Brain,*[1] Herrmann focused on these areas: planning, job design, supervising, teamwork, training, corporate culture, and communication. He discussed how our brains work in conjunction with understanding and performing day-to-day management functions effectively to meet the demands of customers' needs, organizational challenges, and employees' problems.

> **Whole-Brain Thinking**
>
> "Whole-brain" theory says that the brain absorbs, stores, and recalls materials more efficiently in pictures, images, and events than it does in words.

So my purpose in having you draw your brain is simple. I want you to see it—to become more aware of it, to start to appreciate how your brain works, and to realize the significant energy and power that lie within you as an individual. This practice of using pictures to express oneself dates back to the early cave dwellers, as evidenced in the many cave drawings they left behind.

Before there were words, we had pictures. In our preschool days, images were an influential mode of communication, an effective means of expressing ourselves. The favorite story of James A. Crupis, founder of the International Leadership Center in Dallas, Texas, is of the young schoolgirl drawing a picture. The teacher stops at her desk and asks what she's doing. "Drawing God," the little girl replies. "But you can't draw a picture of God," the teacher says. "No one knows what God looks like." "Well, they will when I'm finished," the girl says.[2]

**NEED AN IDEA
ON THIS?
See T•N•T 19,
One Picture or
One Thousand
Words.**

Images play a central role in our lives. About 85 percent of what we remember comes through our visual channel, the eye, to the brain. Drawings show detail more quickly than verbal descriptions. Visual features give us a perspective that helps us relate each part to the whole. When we become aware of the relationships between different visual elements, we can quickly manipulate those symbols and relationships to generate new ideas or solve problems. However, we have come to rely primarily on words in our day-to-day reality. Now we write long-winded memos to direct our organizations.

Techniques such as mind-mapping, created by Tony Buzan, a brain researcher and author of *Use Both Sides of Your Brain,*[3] draw or "map out" what's going on in your head. Mind-mapping is often used to record what's happening in a current situation. Michael Gelb, director of the High Performance Learning Center in Washington, D.C., offers this idea: "Map a meeting from start to finish, and you'll get a much better sense not only of who said what, but of the real dynamics of the meeting."[4]

A mind map gives a picture of the whole, and with its combined symbols it provides a sense of the group's progress. During a strategic-planning meeting, a national professional association wanted not only to record the events of the three-day retreat, but to obtain a pictorial view of the organization's fifteen-year history. To accomplish this, the facilitator placed against the wall a sheet of white paper, about four feet wide by ten feet long. On the left-hand edge of the paper were written the names of the players, while along the bottom was a time line. Seeking input from the attendees, the facilitator "mapped" out a graphic representation of the events of the early years of the association. It was not only a vivid description clarifying misperceived information about the organization, but a great reference point throughout the three-day retreat.

Maximize Your Brainpower: Pull Together Both Sides of Your Brain

In order to use either drawings or mind maps most effectively, you must understand how the brain works and what it is capable of doing. Even advanced technological devices such as magnetic resonance imaging scanners and positron emission tomography scanners (used to track changes in electrical activity and blood flow in the brain as it works on specific tasks) have not enabled us to determine the brain's total capacity. Einstein said that we only use 5 to 10 percent of our brain's potential. Some scientists estimate that we use much less. Let's take a look at how the brain works by studying three key elements: the left side, the right side, and the bridge in between.

Brain Facts

- Yes, there really is gray matter. The brain cells on the left side are gray. The right side appears to be white.

- The amount of wrinkling on the outer layer of the brain visibly indicates intelligence.

- The average human brain weighs about 3.5 pounds (the size of two fists), *but* size is not important: Einstein's brain was of average size.

- The "jellied walnut-shaped brain"[5] (500 million years under development) takes on a different structure in each person.

Science has determined how the brain functions. As discussed by Ned Herrmann, four key characteristics help to explain the workings of the human brain. They are:

1. *Specialization:* Scientific research finds that the human brain has a left hemisphere and a right hemisphere. It appears that the two hemispheres relate more closely than earlier research findings

indicated and are more compatible than dissimilar. For all practical purposes, every "cerebral" activity you engage in needs the support of both sides of the brain. The left and right hemispheres have distinct functions. The left is verbal, involving logical, analytical, and sequential processing of information, and the right is visual and emotional; its function involves simultaneous processing, pattern recognition, and holistic thinking.

2. *Interconnectedness:* Brain connectors, a vast network of up to 500 million fibers, carry signals to various parts of the brain.

3. *Iteration:* Signals move back and forth among the brain's specialized centers to accomplish a desired mental result.

4. *Situationality:* Depending on the situation, the "best-suited" region of the brain will perform a given task, while the other regions go into a resting state. Therefore, it is necessary to be able to turn off parts of the brain situationally so that the parts that are needed can function without competition or interference.[6] Many times it's hard to use situationality because of the conditioning we've experienced, especially in our early school years. We don't or can't shut off our brains.

Reflecting on the words of Winston Churchill, "The longer you can look back, the further you can look forward,"[7] let's look to our early years to see how we used our brains then. During the first few years of life we used our whole brain; in those early years we used about twenty-five times as much brainpower a day as we do as adults. Then we began to specialize and favor one side of our brains over the other. Most research shows that specialization starts between the ages of five and seven, when formal education dominates the social conditioning process. Roger W. Sperry, father of the split-brain theory, feels that "our educational system, as well as science in general, tends to neglect the nonverbal [right brain] form of intellect." He goes on to say, "What it comes down to is that modern society discriminates against the right hemisphere."[8]

Because of this rigid emphasis on left-brain activity, along with its subsequent rewards, such as grades in school, right-brain skills are often neglected. There is a shift from right- to left-brain dominance that disconnects the two halves, rather than using them together. One study shows that children below age five demonstrate an 80 percent rate of creativity, as compared to children at the second-grade level, who only reveal a 10 percent rate. Eventually, the left hemisphere becomes the dominant hemisphere in nearly all human beings, and we lose the spontaneity of our right hemisphere, along with its abilities and skills in intuition, humor, imagination, and playfulness.

However, Herrmann's four characteristics play an increasingly important role in helping us understand how to continuously develop our brainpower so we can pick up both the loud and the subtle signals. In order to capitalize on your brainpower, you don't need to be another Einstein; instead you need to be a transformed version of yourself with an expanded perspective. The right side of the brain can help.

Our Right Brain—The Expansive Mind

We grew up on the three R's: reading, writing, and 'rithmetic. Solid skills. But today we need more. Today's basic three I's are intuition, inspiration, and innovation. This respectable trio often makes its way into the corporate ethos through paper-and-pencil exercises, but it is rarely backed up by concrete, tangible resources like people, dollars, and facilities. The corporate charge of the nineties needs to reflect the old adage, "Put your money where your mouth is."

The top management of Sharp Electronics Corp. encourages all its employees to create and submit new business ideas. Sharp explores each idea to assess its merit. Then, if the idea is worthwhile, the company commits resources (time, people, and dollars). The company lives its credo, "From Sharp Minds Come Sharp Products," and over the past few years, Sharp's stream of new offerings has included electronic organizers and LCD projection television.[9]

NEED AN IDEA ON THIS? See T·N·T 27, Eggs-straordinaire.

Cosmic Fishing

Remember what happens when you first get a hunch: you feel the nibble of an idea and your perception of it is strong. Unfortunately, what often occurs is that you let it go. Out there in your mind's eye are many possibilities waiting to be hooked. R. Buckminster Fuller, inventor of the geodesic dome, invited us to use our intuition and go "cosmic fishing"—to move deeply into the right side of our brains, expand the thoughts there, and allow them to incubate. Here's how and why it works:

- *Subconscious awareness:* When you have been consciously striving to create an idea or arrive at a solution, your subconscious is also aware of what you are seeking.

- *Random selection:* Your subconscious never rests, even when you're asleep. It is constantly sorting and sifting the trillions of bits of data that it holds. It *incubates* ideas and thoughts.

- *Generation of solutions:* Minutes, hours, or even days after you have stopped mulling over a particular problem, your subconscious will flash a solution to you. You are suddenly struck by an idea, or the answer to a tough problem comes to you while you're thinking of something else. Boom! The answer is created or developed or found and the solution emerges (sometimes pops) from the recesses of your right brain right out of your mouth!

While you are out there cosmic fishing, look for the F.I.S.H.™. My now-famous red plastic fish—a birthday present given to me by Anne Talvacchio, one of our staff—has been the savior of more meetings than I can possibly remember. The F.I.S.H.™ can be instrumental in ensuring that your ideas make it to the surface because its main purpose is to eat attack thoughts, those *Fatally Inappropriate, Slimy Hits* that drown many tadpoles (new thoughts or ideas) before they have a chance to see the light of day. Attack thoughts come in many forms and from the most unpredictable places. Uttered by friend and foe alike, these slimy hits smother fresh ideas before they have an opportunity to breathe.

When we are cosmic fishing, we want to hook on to insights, not insults. Yet it is easy for any of us to slip into an ego-bashing mode of operation. Common attack thoughts are:

"You can't do that."   "It will cost too much money."

"How foolish!"   "Whose idea is this?"

"That's no fun."   "That's a ridiculous statement."

"We have done this before."   "No way!"

"Somehow this doesn't seem   "That can't possibly work."
   to work."   "It's not in the budget."

"That idea is destined to fail."   "Sorry, too late."

"That idea is stupid."

"They'll never buy it."

"You've got to be kidding."

"That's unrealistic."

"The boss won't like it."

"What will people say?"

"Put it in a memo."

"Obviously!"

"I don't know if we can get to it."

"It will never sell."

"You don't understand."

"It doesn't make sense."

Hi! I'm the F.I.S.H. But I'm no ordinary guppy. I'm one of the cool Thunderbolt Thinking tools that can keep your meetings swimming along. Just toss me at anyone who's negative. I love it!

NEED AN IDEA ON THIS?
See T•N•T 11, The F.I.S.H.™

Because any of us may be guilty of shouting out attack thoughts at the most inappropriate times, it is best to have the group voluntarily offer these phrases at the beginning of the meeting. Write them down and post them on the wall. This serves as a good reminder for people not to use them.

Use a B.A.T. to Hit Those Home Runs

From 1990 through 1992, while so much of America was deep in the recession, Johnson & Johnson went cosmic fishing and boasted a 15 percent increase in earnings. When he was asked what made the company soar to such great heights, CEO Ralph Larsen responded, "Creative freedom"; he said that he gave his team inspiration and direction and then the freedom to take the next step. In many cases, innovation emerges from chaos. Johnson & Johnson's controlled chaos suits a company whose raison d'être is innovation. New products introduced over the past five years now account for a hefty 25 percent of sales.[10]

Creative freedom. Chaos. Inspiration. Words that could send a pang of terror through most managers, moms, or schoolteachers, especially if order, productivity, and efficiency rank high on their priority list. That's why, in using the Thunderbolt Model, you want a structure that supports goofing off, acting silly, free floating, and all the rest that is associated with inspiration, intuition, and innovation. A strong B.A.T. can help. Include the B.A.T. approach when you plan strategies to ratchet up raw brainpower.

First, let's define B.A.T. The "B" represents your beta or alert waves, demonstrated during your working situations when concrete mental activities occur. Alpha or "A" waves are produced during more relaxed or reflective periods and are best achieved with your eyes closed. "T" could stand for a twilight or trance state but really means theta brain waves. Twilight learning takes place as you emerge from this drowsy, idea-rich state. So the theta state is a great period for developing creative ideas. Although you are conscious in both the alpha and theta states, you tend to be less judgmental and critical in the theta state and ideas seem to flow more freely.

The brain's wave patterns change a hundred times during the day and night, depending on the state you're in. The purpose of the B.A.T. approach is to capitalize on your brain waves while focusing on what you have to think about. To benefit from the B.A.T. process, you must try to catch your people in the daydream cycle. Did you realize that most people dream every ninety minutes, both asleep and awake?

Create your own dream state by using the B.A.T. approach during a thinking session. Incorporate the following technique into your agenda this way:

1. Dim the lights, put on soft music, and ask the participants to relax by shutting their eyes.

2. Stretch your group's corporate imaginations by creating a new scenario that breaks from the traditional meeting setting. Create a twilight environment. To do this, lead the group through an unrelated dream fantasy rich with visual descriptions that awaken their sensory awareness. Encourage the participants to relax enough to allow their brains to slip into an alpha or even a theta state.

3. Slowly turn up the lights and ask the people in your group to capture on three-by-five-inch cards any thoughts that come to mind. Encourage them to capture *all* thoughts, whether or not they are related to the WHAT, the topic of your meeting.

4. Now, with the lights fully on, move immediately into an idea-generating period. Focus on the meeting topic by writing on a flip chart two to five key words that best capture the essence of WHAT you need to discuss. Then have each individual display the ideas developed during the twilight period.

**NEED AN IDEA
ON THIS?**
See T•N•T 3,
Brain Fantasy.

As they mix and match each of their thoughts from the B.A.T. session with the topic at hand, it is highly probable that the group will come up with suggestions or a solution related to the meeting topic.

Remember to bring the F.I.S.H.™, because the fledgling ideas emerging from the deep water of a relaxed alpha or drowsy theta state need protection from judgment and criticism. While we are fishing, our left side (the logical, judgmental side) needs to be turned off. Competition or interference from the analytical side at this time can be deadly.

Our Left Brain: The Computing Mind

The computing mind assumes responsibility for the more analytical functions of the brain only when exploration and development of the right side are completed. When the left side kicks in, we move into a more linear mode of operation. This is what happens:

- *Sequential patterning:* Thoughts come one after the other, creating a routine or regular way of acting or doing.

- *Systematic application:* In a predictable fashion, thoughts are applied through continued effort.

- *Linear execution:* Thoughts are judged by preestablished boundaries of point-to-point thinking.

Corpus Callosum: The Bridge That Keeps the Balance

With all this expanding and computing going on, every minute millions of sensory stimuli invade our brains. Even with only a small number of those stimuli reaching the brain, the left and right hemispheres communicate at a rate of thousands of impulses per second. The blending process is constant. The corpus callosum, the *bridge,* functions as the chief communicator, connecting the two hemispheres. A thick bundle composed of 200 to 300 million connections that facilitate the back-and-forth flow of electrochemical transmissions, the corpus callosum is the power link that brings the two masses together; it unifies attention and awareness to allow the two sides of the brain to share learning and memory.

As the bridge, the corpus callosum monitors the information stream between the hemispheres. It determines which side's talents are best suited to process specific information or to work on a given task, thus channeling the flow to each hemisphere. Dr. Gabriele Lusser Rico, in *Writing the Natural Way,* points out that once the right-brain patterns are reproducible, the corpus callosum shifts from stop to go, making the right-brain images accessible to the left brain, which in turn gives them sequential, communicable form.[11]

Brainpower remains our most precious resource—the only question is how to best use this amazing tool. To satisfy future needs and see new opportunities, we need both components of the brain to complement each other. We need to retrain the brain to function as an integrated whole that draws on the strengths of both the right and left hemispheres at the appropriate time. Striking this balance produces:

- *Synergy:* In synergy, the combined action of the whole is worth more than the sum of the parts.

- *Energy:* Energy results when the hemispheres collaborate, nurturing each half's activity without hindering the progress of the whole.

- *Power:* Power is released when the brain halves work in unison, with direction.

The Thunderbolt Model focuses on incorporating the functions of both sides of the brain, but stresses the need to keep a delicate balance between them. Because we have played down the importance and value of the right side of the brain for so long, the Thunderbolt Model tends to emphasize the use of this side a bit more. But don't get confused! In order to produce solid outcomes, you need to keep a healthy tension between the expansive thinking process and the computing, sorting, and funneling process. As you practice using the tips and techniques offered in the Thunderbolt Model, concentrate on mastering the skill of switching from one side to the other.

Blend the Brainpower: Create Super-Plus Teams

This is tough. It's tough to master free-floating thinking when you are surrounded by people who are convinced they've had the right answer since yesterday. It's tough to risk and be outrageous around people who judge at the drop of a dime. You may have total control over who will be at your meetings, but more often you don't. However, this may be your chance to enhance your Thunderbolt SPIRIT, using flexibility, awareness, courage, humor, and action to break out and reorganize who attends meetings at your organization. If so, the focus should be on those who can influence the outcome and reach the objectives, those who have a real purpose in being there. Remember that the number of people at a meeting has a direct effect on its length.

The more people you have at a meeting, the longer it takes (each participant needs time to provide input). You also run the risk of the meeting being less candid, because a variety of personalities can set up barriers to open communication. And finally, it's often more difficult to reach specific, well-articulated, and agreed-upon results in larger groups because more points of view need to be factored into the final decisions.

Even when you don't have control over who attends, or when a group is large, it's possible to maximize the brainpower and achieve dramatic advances. "By bringing together people who wouldn't ordinarily exchange ideas—or who may be in competition—we've seen thoughts turn into action," maintains Faith Popcorn, as she describes some of her client sessions.[12] And Ken Iverson, chairman of Nucor Corp., says, "Our success is based on groups working together: 25 to 35 people doing some tasks for which a standard is established. If they exceed that standard, they receive extra pay. . . . We take the philosophy so far that even the officers are a group."[13]

Joe Hudetz, while he was CEO of Solar Press, Inc., said, "There's no way management can control the company's aggressive growth on their own. We need the help of all the employees to do it."[14] One summer, they closed down the printing plant, rented a nearby community

> *It is the supreme art of the teacher to awaken joy in creative expression and knowledge.*

161

**NEED AN IDEA
ON THIS?**
See T•N•T 20,
Regressive
Introductions.

college, and assembled 320 full-time workers for a day of idea exchange and sharing. Top managers gave short speeches, and Hudetz presented a slide show on Solar's projected growth and future plans. The employees then met in departmental groups to discuss production bottlenecks, space and equipment needs, and staffing requirements. The outcome was a list of fifty problem areas, each one to be the focus of an employee task force during the coming months.[15]

Create a Personal Brain Trust

C reate your own: brain bank, kitchen cabinet, joy gang, life board, thinker team, flash bank . . . The name doesn't matter; doing it does. Approach eight to ten of the smartest and most daring individuals you know and get them on your team. Establishing a brain trust may be your most critical design decision for the future of your organization. In mining the human capital that is available, you want to choose not only the right people, but the best mix of people. Regardless of the size of your organization, the vein of talent for your team runs deep. You can use both inside and outside talent to create a cross-functional super-team to solve problems and generate ideas.

Your available brainpower can include: board members, key managers, customers, suppliers, administrative staff, and technical people, as well as your lawyer, accountant, insurance representative, and other business consultants. Why not think about friends, neighbors, delivery people, or your kids! George Clement, CEO of Clement Communications, Inc., feels that "CEOs who don't use outside advice run the risk of internalizing too much. They never realize their full potential and they miss a lot of opportunities."[16]

In developing a brain-trust profile, include members who demonstrate:

- Respect for others' capabilities

- Trust

- Individual autonomy

- Willingness to risk
- An action orientation
- Flexibility and adaptability

Follow these three points to put your team together:

1. Decide what you're trying to do and determine the scope of the think-tank session. Do you want a radically changed vision? A readjustment of the company's mission? Do you want to emphasize growth? Focus on acquisitions? Plan a five-year celebration? Think about a socially responsible project for your community? Discuss effective quality standards? Get a sense of your organization's morale?

2. Then you'll be able to decide how many team members you'll need, what kind of team members you'll need, and what skills they will need.

3. Finally, make sure you've got a good mix. Consider the chemistry between you and each team member. The members of the group must feel comfortable with each other in order to operate freely. Ask yourself what your gut feeling is toward each member: see how your stomach feels. Remember, you want to avoid "yes-people" in favor of those who complement and don't duplicate each other's thinking strategies.

Feed Your Brain: Food for Thought

Einstein had ice cream. Every day he would walk to the ice-cream parlor near his home in Princeton, New Jersey. Is there a connection between food and the brain? Well, there may be something to feeding your group while asking them to sort through some tough problems. This type of social contract relaxes the atmosphere and allows the conversation to flow. Every other month, when Pat Burner was president of T.L.C. Child Care Centers, Inc., she took her twenty-two employees out for pizza. The first hour was open season for criticism about anything and anybody, including management. Protest ranged from "You borrowed my supplies without returning them" to "You get too tense when things get crazy." The second hour was devoted to positive comments and finding solutions to the issues that were raised. It was a great way to ease the tension that often surrounds a situation in which one employee needs to "sound off" with a co-worker.[17]

SynOptics Communications' CEO Andrew Ludwick started a staff-to-staff brown-bag lunch after a manufacturing line supervisor complained that a new circuit board took much too long to assemble. Ludwick sat the supervisor and an engineer down at the same table to figure out how they could work together to make the product easier to assemble. The company decided to buy lunch for two related divisions. All the key people from both divisions would sit down together at five tables in the company's Mountain View, California, headquarters. Each table was assigned a problem to solve over lunch; it would then present its results to the rest of the group. On the surface the focus was on solving the problems, but beneath the talk a real chemistry and team spirit developed.[18]

Jay Johnson lets his people's palates do the talking. Every month, he holds a communication session for the seventy employees of Crest Microfilm, Inc., in Cedar Rapids, Iowa. If it's been a so-so month, he orders pizza and soft drinks. But if the company has done well, he lets the employees choose the cuisine. "In a bad month, we'll spend $75 or $80," says Johnson, "and in a good month, $250. At year end, we may spend $450 if we've had as good a year as we'd hoped for." The principle is celebration, but the outcome goes far beyond that. Although the formal purpose may be the dinner, the occasion is a great way to informally discuss the company's performance, as well as to go over problems and suggestions from the employees.[19] Prime ribs or pizza really says it all.

**NEED AN IDEA
ON THIS?**
See T•N•T 5,
Brain Stretch.

Brainpower is your greatest resource.

Step 2 Fast Summary

For Thunderbolt Thinking, remember:

1 Drawings are powerful. They can move a group quickly and provide a lot of detail. Start to retrain your group's thinking: have them draw their brains. Individuals who draw their brains begin to have beyond-the-norm discussions that break gridlock thinking, leading to extraordinary outcomes.

2 The group should be stretched to think beyond the corporate boundaries. Leverage the brainpower available by encouraging everyone to participate. Remember the power of the subconscious mind; foster each person's emerging idea and encourage participants to build on each other's thoughts. Catch your people daydreaming.

3 Everyone processes information differently. Make sure to use the B.A.T. technique to capture each individual's potential to hit a home run.

4 Your most critical design decision will be the mix of participants. Consciously think about who is going to be there and how you can maximize their talents, whether you have selected them or not.

For Thunderbolt Thinking, ask yourself:

1 What is the level of trust among these group members?

2 How would I describe this group's flexibility?

3 What types of action-oriented people do I need at this meeting and who will carry the ideas to completion?

4 Do I have a good mix of people?

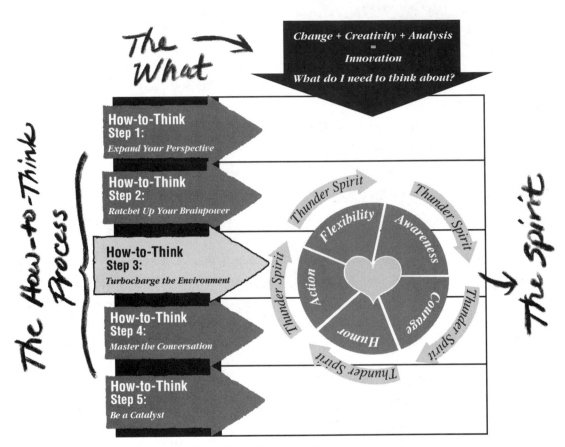

The Thunderbolt Thinking Model

Step Three:
Turbocharge the Environment

Spearheading a lightning bolt right through the heart of a meeting table is not too outrageous an idea. The third step in our how-to model asks you to do just that—to recharge your thinking process by turbocharging the environment. For Anita Roddick,

D R A W - A - P I C T U R E

How Do Your Meetings Look?

Take a few minutes and think back to your last meeting. Can you remember all the objects around you? Picture all the tangible items surrounding you on the table or on the walls. Also, what intangible conditions existed? Was it a formal environment or a more relaxed setting? Draw the images that come to mind from your last meeting environment and capture the essence of that meeting. Again, probably none of your colleagues have ever done this, so go ahead—be the first. Try to capture as much detail as possible. Don't forget about the lighting, the air conditioning, the chairs, the food served, the mood of the other participants, the hour of the meeting, the location, and so on.

Our Last Meeting Environment Looked Like This:

THOUGHT ATTACK!

Write down all the things you *liked* about the environment in your last meeting:

_____

_____

_____

_____

Write down all the things you *didn't like* about the environment:

_____

_____

_____

_____

the very aesthetics of an office can be a stimulant to the imagination. She says, "I used to be a teacher, and I know that one way to encourage creativity is to make the environment stimulating, even entertaining. So walking around our office is a visual and sensory experience unlike most any other office at a normal company."[1] Isaac Levanon, president and CEO of Arche Technologies, Inc., manufacturer of an IBM PC clone, reports that informal environments help employees loosen up in what could otherwise be a tense meeting. He says that most staff meetings are held on Fridays, their dress-down days. He feels that as a result, the exchange of information is more free. Levanon adds, "People don't say, 'Here's the boss, let's think about what I can say.' It's a nonthreatening environment."[2]

How can you transform your thinking environment to turn your next sales meeting, resolution-conflict discussion, or soccer-planning meeting into a think tank?

- Be aware: get in touch with the signals.
- Turn the meeting room on its ear.
- Break out the Toys for Thinking.

Be Aware: Get in Touch with the Signals

Earlier, we discussed five signals—"stuckness," lack of insight, no time, globalization, devalued workers—that set off warning alarms on a daily basis. Meeting environments are no different; they are often full of barriers that block productivity. These barriers stifle innovative and intuitive potential, actually sanctioning mindlessness as an acceptable mode of operation. To experience a transformational shift, you need to be in tune. In many cases, a "crash of thunder" is the only way to jar loose the barriers in these business environments.

There are three persistent conditions that create mindless environments:

1. *Visionus myopius* occurs when normal day-to-day interactions temporarily blind individuals to new opportunities, or when a "We know what's best" attitude develops, preventing new ideas from ever being envisioned.

2. *Idearial arcticosis* is prevalent in organizations that build strength over time, but also build resistance to change, and often is noticed when a "That's not how we do it around here" attitude develops, placing limits on the flow of ideas.

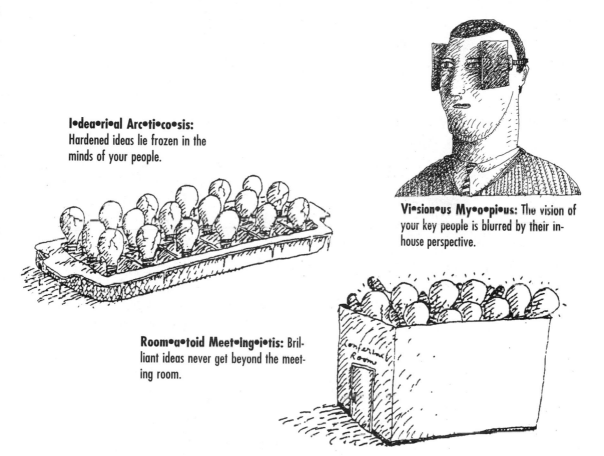

I•dea•ri•al Arc•ti•co•sis: Hardened ideas lie frozen in the minds of your people.

Vi•sion•us My•o•pi•us: The vision of your key people is blurred by their in-house perspective.

Room•a•toid Meet•Ing•i•tis: Brilliant ideas never get beyond the meeting room.

3. *Roomatoid meetingitis* happens when ideas leave the drawing board but organizations don't have a system in place for implementing them, or a "We'll take this up at our next meeting" attitude develops, losing the momentum and the valuable ideas generated in today's meeting.

Turn the Meeting Room on Its Ear

Probably one of the simplest things you can do to counteract these common problems is to turn the meeting room on its ear. At Apple Computer, they name their meeting rooms "Dorothy,"

"Toto," and so on to stress that there's a wizard in everyone, a powerful resource worth exploring.[3] Faith Popcorn creates "communities for thinking," while Dr. NakaMats has a static room and a dynamic room.[4] Creating esprit de corps and a free-flowing environment does not come without risk. Understanding the thinking process goes hand in hand with developing the ideal backdrop, a conducive environment for producing results.

At the outset of his career Ernest Hemingway wrote sitting in cafés during the early morning hours. After a stint of five hours a day, he quit. Duke Ellington composed many of his pieces on trains, evidently taking advantage of the rhythmic clacking and motion of the cars. And when he was in the throes of a project, Thomas Edison slept in his laboratory, sometimes on a table, so that he could start right up when he awoke.[5] Are you ready to turbocharge your meeting?

Imagine your eighteen-foot mahogany boardroom table scattered with bags of bee pollen—not set up with your typical executive tools of legal pads and sharpened pencils—and on the walls around the table are pictures of fat bumblebees. Every time the participants look at the bee pollen, they remember the purpose of their think tank—to cross-pollinate each other's ideas. The bee motif reinforces their purpose and adds an energizing, humorous theme. This deliberately prepared environment frees the participants to banish their adult stuckness and release their more spontaneous, creative selves.

Many boardrooms are judged by the style of the chairs around the table rather than the results produced by those sitting in them. Those days are gone! The speed with which you accomplish your objectives directly relates to your energy level. So don't look toward those soft, cushy chairs for help. Eye contact is a source of energy. When eyes meet eyes, we're better off. Arrange your chairs to give each person as much eye contact with others as possible. Remember, you want to maximize the energy, not stifle it.

Be proactive, aware of and prepared for change. Plan to deliberately transform the environment of your next meeting. Think about freeing individuals from their "institutionalized conditions" so that they

can think differently. One way to do this is to look at the hundred small changes you could make to affect your meeting environment. Start with the chairs and consider these ideas:

- Only have enough chairs in the room for the number of people present. *Rationale:* A full table diminishes the gaps in the group caused by empty chairs.

- Use stacking chairs; place them outside the meeting and ask the participants to carry them in themselves. *Rationale:* This allows the group to determine the design space of the meeting.

- For the fun of it, have the participants switch chairs from the right side of the table to the left side. *Rationale:* When you want people to think expansively, go over to the right side; if you want a logical pattern, move back to the left.

- Don't have any chairs! *Rationale:* It keeps people's thoughts crisp, clean, and to the point. More meetings finish on time (often the biggest meeting pitfall) when the chairs are removed. Corning Inc., Equitable Companies Incorporated, and Johnson & Johnson have also joined the stand-up-meeting brigade. "It does work," said one Corning vice president. "No question about it. People don't b.s. They get right to the point because they hate to stand."[6]

Stand-up meetings have become part of the culture at Ritz-Carlton Hotel Co. Every morning at precisely 9:00 A.M., about eighty of the company's top executives gather for a ten-minute stand-up meeting in the hallway outside the office of president and COO Horst Shulze. "The meeting is part training, part operations, part philosophy—all conducted with drill-like efficiency," says Leonardo Inghilleri, senior vice president, human resources. "We work in a 7-days-a-week, 24-hours-a-day business, and our customers are diverse. Employees need to know how to think on their feet to solve a problem."[7]

Break Out the Toys for Thinking

As you work more with the Thunderbolt Model, you'll notice that many of the tips and techniques ask you to simulate a preschool setting, so it's only fitting to bring toys—also known as Toys for Thinking—to the boardroom table. Some successful toys—I mean tools—I have used include crystal balls, brightly colored tissue paper, metallic confetti shaped like stars or numbers, gold-covered chocolate coins, magnifying glasses, magic wands, noisemakers, and clear balloons that you can write on. Once you start, the ideas are limitless. Almost anything can be used.

"Never lose a holy curiosity."

Mindfully, I have used these toys to effectively accomplish the stated purpose of the meeting. Toys for Thinking trigger individuals back to their younger days. Acting as transformers, they serve as a means to bring play into the environment and release the inhibitions that we have created as adults. Toys for Thinking strengthen the link between play and energy, increasing the flow of blood to the brain and releasing energizing natural chemicals that stimulate fresh thinking.

Finally, Toys for Thinking become instrumental in releasing tension. Designed to help participants through difficult periods, they are often just the thing to break the ice, cool off the boiler, ease through a tough issue, free the logjam, kick-start the engine, diffuse the anger, ease the confrontation, and curb the egos.

With toys on the table, the group can't help but work well together, producing effective results from the informal and relaxed atmosphere. The success of most groups depends on the way the individuals feel

✓ **CHECKLIST**

DELIBERATELY CHANGING THE ENVIRONMENT

Check off the items below that you need to act on in order to turbocharge the environment:

_____ I actually think about the physical layout of the location of the meeting. I sketch a diagram and see if the room's layout enhances or detracts from our easy communication.

_____ I decide how to best design the room. I focus on the tables, lights, windows, air conditioning, and so on to maximize Thunderbolt Thinking.

_____ I list all the barriers that currently exist. I think of both tangible and intangible barriers (i.e., time of day, current business climate, and the topic itself).

_____ I determine what Toys for Thinking would break the barriers and energize the environment. I look around the office or at home to see what toys would match our project, topic, or issue.

_____ I create an outrageous theme that will directly reinforce the purpose of the meeting. I review the main concepts we want to cover and look for the threads that will hold it together.

_____ I think about how I can deliberately involve and energize the participants both before and after the meeting.

**NEED AN IDEA
ON THIS?**
See T•N•T 24,
Thunderbolt
Show and Tell.

about each other, whether or not they trust each other, and how enthusiastic they are about the stated purpose and the generation of outcomes.

During one of our projects with American National Bank, we brought together a mix of senior vice presidents from various functional areas to discuss how to manage the transition period as the bank worked through a major merger. Because of the dynamics created by the merger, we decided to lighten up the event by dubbing the session "The Meeting of the Chiefs," playing on the "powwow" motif. The theme was completed with bubble pipes and bubbles for each chief. Another example of how this can work happens at Enator, a Swedish consulting firm, where the rooms break with convention. How? In one meeting room, people have their conversations and meals at a table made from a grand piano. As a matter of fact, there's no space within the company where one's eyes don't meet the unexpected. Breaking with tradition forces the unpredictable to spring forth.[8]

Revitalize the thinking atmosphere.

Step 3 Fast Summary

For Thunderbolt Thinking, remember:

1 It's important to be aware of and prepare for change. Be proactive: look for the hundred small changes you could make in the environment (e.g., moving chairs, adjusting start and stop times, adding music, or serving interesting snacks).

2 Mindlessness creeps in slowly and deadens most of us. Don't get caught. Be mindful of opportunities that could turn your meeting around 180 degrees, such as bringing in a client to help solve the problem.

3 The three most common barriers to successful meetings are:

- *Visionus myopius:* The vision of your key people is blurred by their in-house perspective.

- *Idearial arcticosis:* Hardened ideas lie frozen in the minds of your people

- *Roomatoid meetingitis:* Brilliant ideas never get beyond the meeting room.

4 Toys for Thinking can break through barriers. They can bring out playfulness, release inhibitions, and energize the group and will free individuals from their institutionalized conditions to establish a new mind-set.

For Thunderbolt Thinking, ask yourself:

1 What barriers do we need to break down?

2 How can I energize the members throughout the meeting?

3 What outrageous toys (tools) could I bring to the meeting to expand our perspectives?

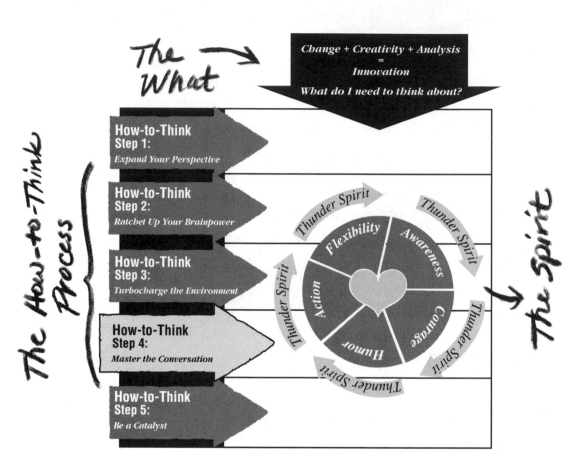

The What → Change + Creativity + Analysis = Innovation. What do I need to think about?

The How-to-Think Process

How-to-Think Step 1: *Expand Your Perspective*

How-to-Think Step 2: *Ratchet Up Your Brainpower*

How-to-Think Step 3: *Turbocharge the Environment*

How-to-Think Step 4: *Master the Conversation*

How-to-Think Step 5: *Be a Catalyst*

The Spirit — Thunder Spirit: Flexibility, Awareness, Courage, Humor, Action

The Thunderbolt Thinking Model

Step Four:
Master the Conversation

So far, we have talked about three elements of the Thunderbolt Model: perception, brains, and environment. We have discussed ideas to maximize our brainpower and have seen the effect the environment has on the success of a meeting and how it frees the brain to see things differently. Now, by deliberately guiding and explaining a conversation, we will also send the brain a very direct message. This fourth how-to step shows you how to master a conversation to get the best from a group.

How can you capture a conversation's power to turn your next budget review meeting, anniversary planning meeting, or food co-op update meeting into a think tank?

- Start by challenging the status quo.

- Jump-start your imagination.

- Understand how conversations flow.

- Master a discussion technique.

- Release the group's creative juices.

- Focus and narrow down the ideas.

- Orchestrate the conversation.

Start by Challenging the Status Quo

❝Not everything that counts can be counted, and not everything that can be counted counts. ❞

❝To me, what is wonderful about The Body Shop is that we still don't know the rules," Anita Roddick says. She adds, "Instead we have a basic understanding that to run this business you don't have to know anything."[1] Roddick honestly believes that having an MBA degree would have lessened her chances for success: she says that she went her own merry way working from gut instinct. However, The Body Shop did more than "go on its merry way." It now ranks as the largest and most profitable British cosmetics company.[2] Likewise, The Price Club, a billion-dollar retail discount warehouse chain, shattered all the basic rules: do anything to lure in the customers, focus on location, and offer long hours. Personally, I'm a member and I love the club. I'll travel to its offbeat location and don't even mind paying an

D R A W · A · P I C T U R E

How Do Your Meetings Flow?

For this exercise, think forward. Next week, you lead a strategy session, Girl Scouts' summer camp planning meeting, new-member orientation group. Picture yourself in front of your group. What would you like to happen? What breakthroughs in people's behaviors would you like to see? What are the things you want to do to generate powerful outcomes? Either draw a picture or write in your ideas below. As you think about this, gaze into the future; don't focus on the past. Really stretch to imagine the ultimate flow of your thinking and that of your group.

I Can Enhance the Flow of Our Thinking by:

THOUGHT ATTACK!

Think about potential barriers that could inhibit your thinking. Now write down all the ways you can think of to break those barriers.

_____

_____

_____

_____

_____

_____

_____

entrance fee because their prices are rock bottom. Besides, the crowds are just amazing to watch. It appears to be a real event for them.

Breakthroughs are experimental. They don't come from intellectual analysis. In most cases, it's a matter of finding the key and unlocking the door to your own perception.[3] With every breakthrough comes change and a new way of thinking. "The unconscious seems to take delight . . . in breaking through—and breaking up—exactly what we cling to most rigidly in our conscious thinking," according to Rollo May, author of *The Courage to Create*.[4] When breakthroughs alter what people consider to be the norm, they adjust slowly, so as change occurs, you'll need to help your people deal with it. The arrival of new thinking patterns and breakthroughs doesn't mean that everything you thought about yesterday is wrong, only that from today on, a greater share of the issues on which you spend time will be novel.[5] It means staying out of thinking ruts, becoming more aware, and developing a mindful state.

It is also important to understand that *breakthroughs don't always demand radical action;* sometimes the slightest shift in normal patterns (even if it goes against standard policies) can work wonders. Think for a moment about simple ways you could challenge the status quo, such as the ones shown in the table.

"The Way We've Always Done It":	Slight Shift:	Radical Action:	Desired Outcome:
9:00 A.M. Monday staff meeting	Start at 8:42 A.M. and only go to 9:00 A.M.	Don't hold meetings for a month	Evaluate whether you really need to meet at all
Paychecks issued every Friday	Select a "surprise payday" at least once per quarter that occurs before Friday	Pay a full month in advance	Demonstrate appreciation of employees

Jump-Start Your Imagination

Earlier we mentioned that even if your imagination was stifled in younger years, the good news is that your grown-up brain retains the same resilience and capability to imagine and be intuitive that it had in your childhood. Now, "You need to shake your mind free from the routines and conventions of adult thinking that can so easily enslave it," suggests Jack Maguire in *The Care and Feeding of the Brain*.[6] For the Thunderbolt Model to work, this is very true.

Unfortunately, not realizing the imagination's incredible value, we don't call upon it as a vital business tool. We rarely capitalize on the power of the human imagination to leap forward and create a solution that makes sense in the business environment. We're way too sophisticated. Business as usual means only examining the realities you see and confront every day. This mind-set typically halts a breakthrough before it begins. Opportunities to explore options using our imagination are often squelched by someone who has the "answer" already.

Capitalizing on the powerhouse of imagination by using the Thunderbolt Model should be a critical task for all managers. For the fun of it, conduct an informal survey with your people and see when their imagination is most alive. Headlines, USA, a Houston-based advertising firm, did this and found that sitting on the toilet was number one. Responding to the needs of a new market niche, they now place printed advertising in public restrooms. Headlines' president got the idea while reading a newspaper posted above the facilities in a Houston restaurant.[7] Here are some ways to jump-start managers' imaginations:

- As soon as a meeting starts, have the managers draw a picture of what they think the outcomes of the meeting will look like. Revealing what they *imagine* will occur by the end of the meeting often results in some interesting agenda adjustments, and a lot of buy-in from the group.

- Ask the group to recycle common, everyday *dust* into a real money-making venture. Because this is so completely ridiculous, groups usually feel it's okay to let go, and energy starts to flow. Just at that moment, capture that energy and deliberately move the group toward their real purpose by asking them to focus the energy on the topic of the meeting. This process creates a fertile environment to explore the issues at hand and often shakes up the results.

- Give this quick overview to the group: How do you light up a room? Basically, a turbine takes an energy source, heat, and drives a generator to produce another form of energy, electricity, delivered through power lines to a switch. However, it's not until you flip the switch that the light comes on, the room is illuminated, and you can see. Now ask: How can we Thunderbolt our organization? Basically, we tap into the power of the group, allowing our ideas to flow and grow in a process that turns raw thought into solid out-

NEED AN IDEA ON THIS? See T•N•T 4, Brain Jolts.

comes. However, it's not until we add a catalyst that the group experiences its real power. Ask what catalyst can be added to your situation, solution, or ideas.

When we transcend and break through our normal thinking patterns, a flow state emerges. We become focused and emotionally involved, we see more sharply, and Boom!—a solution arrives. The idea emerges and the group gels. In this flow state, you are Thunderbolting.

Understand How Conversations Flow

During most interactions, as thoughts and energy flow between the participants, you must know when to let loose and break out wildly, outrageously, and ridiculously and when to curb the whimsical, channeling your thought patterns and turning off your curiosity. It takes a delicate balance to create the optimal blend of both creative and analytical thinking. It is important to sense the point when

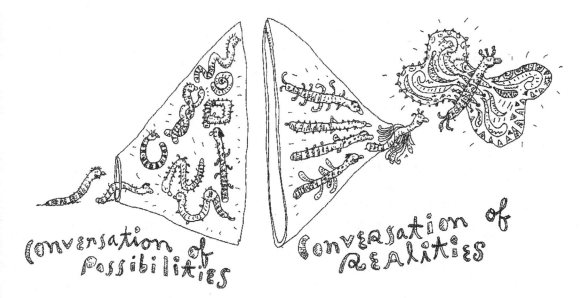

conversation of Possibilities

Conversation of REALities

all the pieces fall together: the group is at its peak, Thunderbolting, and its momentum carries it to a new plateau. This can't happen if the faucet shuts off too quickly, if the germs of ideas are trampled before they are given a chance to mature, or if people's emotions are bruised because egos get in the way. Mastering the conversation calls for you to walk a tightrope, with both arms open and extended to keep your balance.

The flow of conversation usually starts with free-form idea generation and then moves on to point-by-point analysis of each step. Being aware of both the *conversation of possibilities* (creative thinking) and the *conversation of realities* (analytical thinking) during the interaction, and being skilled in directing those conversations, are essential to mastering the fourth step of the Thunderbolt Model.

NEED AN IDEA ON THIS?
See T•N•T 15, Hidden Communication.

Creative thinking, an expansive activity, takes what we already know and combines it into new relationships, bringing to life new images and new ideas. It is not orderly, reasonable, or predictable. We know creativity when we see it in art, science, and other fields, but it seems like a mystery to most of us. Yet this ability to be inspired, innovative, or inventive has caused civilizations to evolve. Analytical thinking, a narrowing-down activity, draws upon known facts and principles to produce conclusions. Logic causes us to ask, Of all the known methods, which is best? It is a powerful tool for classifying and evaluating information, providing a way for us to pull our intuitive ideas together. Through analytical thinking, we connect the gems produced during creative, expansive thought.

Allowing participants to expand and develop all their fresh ideas *before* the final selection or analysis is made is essential, yet difficult. The distance between the master and the fool is a powerful space. It takes courage to walk the tightrope over the vacuum of the unknown. For effective thinking to take place you need guts. Allow your people to have both the conversation of possibilities and the conversation of realities. Remember, the successful meeting drives toward the most effective outcome, *not* just the answer as it is defined by a select few.

Master a Discussion Technique

Leonardo da Vinci invented a whole-brain discussion technique called displayed thinking—also known as storyboarding—to aid him in managing his network of enterprises and directing his zigzag thinking as he simultaneously immersed himself in architecture, painting, city planning, science, and engineering. This technique has been further enhanced by The Walt Disney Company in the planning, development, and operation of its theme parks and resorts; today many national and international organizations use storyboarding.

In 1985, I was trained by Jerry McNellis of the McNellis Group, Pittsburgh, Pennsylvania, and since then I have used displayed thinking as a technique to direct conversations that involve strategic planning, project evaluation, the development of new products, and other areas. So technically, I'm a direct descendant of Leonardo da Vinci! As a dynamic give-and-take technique, I like displayed thinking because it allows you to incorporate both the conversation of possibilities and the conversation of realities.

With displayed thinking, each participant's ideas and suggestions rate equally; they are recorded on color-coded index cards, then posted on large panels. Because no one's thoughts are ignored or bypassed, the process encourages everyone to contribute freely: this is the conversation of possibilities. During subsequent discussions, the group sifts, funnels, and reorganizes the cards as they work through the process to find the usable outcomes: this is the conversation of realities. Thunderbolting shines here because displayed thinking guides the participants to choose the most effective approach, not just the one that might have seemed "right." Visual representation keeps the conversation and participants focused, stimulates the flow of new ideas, and encourages participation.

In the end, it doesn't matter what techniques you use. The important thing is to allow the participants to expand and develop their ideas *before* selecting the ideas you will use. Being aware of both conversa-

Leonardo da Vinci

A true Renaissance man, Leonardo was an incredibly versatile, far-reaching, and talented genius. He not only had a penetrating influence on sixteenth-century art, but his scientific research and observations were considerably more advanced than others of his time.

Leonardo, with his keen powers of visual acuity, left us a magnificent legacy in his fabulous notebooks. His exceptional talent and brilliant imagination were demonstrated through thousands of exquisite illustrations, sketches, and designs documented by detailed notes. Outlined in his drawings are streams of consciousness, illustrating "patterns of flow and counterflow," which give us insight into his imaginative abilities as he was inventing and creating.

There was ultimate unity in Leonardo's work, driven by his "process of vision." Working first with his eye and mind, he then went on to complete his projects with his hands. Captivated by creative power, he alternated between bursts of intense activity and periods of contemplation. His intellectual powers were stimulated and enhanced by his immense world of visional phenomena, leading to a legacy of influential achievements.

Displayed Thinking Discussion Technique

1. **Participants are presented with a topic to explore.**

2. **Discussion proceeds until all of the participants have an opportunity to express their opinions, ideas, and suggestions.**

3. **Options are reviewed and discussed.**

4. **Participants select the ideas they think are most workable.**

5. **Thunderbolt outcomes result.**

tions prepares you to direct the thinking most productively. I have used the displayed thinking technique successfully for years. However, other techniques work just as well. Remember, the key is to *first* expand and collect ideas, *then* direct your group members toward the final selection of ideas.

Release the Group's Creative Juices

Listed below are tips that will assist you in directing a conversation. No matter who the group is or what its size, three helpful rules apply: (1) always do something to loosen up the group, (2) include a specific way to create a team spirit, and (3) encourage the group to produce concrete, specific ideas so you come up with solid suggestions and not vague ones. When people are talking, make sure to capture the verb when you write down the thought. The idea or thought will be more complete because it includes an action. And afterward, it will be easier to summarize the ideas that were developed.

For a conversation of possibilities, try these mind-expanding suggestions:

NEED AN IDEA ON THIS?
See T•N•T 30, The Flash Cap.

Breakout Inventory

Call a break between the possibility and reality conversations. Don't go more than ninety minutes without taking some type of break. Here are some ideas:

- Offer food that echoes the theme (not *too* much sugar). During a "Famous Partners" session, we served fish and chips, cream cheese and bagels, strawberries with cream, and peanut butter and jelly. The purpose of the session was to maximize the unique talents of the staff members by having them partner with each other.

- Bring along a tape recorder and play lively music. We've had selections that ranged from Jane Fonda exercise tapes to custom-tailored music like "On the Road Again" for a group of commercial truck and bus drivers.

- Move the break outdoors and encourage people to get fresh air.

- Offer simple ways to stretch and increase blood circulation. A child's jump rope adds a whole new dimension to a fifteen-minute recess.

"Whoever undertakes to set himself up as a judge in the field of Truth and Knowledge is shipwrecked by the laughter of the gods."

- *Limit releasing:* Accept a continuous flow of ideas regardless of their relevance to the matter under discussion, validity in your own thinking process, or correctness as applied to the topic.

- *Thunder wondering:* Let the "raw ideas" cook by building in relaxation periods so you can invite and explore daydreams. During this wondering period, the brain unconsciously transfers solutions, designs, or characteristics from unconnected objects to the problem or situation. Then there comes a moment of inspiration when the idea or solution bubbles up to your consciousness.

- *Strategic humor:* Establish a "play framework" so imagination, flexibility, and risk taking can flourish.

- *Common insight:* Encourage new ideas stimulated by the ideas of others, add new ideas to a current situation, or build and refine ideas into a concrete state. Intensify the conversation by allowing the power of each member's unconscious to work within the group dynamics.

- *Opportunistic visioning:* Look for new patterns, such as uses for failed ideas; see in nontraditional ways; see opportunities in unexpected events. Encourage brain patterns to go across, under, around, and over the situation and explore all possible ideas. Force the group to interrupt its habitual, organized thought processes and leap sideways out of the ingrained patterns. When that happens, the brain often links unrelated patterns to solve problems or come up with new ideas.

Focus and Narrow Down the Ideas

A conversation of realities occurs when you are evaluating ideas, narrowing in on workable solutions, running risk analyses, and preparing to carry the ideas into action in a linear way. In directing the conversation of realities, you need to establish:

- *Agreed-upon criteria:* These are evaluative measures that identify the stated parameters of the project, program, or outcome. Use them to select, test, and revise one or more ideas from all the ideas generated.

- *A search for the principle:* Begin this by evaluating an idea—"objecting to it"—and examining its weak points, faults, and fallacies.

Comic Relief

Mark Twain's dry wit often adds comic relief to many of my clients' thinking sessions. Here is why. Sometimes a few participants are hesitant to jot down their ideas on the index cards. After years of experience, I realized that their reluctant behavior is really a fear of misspelling. When you think of it, this shouldn't be a major surprise. The overriding fear of getting it wrong comes directly from our educational system. When I suspect this, I quickly quote Twain: "I don't give a damn for a man that can spell a word only one way." Immediately, the tension evaporates and group members feel free to express their ideas and worry about spelling later.

Then return to the principle behind the idea and see if you can work with it to build something useful.

- *Point-to-point thinking:* In point-to-point thinking, one thought directly follows another. Draw conclusions based on logic: one thing following another in logical order for systematic application.

Orchestrate the Conversation

Working with SmithKline Beecham Pharma Inc., I developed a series of strategy sessions to help them work through a major product repositioning and development initiative. The sessions incorporated a lot of freewheeling idea generation, often using toys and other resources to stimulate ideas. Throughout the process, the participants wrote down their ideas on three-by-five-inch cards and then displayed them on large wallboards around the room. Then, in order to get them involved, I broke them into small groups where ideas were developed more fully and presented to the larger group.

Since this was such an intense project, I deliberately peppered the sessions with fun activities to keep the participants' thinking fresh. During one exercise, as a debriefing, I had them use toothpaste to "draw" how they felt about the outcomes achieved during the day. What ensued was a dynamic discussion that provided some valuable insights for the follow-up session. By using both creative and analytical techniques, participants were able to analyze major trends in the marketplace, generate ideas, formulate an action plan to better position them against their competitors, and ultimately move their product back on target. In the end the president reported that the initiative was one of the most successful he had seen in the company.

Humor is power—use it strategically.

Step 4 Fast Summary

For Thunderbolt Thinking, remember:

1 The distance between the master and the fool is a powerful space. All creation springs from this empty vacuum. It takes courage to walk this distance.

2 The brain absorbs, stores, and recalls information more efficiently in pictures, images, and events than it does in words. Make sure to use a visually dynamic technique to direct your conversations. Capture individual responses and display them so others can build on the idea.

3 Analytical thinking inhibits creative thinking, but creative thinking is useless without analytical thinking. For extraordinary results you need both. Encourage your group to have both conversations of possibilities and conversations of realities.

4 The key to successful thinking is driving toward the most effective outcome, not just the "right" answer as defined by a few.

For Thunderbolt Thinking, ask yourself:

1 What is our purpose? What do we need to know by the end of our time together?

2 How can I make sure that both conversations of possibilities and conversations of realities take place?

3 What visual discussion technique am I most comfortable using to direct the conversation?

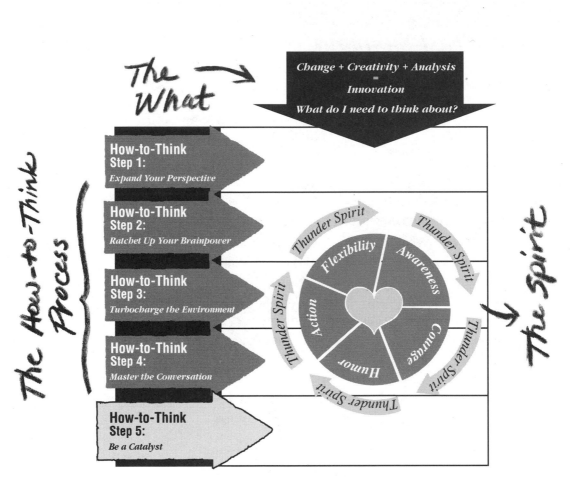

The What

Change + Creativity + Analysis
=
Innovation

What do I need to think about?

The How-to-Think Process

How-to-Think
Step 1:
Expand Your Perspective

How-to-Think
Step 2:
Ratchet Up Your Brainpower

How-to-Think
Step 3:
Turbocharge the Environment

How-to-Think
Step 4:
Master the Conversation

How-to-Think
Step 5:
Be a Catalyst

The Spirit

Thunder Spirit

Flexibility

Awareness

Action

Courage

Humor

Thunder Spirit

Thunder Spirit

Thunder Spirit

The Thunderbolt Thinking Model

CHAPTER

Step Five: Be a Catalyst

In alchemy, salt is the final distilling agent cited as essential to the transformation of primitive matter, the *prima materia,* into the philosophers' stone, which has the power to transmute baser metals into gold. In its common form salt symbolizes the original raw

"The bitter and the sweet come from the outside, the hard from within, from one's own efforts. "

material and brings the distilling process full circle. Adding salt to the raw material in the presence of mercury and sulfur makes the transformation complete. From the salt grain grows the philosopher's stone. From a creator's germ grows a work of genius.[1] This final how-to step brings the WHAT, HOW, and SPIRIT full circle. The blending of each component depends on the ultimate actions taken by you—the catalyst.

How can you achieve extraordinary outcomes as a catalyst to turn your next board of directors' meeting, neighborhood watch meeting, or vacation planning meeting into a think tank?

- Blend the catalyst with the facilitator.
- Invent your own catalytic style.
- Cultivate your skills as a catalyst.

Blend the Catalyst with the Facilitator

The catalyst serves as a change agent, speeding something up or slowing it down. He or she is as essential to the group's thinking process as a conductor is to a symphony, a coach to a team, a general to an army. This person first breaks down environmental barriers, then eases the group through the process, and finally builds bridges toward productive results. The catalyst is the one who steps out in front and uses the Thunderbolt Model to promote the transformational shift, essentially igniting the thinking. This change agent helps to unstick group members by creating a thinking environment with the Thunderbolt Model, activating the shift that revolutionizes thinking.

The catalyst uses Toys for Thinking—tools that trigger individuals back to their school days and allow them to think freely—without reprimanding them as their teachers once did. Through the catalyst, a free, safe climate invites humor and encourages people to have fun, allowing them to delve into the recesses of their brains where they normally don't go. Finally, the catalyst must obliterate the traditional

D R A W · A · P I C T U R E

How Does a Catalyst Look?

Cat·a·lyst *n.* a substance that speeds up or slows down
a chemical reaction but that itself is not changed.

Draw a picture of yourself as a catalyst. Definitely let yourself experiment with this. Focus on being a change agent, and allow your hand to flow. For the fun of it, draw this picture with your opposite hand. To help you, think about people (a co-worker, support staff, your kids), places (your office, a particular space in your building, your home), and things (time of day, music you like) that can slow down or speed up your thinking.

Me as a Catalyst:

THOUGHT ATTACK!

Write down five things, words, or phrases that come to mind when you think of a catalyst:

1. _____

2. _____

3. _____

4. _____

5. _____

schoolroom mode and liberate individuals to move beyond their wildest expectations and fully use their brainpower. He or she shatters the prevailing cultural trance of "business as usual" so prevalent in many organizations.

The catalyst is you. However, when you have too large a stake in the outcome to be bias-free, you will need to blend in the skills of a facilitator. This outside person could be a colleague acting as the chairperson, an appointed inside facilitator, or an outside consultant. As an "honest broker," this bias-free person should not have a stake in the outcome and should become transparent as the group moves toward its stated purpose and produces outcomes. The facilitator will help you and the group through the process while remaining detached from the outcomes.

As a nonpartisan guide, this facilitator reinforces the need to listen, focus, and hear one another out; it is within this atmosphere that

NEED AN IDEA ON THIS? See T•N•T 13, The Garbage Bag Dump.

ideas, solutions, and answers emerge. The facilitator continuously reads the group's feedback signals and fosters collaborative teamwork, but intervenes only when needed to help the group achieve its purpose.

Invent Your Own Catalytic Style

S ince kindergarten, schooling has been aimed at achieving goals, rather than being mindful of the process by which they were achieved. We were taught to squelch curiosity, fear failure, and prevent any new nontraditional ideas from popping out; eventually we conformed, because creative thought became uncomfortable. We became *stuck*.

Our school experience may have been profound, but as a catalyst, you can reverse the cycle and rekindle the creative juices in your organization. You can inspire the shift from "We can't have fun and must be businesslike" to "We can have fun and produce even more meaningful results," a shift from rigid rules and regulations to relaxation and a freewheeling spirit, a shift from one right answer to exploring all possibilities, a shift from holding back to breaking out.

NEED AN IDEA ON THIS?
See T•N•T 23, Thought Walk.

Cultivate Your Skills as a Catalyst

There are two types of skills that will help you develop a Thunderbolt catalyst style: *group process skills* and *personal development skills*. Group process skills involve seeking information, clarifying, negotiating, planning, organizing, and facilitating. Personal development skills are maturity, bias-free attitudes, a sense of humor, and whole-brain thinking.

The following ideas can enhance your group process skills:

- *Seek information, thoughts, and ideas from the group:* Involve others by seeking information before reaching a conclusion, encouraging others to make contributions, and developing cooperation and openness.

"Peace cannot be kept by force. It can only be achieved by understanding."

- *Clarify:* Reach an understanding of what others are saying by asking questions and/or summarizing to check the accuracy of what has been said or implied.

- *Negotiate:* This is done through a give-and-take process and brings about consensus, often with divergent positions being traded between individuals; obtain commitment on clear, achievable goals.

- *Plan and organize:* This is used for a system and for identifying the group's actions, risks, and responsibilities; use this skill in planning the how-to step to run the meeting as well as to sort through the content (the WHAT) to be covered.

- *Facilitate:* Help others to focus and provide insight and direction; this skill allows you to think on your feet and use supportive behaviors to handle group dynamics.

These ideas can strengthen your personal development skills:

- *Display maturity:* You must be experienced and stable enough so that your ego does not ride on the outcome of the meeting, and you should be able to show genuine caring for people and ideas.

✓ **C H E C K L I S T**

IGNITING THE PROCESS

Put an "X" next to the statements that best describe the action steps you need to take.

_____ I will determine if I should facilitate, or if I should ask an independent inside or outside person to be the facilitator.

I will review the list of group process or personal development skills and determine which ones I need to brush up on or learn so that I can be an effective catalyst.

_____ I will list all the techniques that have worked well in past meetings. I plan to use them again.

_____ I will develop my sense of humor. Where do I need to lighten up?

_____ I will visit my humor library before I go to the meeting.

Need a T•N•T power boost to get your spirit moving? See Matrix 2.

- *Remain bias-free:* Stay free from emotional ties to the topic to be discussed and distanced enough from the topic to handle and ensure both the positive and negative sides of the conversation. If you are not, get an outside facilitator.

- *Use whole-brain thinking:* Combine techniques of both left- and right-brain thinking.

Add the salt and trigger results.

FLASH ⚡

Step 5 Fast Summary

For Thunderbolt Thinking, remember:

1 A catalyst ignites the process; get your group energized to go the extra mile. Break down barriers and then build bridges.

2 A catalyst knows when to blend with a facilitator who is:

- A nonpartisan guide
- An honest broker
- Bias-free

3 Even if you feel creatively stifled, the wonderful potential within you can be awakened! The best way to unleash your potential? Use Toys for Thinking.

4 Practice, planning, and preparation are three critical factors in developing both group process and personal development skills.

For Thunderbolt Thinking, ask yourself:

1 What is my personal investment in the meeting's outcome?

2 Am I bias-free? Can I be the facilitator?

3 Who else demonstrates the right personal and group process skills to be our catalyst? Is he or she an inside person? An outside person?

PART FOUR

Thunderbolting:
When and How to Use It

A Zero-Based Meeting Attitude— Here's How

In the seventeenth century, an edict was passed by the lord protector of England, Oliver Cromwell, that in order to curtail the savage practices of some of his troops (ranging from pillaging to murder), a new procedure would be initiated. The offending soldier and his entire company would assemble underneath the local gallows and hold a meeting. This meeting would consist of rolling dice. Everyone would participate. The man who lost would be hanged. Not necessarily the instigator of the crime, but simply the man who lost. The results were fewer crimes, fewer troops—and fewer meetings.[1]

Tame the Meeting Monster

Do you suffer from meeting mania? Is the meeting you just scheduled really necessary? What are your alternatives? Do you need to convey a message? Put it in a memo. Do you have to make an urgent decision? Take executive action yourself. Do you need group input? Call one or two individuals and survey their feelings. At Doublet Manufacturing, Inc., the executives don't have formal meetings because they get together to

Break These Seven Meeting Myths

1. Meetings are powerful when the meeting leader is successful.

2. Meetings are beneficial when the participants are courteous.

3. Meetings are inevitable; poor meetings are a fact of life.

4. Meetings are a way to resolve conflict for a difficult situation.

5. Meetings are a valid method for getting an immediate response.

6. Meetings are good management because they "touch base" with everyone.

7. Meetings are a sound vehicle for developing a sense of belonging.

open the mail every day. "It only takes half an hour, forty-five minutes at most. And we never have to have formal meetings, because we get together every day," says past president Christophe Morin. The idea came from their $30 million French parent company, whose executives also get together every morning at mail time.[2]

Since there is often a huge time commitment involved, meetings either add something to a person's life or take something away. Sadly, for many people, meetings take something away, and too often, when the meeting is over, the feeling is one of relief.[3] At Motorola, consultant Philip Thomas not only tames the monster, but tries to encourage a higher level of performance with freed-up meeting time. He says, "I tell people—why not chop your staff meetings in half and accomplish the same thing? . . . If you used to have a six-hour staff meeting—cut it down to two hours. And tell everyone there, 'I just gave you four hours. . . . I want you to go back and do the same thing with your people.' "[4]

A Virginia Beach, Virginia, company, Linda L. Miles & Associates, which gives more than one hundred training seminars a year to health care professionals and their staffs, dreamed up the Tardy Kitty: for every minute someone is late to a meeting, the culprit must pitch one dollar into the kitty. At the end of the quarter, the accumulated fines fund a night out for the staff. Grateful seminar attendees tell Miles that chronic latecomers are now prompt. "The key to its success is that there are no exceptions, because it is usually the leader who is coming late," Miles observes.[5]

66I believe, on the whole, that love is a better teacher than sense of duty. 99

In this fast-paced world, meetings can be an ideal forum for making decisions. Yet meetings often end up as buffers, as a convenient way to avoid making a choice, taking a stand, or reaching a decision. "In [PepsiCo's] freewheeling culture, a committee is defined as 'a dark alley down which ideas are led . . . to be strangled.'"[6] When meetings at a software company were multiplying geometrically, the programmers stepped in to control the monster. They said, "We're fed up with meetings. In fact, we're so fed up with interminable meetings that waste our time, we've begun to take drastic measures to show how useless they are."[7] The company introduced a taxi-type meter that pops up on the computer screen to show participants how much the meeting is costing per minute—accounting for individuals' billable time and overhead cost.

Provide Relief from the Pressure Cooker

Our goal is to build productive, healthy companies. Not to do more of the same. Meetings that stretch beyond their point of productivity, meetings that are held "just because," and frequent, important "sacred cow" meetings steep us deeper in time's pressure cooker. Watch out, because the lid at your place could blow off!

The late Melia Peavey, while she was COO of Peavey Electronics Corporation, a 2,400-employee electronic musical instrument manufacturer in Meridian, Mississippi, cut down on unproductive meetings by taking her staff meetings directly to the trouble spot. "When you're cooped up in a meeting room the problem seems remote," she said.

"By going to the site you get decisions rolling quickly. The different managers can pick up on what needs fixing. You can stop and question employees on the spot, rather than hearing second-hand what's going on."[8]

Here are eight more innovative ways *not* to hold a meeting:

1. Institute a "meeting patrol team" to inspect the conference room hourly. Fine any groups that overstay the hour limit.

2. Create an outrageous reward system for the person or department holding the fewest meetings per week.

3. Purchase a nifty phone system that makes it easy and fun to receive and leave messages. Get creative with your voice-mail system by rotating greetings that "spoof" the boss.

4. Fax the information and ask for a faxed reply.

5. Draft a summary memo, including three to four thoughtful, straightforward specific questions that recipients can respond to via a written message.

6. Invest in the new computer-conferencing software that stages a "meeting" in real time, while each individual interacts from his or her own office setting.

7. Create a daily electronic newsletter. Fargo Electronics, a Minnesota-based specialty manufacturer of printers, countered employees' threats of daily meetings with a charged idea: a daily electronic newsletter. The president was sure it would be faster and more informative. "It's been great for eliminating surprises," he commented. "If problems with a product keep coming up in the newsletter, no one's shocked when we discontinue it."[9]

8. Do it! It's all right to take action yourself instead of calling a meeting.

THUNDER METER

THUNDER MEETINGS

After reading each statement below, rate your performance as a leader at your last team meeting, audit committee, or marking review session. Using a scale from 1 to 10, fill in the blanks and add up your score. Then look at the Thunder Meter for an instant flash reading of your performance.

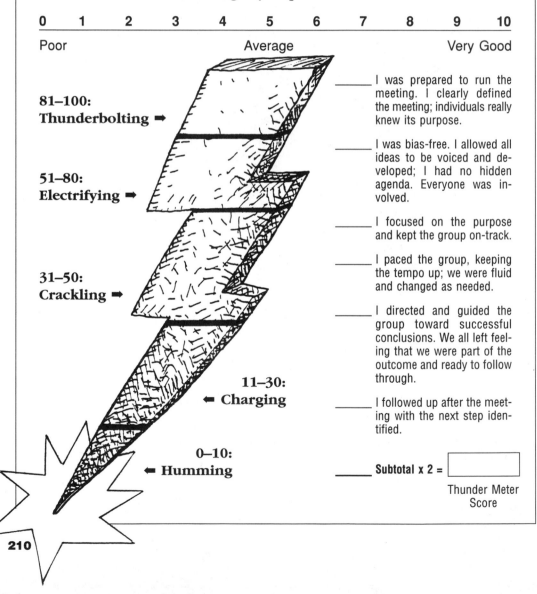

| 0 | 1 | 2 | 3 | 4 | 5 | 6 | 7 | 8 | 9 | 10 |

Poor   Average   Very Good

**81–100:
Thunderbolting** ➡

_____ I was prepared to run the meeting. I clearly defined the meeting; individuals really knew its purpose.

_____ I was bias-free. I allowed all ideas to be voiced and developed; I had no hidden agenda. Everyone was involved.

**51–80:
Electrifying** ➡

_____ I focused on the purpose and kept the group on-track.

_____ I paced the group, keeping the tempo up; we were fluid and changed as needed.

**31–50:
Crackling** ➡

_____ I directed and guided the group toward successful conclusions. We all left feeling that we were part of the outcome and ready to follow through.

_____ I followed up after the meeting with the next step identified.

**11–30:
⬅ Charging**

**0–10:
⬅ Humming**

_____ **Subtotal x 2 =** [   ]

Thunder Meter
Score

Centuries-Old Pitfalls

Whether you are observing through the "looking glass" or facing meetings on a daily basis, you will notice that common traps plague most meetings. Let's take a look at the most-cited drawbacks of meetings as reported in a survey we conducted with executives across the United States and Canada. Are any of these common barriers evident at your meetings?

- Apathy and boredom

- Running overtime

- Straying from one subject to another

- Talking at the same time

- Disruptions and personal attacks

- Win-lose approaches in decision making

- Unclear roles and responsibilities

- Chaos

- Lack of preparation and/or follow-up

Keeping participants focused on the meeting's purpose is a challenge even for the most skilled meeting leader. So it wasn't too much of a surprise, when we reviewed the survey data as reported by meeting leaders, to find that "straying from one subject to another" was their number-one pitfall. We also learned that 70 percent used written agendas "sometimes," "rarely," or "never." In addition, only 12 percent of the total respondents checked "always" when asked if they develop specific questions for each issue to be covered during the meeting. I can't help but think of the haunting lines from *Alice's Adventures in Wonderland,* when Alice asked the Cheshire-Cat, " 'Would you tell me, please, which way I ought to go from here?' 'That depends a good deal on where you want to get to,' said the Cat." [10] Questions guide and direct the group's thinking.

Meeting Images

When they were asked, "What one word best describes your meetings?" executives told us:

Let's hear it for meetings that are . . .

Accomplished
Concise
Constructive
Directional
Disciplined
Efficient
Fast
Focused

Stop, not another meeting that's . . .

Constipated
Disorganized
Dull
Endless
Frenzied
Frustrating
Imbalanced
Inefficient

"Mad as Hell" About Meetings?

Just how upset were executives, managers, consultants, and board presidents about meetings? I wanted to know, so we questioned them and found an enlightening answer. Although I thought my desk would be burning with red-hot anger pouring from the survey sheets, surprisingly, I found that not to be the case across the board.

SELF-ASSESSMENT

Mad as Hell

How mad are you about meetings? (Circle the number that applies.)

0	1	2	3	4	5	6	7	8	9	10

Not at All   Somewhat Mad   Mad as Hell!

Write down three reasons why you are mad and beside each one list the ways the Thunderbolt Model can help change your attitude:

1. _____

2. _____

3. _____

Instead, there was almost a counterbalance on each end of the scale. Eighty-one percent of the executives from small companies (0–10 employees) felt "not at all" to "somewhat" mad about meetings, while 53 percent of executives from large corporations (500+ employees) ranged from "somewhat" to "mad as hell" about meetings. It appears that in small organizations the meetings are better focused, are more efficient, and provide consistent ongoing follow-up to the participants, thus producing more powerful results.

Go Ahead and Hold a Meeting, But . . . !

"Although meetings should be a management tool," states George David Kieffer in *Success Magazine*, "they sometimes become weapons in the hands of terrorists, holding hours of

Meeting Basics

Which of these meeting basics do you use? (Place an "X" in the box that best describes your behavior.)

Meeting Basic	Never	Rarely	Sometimes	Always
Define the purpose: limit the scope of the meeting.				
Have a written agenda (with time frames outlined).				
Develop specific questions for each issue.				
Invite only those *essential* to the decisions.				
Address each item on the agenda.				
Provide all participants with an opportunity to contribute.				
Record the discussion and note the outcomes.				
Assure that follow-up action is assigned.				

salaried time hostage." [11] Understanding and applying the basics of the Thunderbolt Model can help to alleviate the threat of holding your employees or anyone else hostage. I summarize the basics this way:

1. Prepare, then tighten your focus on exactly what you want to accomplish.

2. Construct a blueprint to follow and have a timepiece handy.

3. Mix the right brains together, splashed with a dash of fun.

4. Call them into action.

This really boils down to one essential for me: *preparation.* Mark McCormack, business owner and author of *What They Don't Teach You at Harvard Business School* [12] and *The 110% $olution,* [13] is a planning fanatic. He's a wheeler-dealer who runs tight meetings. In an interview, he revealed this: "I never met a successful person who wasn't 100 percent prepared. Once you've learned the edge exceptional preparation gives, it becomes a lifelong habit." [14] Don't get confused; preparation is not just a before-meeting task. You must continually "prepare" for each stage of the meeting: before, during, and after. In our "Mad as Hell" survey, I was pleased to see the distribution of time spent on meetings. The results indicated that of the 49 percent of overall time people spent in meetings, 12 percent was spent in preparation; 25 percent was spent in the actual meeting, and 12 percent was invested in the follow-up.

"Invested" is exactly what I mean, because every meeting sends a message. The message you want to transmit is: "It was worth it to attend." Preparation ahead of time ensures that you'll have strong follow-up on the agreed-upon actions. Transforming meeting hours into action steps becomes an exceptional investment for those who attended, you and others in your organization.

NEED AN IDEA ON THIS? See T•N•T 18, A Name Tag Is a Name Tag Is a Name Tag.

Prepare More, Excel More

The following are ideas for polishing your preparation skills:

- Establish this "golden rule" for all meetings: know precisely what you want to accomplish in every single meeting you run or attend.

- Create a solid agenda, but not one set in cement. Keep it pliable so you can adjust, flex, and stretch it as needed. Keep a flexible focus.

- Put as much information into a visual format as possible. We retain visual stimuli about 85 percent more effectively than if we just hear it. Draw pictures, diagrams, charts.

- Visualize. Mentally walk through the various scenarios for each stage of the meeting. Picture the outcomes you want.

- Help others: send out the agenda and other pertinent documents prior to the meeting, formulate key questions that will help prime the participants' thought processes, and deliberately ask for their commitment to action before they enter the room.

- Hold a dress rehearsal. A CEO of a graphics-imaging company in Dallas, Texas, wanted to stop employee gossip about his monthly board-of-directors' meetings, so he decided to hold dry runs of the meetings with his staff of ninety. "It goes over like gangbusters," he said. "Delivering the same spiel we give the board shows we respect employees' participation." Employees ask tough questions, which gears management up for the real McCoy the next day.[15]

Let me stress it again: planning is everything! Especially review the following two areas:

1. *Preplanning preparation:* Clearly define the problem or needs; outline all the topics that should be addressed. Make sure all your attendees agree.

2. *Tracking and monitoring:* Establish a system to make sure that results get put into action. Don't fall prey to the "nothing ever happens" syndrome. Make sure to plan ahead so that you can develop an action plan to carry your ideas forward.

Create a "Rules of Trust" Model

Many employees work their entire lives and never experience a positive meeting. What a waste! Not just of time, but of the valuable information that could have been communicated in each one of them. Every year during their birthday month, the 7,000-plus employees at Cisco Systems' headquarters in San Jose, California, receive an E-mail invitation to a "birthday breakfast" with CEO John Chambers. Several dozen employees show up each month to put their toughest questions directly to the CEO. "The birthday breakfast is the most effective vehicle for getting candid feedback from employees and for discovering potential problems," says Chambers. "If there's a gap between what the leadership says it's doing and what's actually happening, I'll find out about it at the birthday breakfast."[16]

Once a quarter, Valarie Wilson, while she was chair and CEO of Wilson Sculley Associates, Inc., would lift sagging spirits with a Saturday-morning QUIT (quarterly internal talks) meeting. Wilson believed that by seeing the numbers and plans typically reserved for board members, employees knew exactly where they fit in. But she's convinced that it was the entertaining and often offbeat presentations that really made the Saturday-morning meetings work. At one quarterly meeting that used a sports motif, managers announced lineup changes in the organizational chart; posted scores for profitability, sales, and overhead for the first half of the year; and unveiled the strategy for the second half of the year.[17]

Think about it, then wipe the slate clean. Now is when you have the opportunity to break the "monotonous meeting syndrome." Put away the *Robert's Rules of Order* and install Rules of Trust that focus on building on each other's ideas, instill commitment, and call for action.

“Science is the attempt to make the chaotic diversity of our sense-experience correspond to a logically uniform system of thought.”

NEED AN IDEA ON THIS?
See T•N•T 26,
The Shape of
Things to Come.

Start Now—The Power Is in the Moment

For your next meeting, make a mental note of these eight items and weave them into your thoughts as well as into the actual agenda. Well-functioning groups have:

1. *Clear role definition:* Participants know why they are together, what their purpose is, what the organization expects of them, and what they need to do.

2. *A high level of sensitivity:* Members demonstrate sensitivity and understanding of others' needs and expressions. They listen to and respect others' opinions.

3. *A relaxed atmosphere:* An informal exchange occurs between members. The discussions flow freely rather than tensely or formally.

4. *Good time control:* The leader pays attention to time. The meeting stops and starts as scheduled, unless participants have willingly agreed to extend the time.

5. *An interruption-free environment:* Participants have committed their attention to the meeting. There are few delays or interruptions.

6. *Acknowledgment of contributions:* The leader and participants recognize the individual contributions being made.

7. *Group check-ups:* Participants and the leader continually evaluate group performance. They adjust the agenda as needed.

8. *Lots of laughter:* All the members of the group are able to have a good laugh at themselves and others.

Notable Meetings in History

Listed below are whimsical accounts of meetings that each illustrate a simple lesson. Use them as a potential resource in your own meetings to drive home key points.

The First Officially Recorded Meeting

It was in a great setting, by today's standards; we would surely call it a resort. Some may even say it was ideal because only the decision makers were present, a small, tightly knit group of key individuals. In the garden, all was going according to plan until the break—whoever ordered the forbidden fruit didn't realize the weakness of the attendees. Well, the rest is history.

Lesson: *Be aware of snakes at your meetings.*

The Meeting Table

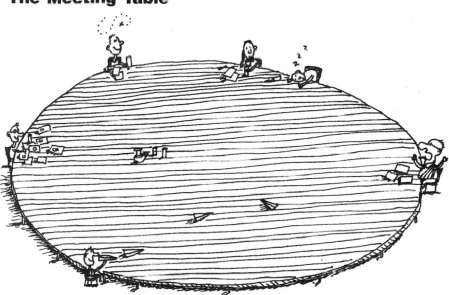

The meeting table often goes unnoticed and is taken for granted; it has been given little consideration over the years. But let's peek back into history. Where has the table made its mark?

The most noted table design was King Arthur's Round Table. But if the truth be known, it wasn't the shape that did Arthur in. The Round Table concept failed because Arthur was unable to hold together the alliances necessary to fulfill his objective of peace and unity throughout his kingdom. Objectives became clouded, leadership faded, and King Arthur's cause fell into oblivion.[18]

Lesson: *Articulate clearly the purpose of your meeting.*

Most of us consider the meeting table the place to do business. And that usually means that we sit around it. Well, history recounts a famous meeting where the table became an integral part of the message delivery system. In the late 1950s, international relationships were strained. The Cold War was in full swing and so was Khrushchev's arm as he pounded the meeting table with his shoe, while declaring aloud, "We will bury you." I never could quite figure out if he was addressing our country or an ant crawling across the table. I'd better look at those meeting minutes again.

Lesson: Understand the expectations of those who will attend.

Back in the spring of 1991, table design was still the main focus in a tremendously important meeting: the Middle East peace talks. If I recall correctly, it took weeks to decide the shape, size, and seating arrangements. If only he were here, King Arthur would have relished his circular table compared to the triangular design U.S. secretary of state James Baker had to deal with.

Lesson: The environment does affect the process and thus the outcomes.

Today, the Round Table is back, used in Canada as a radical political concept. The National Round Table has the potential of bringing undiluted thinking directly to the prime minister and the cabinet, circumventing the traditional route along which proposed laws usually travel. But the acid test for these Round Tables, within the next year, will be whether they can translate all their talk into action.

Lesson: Build in time to create a next-step action plan.

Look at Who's Coming and Who's Not

"Once upon a time a baby girl was born to a king and queen. In their joy, the royal couple invited the three good fairies of their kingdom to bestow magical gifts upon the tiny princess. At the cradle, the first fairy blessed the infant with incomparable beauty. The second fairy promised that the child would grow up to be as wise and good as she was beautiful. But before the third good fairy could present her gift, the witch Malevolent burst into the nursery. Furious at not having been invited to this event, she swore that when the child reached her sixteenth birthday, she would prick her finger upon a spinning wheel and die." Fortunately, the third fairy could countermand this evil curse. She decreed that the princess would prick her finger, but instead of dying, she would sleep for one hundred years, until Prince Charming awakened her with love's first kiss.[19]

Lesson: *Understand the impact on those who don't attend the meeting and the effect they can have on the outcomes.*

Obviously, Winston Churchill, Franklin D. Roosevelt, and Josef Stalin were three key guests at the crucial meeting in Malta where they sealed the Allies' final pact to defeat Hitler. What would have occurred if one of the three had not shown up?

Lesson: *Be aware of who the decision makers are, and make sure they are present.*

Speaking of not showing up, that's exactly what happened to one of our clients. However, it was done on purpose; *her* client "uninvited" her to a meeting after the initial invitation had been made. Teasingly, we call this the Meeting from Hell. Apparently, after reviewing the report our client was to deliver, the president of her client's firm couldn't deal with the conclusions drawn from the study and determined that "it would be best" for the company to withhold the information. In retrospect, my client was glad she didn't attend. However, she did report to me that the opportunity to really effect change would have been worth the challenge of facing the president head-on. On reflection, if she had attended, we would have renamed it the Meeting from Hell—with Fireworks.

Lesson: *It takes courage to deliver a strong message.*

The One-Minute Meeting:
It's Often Fatal

In the 1800s, we had Custer's Last Stand. Duration: seven minutes. Results: deadly. In the 1920s, we had the St. Valentine's Day Massacre. Duration: three minutes. Results: lethal. In the 1930s we had the final meeting between Rhett and Scarlett in *Gone with the Wind*. Duration: forty-five seconds. Result: hurtful. Should I continue, or are you getting a picture of the quick, on-the-run meeting?

Lesson: *Timing is everything.*

The Meeting Hall of Fame:
An Infamous Classic

Scene: The Mad Hatter's tea party. The innocent meeting in Wonderland turns into total confusion as "the seating arrangements are chaotic, the Mad Hatter speaks nonsense, the March Hare is rude, and the Dormouse sleeps through the proceedings. Nobody takes charge, the conversation goes in circles, nothing is accomplished, and the Dormouse ends up stuffed into the teapot."[20]

Lesson: *Preparation, preparation, preparation.*

Don't waste your people's brainpower—use meetings as effective business tools.

CHAPTER

18

On-the-Job
Thunderbolting

Remember,
Thunderbolt Thinking transforms your insight and options into powerful results.
Don't limit yourself now! The
idea is for you and those you
work with, live with, and
socialize with to think more
effectively. Ask yourself:

- Do we stay fresh while implementing new programs or completing old ones?

- Do we remain charged up to deliver quality services?

- Do we look for ways for each of us to invigorate the organization?

- Do we support being far-out, on the fringe?

- Do we create Thunderbolts when we need them?

"Perfection of means and confusion of goals seem—in my opinion—to characterize our age."

Don't forget that you and your people need time to think, especially when your organization's thinking has become stale or the people on your team are "experts" in their fields and have been on the job at least three years.

On-the-job Thunderbolting can be effective in a number of ways. Use the Lucky 13 strategies to help you build an innovative workplace. Keep your teams highly charged, with lots of activities. Plan specific ways to exercise your people's brains and to break out of old ruts. Try using the Thunderbolt Model the next time you need to plan, generate ideas, communicate, solve problems, or rekindle the energy on your team, in your family, or in your community.

The Thunderbolt Model: A Summary

The Thunderbolt matrix, with a dash of SPIRIT, makes the Model a viable tool you can easily use. It has three components:

- *WHAT you need to think about* focuses you on your current need, issue, problem, or situation, directing you toward the content you need to consider. WHAT you need to think about can be anything you want it to be.

- *How you think* guides you to think differently, to think on purpose, to be aware of the power you have to direct the thinking of yourself and others. How you think follows a five-step format that directs you to:

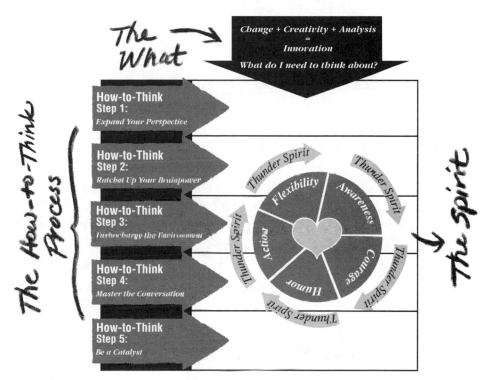

The Thunderbolt Thinking Model

1. Expand your perspective by looking at alternatives.

2. Ratchet up raw brainpower by tapping into your hidden resources.

3. Turbocharge the environment by creating surroundings that stimulate thinking.

4. Master the conversation by identifying both parts of the conversation.

5. Become a catalyst by moving to action with a system in place.

- *SPIRIT, the heart of the Model,* recharges your thinking, strengthening the WHAT and the HOW by blending five critical ingredients into the process to accelerate the group's thinking, producing outcomes that move from good to extraordinary. The SPIRIT is a combination of your attitudes:

1. *Flexibility:* Another name for change

2. *Awareness:* Inside and outside

3. *Courage:* Risk and vulnerability

4. *Humor:* More than the frosting

5. *Action*: A can-do attitude

As the core components of the Model, the WHAT, the HOW, and the SPIRIT are all driven by the Formula for Innovation. The formula reflects the way the elements of change, creativity, and analysis combine, leading to innovation.

Change + Creativity + Analysis = Innovation

Applying Thunderbolt Thinking

Following are suggested ways to apply the Thunderbolt Model to specific situations.

Vision or Mission Development

Think of using the Thunderbolt Model when: your organization's vision or mission is vague and lofty, it consists of a cut-and-paste effort from last year's annual meeting, or your vision leaves your people facing a vision gap preventing them from connecting the orchestrated statement with what to do on Monday morning.

Expand your group's perspective by including: a well-known futurist from your community, a graphic artist, a musician, a juggler, other successful organizational leaders, or people from a different country or culture, especially if they are fluent in a second language.

Suggested framework for the visioning or mission session:
Make sure your purpose is crystal clear. The group should understand
that they are creating a vision. It is always good to define it as an integrated image—a picture—painted in words that are very explicit in
emotionally or behaviorally capturing your organization's purpose. Hold
this type of session separate and apart from all other meetings. Allow
ample time; do not rush this process.

Trigger questions to ask:

- Why do we exist?

- What is the real purpose of our organization?

- What is the key, underlying essential element of our organization?

- What is the one common element that
  builds a shared experience in our organization?

- How can we best draw the future view of
  our organization?

Strategic or Long-Range Planning

**Think of using the Thunderbolt Model
when:** the financial officer is planning to run
the meeting, the budget has dictated the strategic direction of the organization for the last two
years, or the same group of people is involved
that ran the last strategic planning process.

**Expand your group's perspective by in-
cluding:** members of the crew that cleans
your offices at night, members of your board

of directors, a few customers, your competitors, someone who knows nothing about your organization or your business, or someone from the past—invite Einstein, Edison, or Plato!

Suggested framework for the strategic or long-range planning session: Make sure you define the purpose and distinguish between what you'll be in three to five years and how you'll get there. Structure the meeting (retreat, session, etc.) with ample time for people to think. Build in enough time so that you can create a tracking and monitoring system to implement the strategic plan. Look particularly at how you will deal with the day-to-day inhibitors so you can get the plan implemented.

Trigger questions to ask:

- What is the single most important thing we should accomplish in three years to reach our vision?

- How can we best draw our future view?

- What questions do we need to answer in order to plan for the next three to five years?

- What is our key driving force?

- How would we rate our current strategic I.Q.?

Marketing Planning Session

Think of using the Thunderbolt Model when: the budget keeps increasing but not your share of the market, you have "sold" your product or service in the same way for the last eighteen months, or a new competitor has moved into your market area.

Expand your group's perspective by including: a thirteen-year-old or several of the product or service users. A must is to have some of the people who create or produce the product or service attend.

"Education is that which remains when one has forgotten everything he learned in school."

Suggested framework for the marketing planning session: Find out all the whys for your current successful marketing efforts. Look at the principles behind the success—the WHAT and HOW. Try to hold the planning session at the place of purchase or use by the customer.

Trigger questions to ask:

- What are some outrageous ways to promote our services that will keep us in the customer's spotlight?

- How can we reach our customers more effectively but spend no more money?

- How can we maximize our marketing dollars to get several hits at once?

- What can we do that will absolutely kill our product? Now think of the opposite.

- What are all the moments of truth we have with our customers?

New Product or Service Development Session

Think of using the Thunderbolt Model when: time is a major factor in getting the new product or service into the marketplace, or you need to maximize your in-house resources by drawing on all your people's brainpower.

Expand your group's perspective by including: highly creative, free-thinking outsiders who are risk takers and are able to ask "dumb" questions.

Suggested framework for the new product or service development session: Hold the meeting in an atypical location. If weather allows, try holding it outside. Create a very open atmosphere with a lot of stimuli.

Trigger questions to ask:

- How can we blue sky this idea?

- What are all the ways to really Thunderbolt this product?

- What are all the reasons why people would not buy the product? Now generate ideas to change this.

- If this product could do one thing, what would it be?

- If we were buying this product, what would we want?

Quality Development Session

Think of using the Thunderbolt Model when: you are losing dollars on the bottom line because mistakes keep occurring all along the "line," or you are losing staff because of frustration or poor morale within your organization.

Expand your group's perspective by including: all those who are involved in the production and delivery of the product or service you're discussing, or someone who provides service every day, such as a waitress, hotel manager, or car dealer's service supervisor. Make sure to select someone who models the "quality" you want!

Suggested framework for the quality development session: Actually plan a quality session—go for the best, really demonstrate what high quality means by the location you choose for the meeting, the food offered, and the service in general. Use this as a backdrop for your session to drive home the idea of quality.

Trigger questions to ask:

- How can we become more aware of quality?

- What unique ways can we use to build the three cornerstones of quality: commitment, competence, and communication?

- What would a well-thought-out review cycle to monitor quality look like?

- What existing barriers inhibit quality at our company?

- How can we measure whether we are providing quality services?

Team-Building Session

Think of using the Thunderbolt Model when: mouths are always open, but minds are closed.

Expand your group's perspective by including: people who are directly involved in the team, group, or staff and those you'd like to have on the team.

Suggested framework for the team-building session: Keep it simple and informal. Let the group create their own parameters and environment. You should not be the facilitator. Use someone from outside or from another internal department to facilitate; you remain as the catalyst. Ask the team for input on designing the session and on the topics or issues they want to explore.

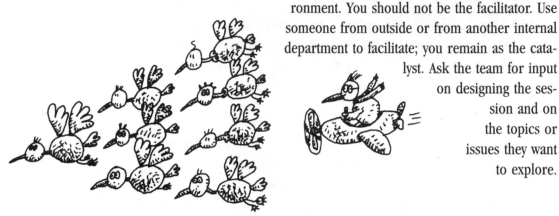

Trigger questions to ask:

- Who are we, really?

- What are the top three reasons someone new would join this team?

- What is the one thing that no one else knows about this team?

- How do we build a meaningful communication network among this team?

- What are all the ways that this team really soars?

- What are all the ridiculous ways to recruit new members to our group?

- What are all the ways to get this team more committed to our work?

- What are all the ways for this team to stay nimble on its feet while working on the project?

- What are the key ideas that will keep this team focused for the duration of the project?

"I never think of the future. It comes soon enough. "

Thunderbolt Think Tanks: Everyday Ways to Use the Model

The awesome power of human interactions overshadows technological advances, forcing high touch to remain a priority for most of us. Look at the millions AT&T spends encouraging us to "reach out and touch someone."

Human interactions consist of people coming together with a shared purpose. They may take the form of bargaining sessions or annual retreats; task forces or staff meetings; family parties, corporate product launches, or anniversary parties—it doesn't matter. What does matter is the interaction: articulating ideas, voicing opinions, listening, and respecting feelings.

What if . . . you could harness the "flashes of insight" from these interactions within your company, your home, your community? What if . . . you could create "communities for thinking" rather than "time slots" where people sit robotically ticking off agenda items? What if . . . you could unstick your employees instead of letting them be stuck in meetings, task forces, and committees? Would taking "time to think" every day be worth it then? Would you be willing to do something about creating your own everyday think tank?

Dispelling the Think-Tank Myth

Traditionally, we've done our thinking in a sterile vacuum instead of in the muddiness of the workplace. Let's dispense with the theoretical, pompous, elitist attributes that describe think tanks. Let's banish the notion that think tanks should remain in the realm of the super-bright who, locked away, focus on esoteric matters that aren't fit for consumption by the common person. Let's reinvent the meaning of think tanks and climb down from the ivory tower, descend from the mountaintop, and move in behind those closed doors at your organization.

Think tanks are a natural. Acting as a "change laboratory," they present the perfect petri dish within which to experiment with change. They offer an environment that can encourage incremental change when we gather on our living room floors, in our eight-by-ten-foot cubicles, around the desks at school, in the church hall, and at your kid's hockey club. The catch is this: while meetings burn up time and people, they are still a resourceful communication and management tool. And predictions are that this tool will continue to act as the link that connects us in our organizations.

Your challenge is to make those interactions more effective. So it doesn't matter if the interaction you're having is with one other person or a group of a hundred—the Thunderbolt Model can be the basis for transforming your "meeting" into a productive think-tank session. Try some of these things: turning an ordinary staff meeting into a thirty-minute, streamlined think tank by focusing on only one key issue, reformatting your family's next vacation-planning discussion by drawing pictures of all the places you'd like to visit, or delivering your next white paper to a group of one hundred people by asking a series of insightful, penetrating questions of the participants.

The opportunity to create a think tank and use the Thunderbolt Model is only limited by your own imagination. There is no end to the possible ways to blend the model's three components (WHAT, HOW, and SPIRIT) to fit your needs. Use the Change Lab Planner to turn your next meeting into a change lab.

Fast Start

For over 200 pages you have been building power, energizing yourself to take action. Using the "Aahs" from your drawing, the insights from your notes, and the specific outcomes from your thought attacks, it's time to create your own Thunderbolt session.

Remember that your passion will lead to breakthroughs and your commitments will be the bridge that carries your results forward. Also remember that the best fertilizer for a breakthrough is consistent, incremental change—even slight shifts can create a difference. Finally, your

Change Lab Planner (Sample)

Part 1

Think about an upcoming meeting you'll conduct at which you'll have flexibility in setup.

What is the main purpose of this meeting? *Increasing assembly line productivity.*

What three topics do you need to cover during this meeting?

- *Our current rate of productivity and current revenues.*
- *Desired changes to the rate of productivity and revenue goals.*
- *Feasibility of suggested changes and time-frame outline.*

Part 2

Which Thunderbolt tools and techniques could you use for each topic in order to create a change lab atmosphere?

Topic	Thunderbolt Tool and/or Technique
Rate of productivity	*Hold a Thought Attack session to generate a lot of ideas about how to improve productivity.*
Desired changes to rate of productivity	*Push the ideas generated by the Thought Attack through the "funnel." Look for connections and links among the ideas for new ways to change the rate of productivity.*
Feasibility of changes	*Spend three minutes per idea creating what-if questions that test the idea's feasibility.*
Establishing time-frame outline	*Have the team put on "visionary" glasses to create their best time-frame outline. Then have them take off the glasses and adjust the plan as needed.*

Change Lab Planner

Part 1

Think about an upcoming meeting you'll conduct at which you'll have flexibility in setup.

What is the main purpose of this meeting? _____

_____

What three topics do you need to cover during this meeting?

- _____

- _____

- _____

Part 2

Which Thunderbolt tools and techniques could you use for each topic in order to create a change lab atmosphere?

Topic	Thunderbolt Tool and/or Technique

brain is always working, so practice asking powerful questions to ensure powerful results.

The power is in this very moment. So begin by assessing what you can do to make your next meeting more productive. As you think about the actions you can take to improve your meetings, try to be as specific as possible. Use the trigger questions below to get you started. Ask yourself:

- What am I willing to change about our meetings to get extraordinary results?

- What is the single most important thing I must do before we meet?

- How can I have fun while designing the next meeting?

Draw new meaning into meetings:
experiment and create change
laboratories—turn them into think tanks.

CHAPTER

Do It Now—
With Action You Get Results

⚡

I wasn't aware of it at the time, but the spark was ignited in 1984. The life-altering challenge I faced then and continue to face each day is how not to get stuck. How not to let one thought be so overwhelming that I can't see another side. How not to let my ingrained thinking patterns drive my brain, but instead to allow myself to break out of the mold and see the situation from another vantage point.

So whether you have just picked up this book or have just finished it, my message remains the same. *The time is now!* The time is now to help break the gridlock of thinking that causes our organizations to get stuck. The time is now to Thunderbolt Think in our homes, communities, and workplaces. And the time is now for you to act, to move into action, and to get *unstuck*.

Become a barrier blaster and a bridge builder. Do it now!

CHAPTER NOTES

Chapter Two

1. Kanter, Rosabeth Moss, "Change Where to Begin," *Harvard Business Review* 69, no. 4 (July–August 1991), p. 8.
2. "Management Focus: Bespoke Factories," *The Economist* 325, no. 7788 (December 1992), p. 71, Business section.
3. Nolan, Richard L., "The Strategic Potential of Information Technology," *Financial Executive* 7, no. 4 (July–August 1991), p. 26.
4. Salter, Chuck, "Fast Change," *Fast Company,* Issue 23 (April 1999), p. 135.
5. Sokol, Reuben, "Gaining a World-Class Edge," *CMA Magazine* 66, no. 7 (September 1992), p. 19.
6. Magnet, Myron, "The Truth About the American Worker," *Fortune* 125, no. 9 (May 1992), p. 65.
7. Popcorn, Faith, *The Popcorn Report* (New York: Doubleday Currency, 1991), p. 21.
8. Magnet, Myron, "The Truth About the American Worker," *Fortune* 125, no. 9 (May 1992), p. 65.

Chapter Three

1. Sinnett, William, *From Direct Labor to Team Player* (Morristown, N.J.: Financial Executives Research Foundation, 1992), p. 8.
2. "Management Focus: Bespoke Factories," *The Economist* 325, no. 7788 (December 1992), p. 71, Business section.
3. Hamel, Gary, and Praholad, C. K., "Corporate Imagination and Expeditionary Marketing," *Harvard Business Review* 69, no. 4 (July–August 1991), p. 83.
4. Garfield, Charles, *Peak Performers* (New York: Avon Books, 1987), p. 203.
5. Sinnett, William, *From Direct Labor to Team Player* (Morristown, N.J.: Financial Executives Research Foundation, 1992), p. 11.
6. Stewart, Thomas A., "Brainpower," *Fortune* 123, no. 11 (June 1991), p. 50.
7. Hamel, Gary, and Praholad, C. K., "Corporate Imagination and Expeditionary Marketing," *Harvard Business Review* 69, no. 4 (July–August 1991), p. 84.
8. Noble, Sara P., ed., *301 Great Management Ideas from America's Most Innovative Small Companies* (Boston: Inc. Magazine, 1991), p. 202.
9. Maren, Michael, "Catch the Age Wave," *Success Magazine* 38, no. 8 (October 1991), p. 19.

Chapter Four

1. Maren, Michael, and Wallace, Don, "Masters of the Impossible," *Success Magazine* 39, no. 1 (February 1992), p. 30.
2. Poe, Richard, "Image Streaming," *Success Magazine* 38, no. 3 (April 1991), p. 72.
3. Stewart, Thomas A., "Brainpower," *Fortune* 123, no. 11 (June 1991), pp. 44–46.
4. Gordon, Jack, and Zemke, Ron, "Making Them More Creative," *Training Magazine* 23, no. 5 (May 1986), p. 30.

5. Byrd, Jack, and Smith, Julie M., "Innovation Revolution: Getting Better Ideas," *Training & Development Journal* 43, no. 1 (January 1989), p. 68.
6. Stewart, Thomas A., "Brainpower," *Fortune* 123, no. 11 (June 1991), p. 50.
7. Goleman, Daniel, Kaufman, Paul, and Ray, Michael, *The Creative Spirit* (New York: Penguin Group, 1992), p. 42.

Chapter Five

1. Arthur D. Little, Inc., *Prism, Tenth Anniversary Issue: Innovation for Business Results* (Third Quarter 1998), p. 35.

Chapter Six

1. Hammerschlag, Carl, *The Theft of the Spirit* (New York: Simon & Schuster, 1993).
2. Kriegel, Robert J., and Kriegel, Marilyn Harris, *The C Zone: Peak Performance Under Pressure* (Garden City, N.Y.: Anchor Press/Doubleday, 1984).
3. Hill, Napoleon, *Think and Grow Rich* (New York: Fawcett Crest, 1983).
4. Goleman, Daniel, *Emotional Intelligence: Why It Can Matter More Than IQ* (New York: Bantam Books, 1997), p. 149.

Chapter Seven

1. Rico, Gabriele Lusser, *Writing the Natural Way* (Los Angeles: Tarcher, 1983), p. 211.
2. Bach, Richard, *Biplane* (New York: Dell, 1966), p. 37.
3. Herrmann, Ned, *The Creative Brain* (Lake Lure, N.C.: Brain Books, 1988), p. 192.
4. Goleman, Daniel, Kaufman, Paul, and Ray, Michael, *The Creative Spirit* (New York: Penguin Group, 1992), p. 44.
5. Saporito, Bill, "What Sam Walton Taught America," *Fortune* 125, no. 9 (May 1992), p. 104.
6. Maren, Michael, and Wallace, Don, "Masters of the Impossible," *Success Magazine* 39, no. 1 (January–February 1992), p. 22.

Chapter Eight

1. Davis, Stanley M., *Future Perfect* (New York: Addison-Wesley, 1987), p. 85.
2. Langer, Ellen J., *Mindfulness* (New York: Addison-Wesley, 1989), p. 4.
3. Ibid., p. 44.
4. Ibid.

Chapter Nine

1. May, Rollo, *The Courage to Create* (New York: Bantam Books, 1976), p. 13.
2. Kriegel, Robert J., and Patler, Louis, *If It Ain't Broke . . . Break It!* (New York: Warner, 1991), p. 9.
3. Noble, Sara P., ed., *301 Great Management Ideas from America's Most Innovative Small Companies* (Boston: Inc. Magazine, 1991), p. 204.
4. Rico, Gabriele Lusser, *Writing the Natural Way* (Los Angeles: Tarcher, 1983), p. 211.
5. Goleman, Daniel, Kaufman, Paul, and Ray, Michael, *The Creative Spirit* (New York: Penguin Group, 1992), p. 20.

Chapter Ten

1. Davis, Stanley M., *Future Perfect* (New York: Addison-Wesley, 1987), p. 85.
2. "The Lost Art of Practical Joking," *The Laugh Connection Newsletter* 2, no. 2 (Spring 1992), p. 1.
3. Ontario Science Center, "But Seriously," *Newscience* 16, no. 7701 (1991), p. 1.

4. "The Lost Art of Practical Joking," *The Laugh Connection Newsletter* 2, no. 2 (Spring 1992), p. 1.

5. Kushner, Malcolm, *The Light Touch* (New York: Simon & Schuster, 1990), pp. 27–28.

6. de Bono, Edward, *Po: Beyond Yes and No* (New York: Viking Penguin, 1972), p. 80.

7. McGarvey, Robert, "Creative Thinking," *USAir Magazine* 12, no. 6 (June 1990), p. 40.

8. Ibid., p. 20.

9. "The Lost Art of Practical Joking," *The Laugh Connection Newsletter* 2, no. 2 (Spring 1992), p. 1.

10. Rice, Faye, "Champions of Communication," *Fortune* 123, no. 11 (June 1991), p. 112.

11. Metcalf, C. W., "The Good Humor Man?" *USAir Magazine* 14, no. 4 (April 1992), p. 61.

12. Kushner, Malcolm, *The Light Touch* (New York: Simon & Schuster, 1990), p. 211.

13. Ibid., p. 146.

Chapter Eleven

1. de Bono, Edward, *Tactics* (London: Pilot Productions, 1984), p. 117.

2. Saporito, Bill, "What Sam Walton Taught America," *Fortune* 125, no. 9 (May 1992), p. 104.

3. Ibid., p. 106.

4. Roddick, Anita, *Body & Soul* (London: Ebury Press, 1991), p. 187.

5. Ibid., p. 27.

6. Lev, Michael, "Give Me Your Tired, Your Rusty . . . ," *New York Times,* October 6, 1990, p. 18.

7. Saporito, Bill, "What Sam Walton Taught America," *Fortune* 125, no. 9 (May 1992), p. 106.

Chapter Twelve

1. Briggs, John, *Fire in the Crucible: The Alchemy of Creative Genius* (New York: St. Martin's Press, 1988), p. 275.

2. Ibid., pp. 274–275.

3. Briggs, John, *Fire in the Crucible: The Alchemy of Creative Genius* (New York: St. Martin's Press, 1988), p. 167.

4. Goleman, Daniel, Kaufman, Paul, and Ray, Michael, *The Creative Spirit* (New York: Penguin Group, 1992), p. 137.

5. Grudin, Robert, *The Grace of Great Things* (New York: Ticknor and Fields, 1990), p. 15.

6. Tzu, Sun, *The Art of War* (Boston: Shambhala Publications, 1988).

7. Walton, Donald, *Are You Communicating?* (New York: McGraw-Hill, 1989), p. 234.

8. Tobia, Peter M., and Becker, Martin C., "Making the Most of Meeting Time," *Training & Development Journal* 44, no. 8 (August 1990), p. 38.

9. Butler, Charles, "On the Mark," *Successful Meetings* 41, no. 1 (January 1992), p. 54.

10. Noble, Sara P., ed., *301 Great Management Ideas from America's Most Innovative Small Companies* (Boston: Inc. Magazine, 1991), p. 20.

11. Larson, Gary, *The Far Side Gallery* (Kansas City, Mo.: Andrews, McMeel & Parker, 1986).

Chapter Thirteen

1. Herrmann, Ned, *The Creative Brain* (Lake Lure, N.C.: Brain Books, 1988).

2. Skillman, Keith C., "Leadership Close-Up," *Association Management* 43, no. 9 (September 1991), pp. 60–61.

3. Buzan, Tony, *Use Both Sides of Your Brain* (New York: Dutton, 1983).

4. Grossmann, John, "Mind Mapping," *USAir Magazine* 10, no. 9 (September 1988), p. 79.

5. Maguire, Jack, *Care and Feeding of the Brain* (New York: Doubleday, 1990), p. 5.

6. Herrmann, Ned, *The Creative Brain* (Lake Lure, N.C.: Brain Books, 1988), pp. 31–39.

7. Ibid., p. 29.

8. Ibid., p. 9.

9. Hamel, Gary, and Praholad, C. K., "Corporate Imagination and Expeditionary Marketing," *Harvard Business Review* 69, no. 4 (July–August 1991), pp. 89–90.

10. Weber, Joseph, "A Big Company That Works," *Business Week,* no. 3264 (May 1992), pp. 125–127.

11. Rico, Gabriele Lusser, *Writing the Natural Way* (Los Angeles: Tarcher, 1983), p. 71.

12. Popcorn, Faith, *The Popcorn Report* (New York: Doubleday Currency, 1991), p. 13.

13. Maren, Michael, and Wallace, Don, "Masters of the Impossible," *Success Magazine* 39, no. 1 (January–February 1992), p. 28.

14. Noble, Sara P., ed., *301 Great Management Ideas from America's Most Innovative Small Companies* (Boston: Inc. Magazine, 1991), p. 188.

15. Ibid.

16. Ibid., p. 191.

17. Ibid., p. 21.

18. Ibid., p. 18.

19. Ibid., p. 29.

Chapter Fourteen

1. Goleman, Daniel, Kaufman, Paul, and Ray, Michael, *The Creative Spirit* (New York: Penguin Group, 1992), p. 136.

2. Noble, Sara P., ed., *301 Great Management Ideas from America's Most Innovative Small Companies* (Boston: Inc. Magazine, 1991), p. 200.

3. Thompson, Charles, *What a Great Idea* (New York: Harper Perennial, 1992), p. 150.

4. Ibid., p. 11.

5. Briggs, John, *Fire in the Crucible: The Alchemy of Creative Genius* (New York: St. Martin's Press, 1988), pp. 272–273.

6. Kriegel, Robert J., and Patler, Louis, *If It Ain't Broke . . . Break It!* (New York: Warner Books, 1991), p. 128.

7. Olofson, Cathy, "The Ritz Puts On Stand-Up Meetings," *Fast Company,* Issue 17 (September 1998), p. 62.

8. Goleman, Daniel, Kaufman, Paul, and Ray, Michael, *The Creative Spirit* (New York: Penguin Group, 1992), p. 139.

Chapter Fifteen

1. Roddick, Anita, *Body & Soul* (London: Ebury Press, 1991), p. 21.

2. Kriegel, Robert J., and Patler, Louis, *If it Ain't Broke . . . Break It!* (New York: Warner Books, 1991), p. 108.

3. Capacchione, Lucia, *The Power of Your Other Hand: A Course in Channelling the Inner Wisdom of the Right Brain* (Hollywood, Calif.: Newcastle, 1988), p. 85.

4. May, Rollo, *The Courage to Create* (New York: Bantam Books, 1976), p. 62.

5. Ibid., pp. 63–67.

6. Maguire, Jack, *The Care and Feeding of the Brain* (New York: Doubleday, 1990), pp. 121–122.

7. Thompson, Charles "Chic," *What a Great Idea* (New York: Harper Perennial, 1992), p. 13.

Chapter Sixteen

1. Briggs, John, *Fire in the Crucible: The Alchemy of Creative Genius* (New York: St. Martin's Press, 1988), p. 280.

Chapter Seventeen

1. Frank, Milo O., *How to Run a Successful Meeting in Half the Time* (New York: Pocket Books, 1989), p. 158.

2. Noble, Sara P., ed., *301 Great Management Ideas from America's Most Innovative Small Companies* (Boston: Inc. Magazine, 1991), p. 23.

3. Dunsing, Richard J., *You and I Have Simply Got to Stop Meeting This Way* (New York: American Management Association, 1978), p. 16.

4. Anderson, Duncan Maxwell, "Time Warrior," *Success Magazine* 38, no. 10 (December 1991), p. 40.

5. Noble, Sara P., ed., *301 Great Management Ideas from America's Most Innovative Small Companies* (Boston: Inc. Magazine, 1991), p. 198.

6. Kriegel, Robert J., and Patler, Louis, *If It Ain't Broke . . . Break It!* (New York: Warner Books, 1991), p. 86.

7. Filipczak, Bob, and Thompson, Brad Lee, "Training Today: Managing the Meeting Monster, Video Secrets, the Case for Deductive Learning and More," *Training Magazine* 28, no. 3 (March 1991), p. 10.

8. Noble, Sara P., ed., *301 Great Management Ideas from America's Most Innovative Small Companies* (Boston: Inc. Magazine, 1991), p. 199.

9. Ibid., p. 25.

10. Carroll, Lewis, *Alice's Adventures in Wonderland* (New York: Random House, 1946), p. 71.

11. Kieffer, George David, "The Supreme Agenda," *Success Magazine* 36, no. 10 (December 1989), p. 52.

12. McCormack, Mark, *What They Don't Teach You at Harvard Business School* (New York: Bantam Books, 1984).

13. McCormack, Mark, *The 110% Solution* (New York: Villard Books, 1991).

14. Butler, Charles, "On the Mark," *Successful Meetings* 41, no. 1 (January 1992), p. 54.

15. Noble, Sara P., ed., *301 Great Management Ideas from America's Most Innovative Small Companies* (Boston: Inc. Magazine, 1991), p. 197.

16. Goldberg, Matt, "Cisco's Most Important Meal of the Day," *Fast Company,* Issue 13 (February–March 1998), p. 56.

17. Noble, Sara P., ed., *301 Great Management Ideas from America's Most Innovative Small Companies* (Boston: Inc. Magazine, 1991), p. 22.

18. Frank, Milo O., *How to Run a Successful Meeting in Half the Time* (New York: Pocket Books, 1989), p. 66.

19. Ibid., pp. 34–35.

20. Miller, Robert F., *Running a Meeting That Works* (Hauppauge, N.Y.: Barron's Educational Series, 1991), p. 5.

GLOSSARY

The definitions in this glossary are intended to provide a working understanding of the terms used in this book. They are not precise, technical definitions.

Analytical thinking: A narrowing-down activity that draws upon known facts and principles to arrive at a conclusion.

Brainpower: The sum of the individual intellectual capital within an organization. Properly harnessed, it can be an effective strategic weapon, a competitive edge.

Common insight: The contribution of new ideas stimulated by the ideas of others, then blended into a concrete solution.

Computing mind: Assumes the logical, left-brained brain functions such as sequential patterning, systematic application, and linear execution.

Conversation of possibilities: The situation that occurs when you are searching for new ideas, creatively thinking, or solving problems.

Conversation of realities: The situation that occurs when you are logically evaluating ideas, narrowing in on workable solutions, and carrying out risk analysis.

Corpus callosum: A massive bundle of nerves, containing some 200 million fibers. Also called the "chief communicator," because it connects the two hemispheres of the brain.

Creative thinking: An expanding activity that takes what we already know and combines it into new relationships and therefore into new images, ideas, or solutions.

Displayed thinking: A highly interactive, visual process that combines both creative and analytical thinking. It was originated by Leonardo da Vinci and popularized by Walt Disney. Also known as storyboarding.

Effective thinking: Group thinking that combines both creative and analytical thinking to produce the most *effective* answer, not just the *right* one.

Five-sensing: A sensory-based experience that uses impressions obtained through the five senses. It consists of the ability to perceive something or someone through our sight, hearing, taste, smell, or touch, resulting in a richer, fuller understanding.

Gridlock thinking: A jam in the flow of thought. Essentially ideas are frozen and movement is constricted in all directions.

246

Idearial arcticosis: A situation in which hardened ideas lie frozen in the minds of your people.

Left brain hemisphere: The hemisphere that demonstrates logic, analysis, and language skills, as well as more serious, rational, and linear thought patterns.

Limit releasing: A process that allows creative ideas to emerge without limiting the flow or criticizing the ideas.

Meeting: A gathering of individuals such as a retreat, task force, think tank, committee, focus group, conference, or convention.

Mindfulness: The ability to be open to new categories and ways of interpreting information and to be aware of more than one perspective.

Mindlessness: A state of being trapped in rigid thinking, restricted to one use of information, and unable to think about options.

Opportunistic visioning: The ability to see new patterns such as uses for failed ideas; the ability to see opportunities in unexpected events.

Point-to-point thinking: A state in which one thought directly follows another in a logical order.

Right brain hemisphere: The hemisphere that demonstrates creativity, spontaneity, and random thought patterns.

Roomatoid meetingitis: A situation in which brilliant ideas never get beyond the meeting room.

Storyboarding: See Displayed thinking.

Strategic humor: The purposeful use of humor to break through gridlock thinking, build teams, and motivate creative thinking.

Stuckness: A "don't buck the system" attitude cemented into the corporate pillars of many organizations.

Thunder courage: The ability to go to the core of a situation and transform it *now*.

Thunder Meter: A rating from 0 to 100 assessing the Thunderbolt Power within your organization. The meter consists of: 0–10, Humming; 11–30, Crackling; 31–50, Charging; 51–80, Electrifying; 81–100, Thunderbolting.

Thunder wondering: An incubation period of raw ideas that allows your inspiration to cook up new solutions.

Thunderbolt outcomes: The results of a transformed meeting, consisting of outcomes that directly relate to the business's goals and needs and enhance the organization's performance.

Thunderbolt thinking: Flashes of insight that keep you from getting stuck, refreshing and recharging your thinking.

Thunderbolt Thinking Model: A matrix with three components: WHAT you need to think about, five how-to steps on HOW you think, and five aspects of Thunderbolt SPIRIT.

Thunderbolting: The situation when the group is exploding, flashing, and producing extraordinary Thunderbolt outcomes; passion and commitment are evident among the entire group.

Tools for thinking: "Toys" that are purposely used in a meeting to turbocharge the environment.

Whole-brain thinking: The process by which the brain absorbs, stores, and recalls materials more efficiently in pictures, images, and events than it does in words.

INDEX

Numbers following "T•N•T" refer to item numbers in the center section, not to page numbers.

Action: Action Ladder, 137–138; attitude of, 84; benefits of leaping into, 116; and breakthroughs, 183; and can-do attitude, 64, 115–123; compared with deliberation, 116; and forest paradox, 115; with fun, 120; immediate action encouraged, 118; and immediate start-up of Thunderbolt Thinking, 239–240; with quality, 118–119; quick action encouraged, 119–120; with simplicity, 122; with social conscience, 121–122; in Thunderbolt Thinking Model, 117, 226; tips on developing, 117; To-Do Chart for, 139; and transforming the "nothing ever happens" mood, 117–123

Action Ladder, 137–138

Agendas: hidden agendas, T•N•T 15, T•N•T 21; for meetings, 140–141, 215

Alchemy, 195–196

Alice's Adventures in Wonderland (Carroll), 211, 222

Alpha waves, 157–158

American Honda Motor Company, 28

American National Bank, 176

American Society of Association Executives, T•N•T 4

Amerman, John, 107–108

Analogies, T•N•T 4

Analytical thinking, 64–65, 186, 246

Anger, about meetings, 212–213, 215

Apollo 11, 27

Apple Computer, 171–172

Arche Technologies, Inc., 169–170

Arnn, Larry, 122

Art of War (Sun Tzu), 133

Arthur's Round Table, 219–220

ASAE Foundation, T•N•T 4

Assumptions, challenging, 133–134

AT&T, T•N•T 27

Attack thoughts, 155–156

Attitude: action attitude, 84; and Thunderbolt SPIRIT, 61–64, 81–85; of Thunderbolt Thinking, 61–64

Awareness: awakening internal environment for, 97–98; and barriers in meetings, 170–171; exercises for, 97–98; of humor, 108–110; and managing paradox, 93; versus mindlessness, 94–95; of nature, 94; and sensory awareness, 131–133; and stuckness, 42–43; subconscious awareness, 154; and success, 95–96; in Thunderbolt Thinking Model, 62, 96–97, 226; tips for, 96–97; and turbocharging the environment, 170–171

B.A.T. process, 156–158

Bach, Richard, 88–89

Baker, James, 220

Barry, Dave, T•N•T 9

Beaulieu, Bryan, 39

Beethoven, Ludwig von, 130

Benetton, Luciano, T•N•T 9

Berlin Wall, destruction of, 26

Berryman, Garry, 28

Beta waves, 157

Bias-free approach, 201

Billingsley, George, 91

Biplane (Bach), 88–89

Birth of Bun-Huggers, T•N•T 2

Bodhicitte, 97

Body Shop, Inc., 121, 180

Bowerman, Bill, 133

Brain: beta and alpha waves of, 157–158; bridge between hemispheres of, 159–160; characteristics of, 151–154; corpus callosum of, 159–160, 246; and cosmic fishing, 154–156; definition of brainpower, 246; description of, 41; drawing of, 40, 42, 44–45, 81, 148–150, 153, T•N•T 10; facts on, 151; and food for thought, 163–164; and generation of solutions, 155; hemispheres of, 151–156, 158–159, 247; interconnectedness in, 152; iteration in, 152; left brain, 151–153, 158–159, 247; and random selection, 155; right brain, 151–154, 247; situationality in, 152; specialization in, 151–152; split-brain theory, 152; and subconscious awareness, 154; total capacity of, 151; weight of, 151. *See also* Ratcheting up your brainpower

Brain Fantasy, T•N•T 3

Brain Flossing, T•N•T 1

Brain Jolts, T•N•T 4

Brain Stretch, T•N•T 5

Brain Transformers, T•N•T 6

Brain trust, 162–163

Brainpower. *See* Brain; Ratcheting up your brainpower

Braniff, Ronald, 106

Brazil, 121

Breaking Through Conditioned Responses, T•N•T 7

Breaks: between possibility and reality conversations, 190; Thought Walk for, T•N•T 23

Breakthroughs, 182–183, T•N•T 7

Brian's Song, 104–105
Briggs, John, 130
Bun-huggers as warm-up, T•N•T 2
Burner, Pat, 163–164
Buzan, Tony, 150
Byrd, Jack, 59

C. W. Metcalf & Co., 108
Cabbage Patch Kids, 24
Canada, 220
Cancer Guidance Institute, T•N•T 17
Can-do attitude, 64, 115–123
Care and Feeding of the Brain (Maguire), 183
Carroll, Lewis, 211, 222
Catalyst: blending with facilitator, 196, 198–199; checklist for, 201;
    cultivating skills as, 200–201; drawing of, 197; example of, from
    alchemy, 195–196; and group process skills, 200; inventing
    personal style of, 199; overview of, 60–61, 195–196, 202; and
    personal development skills, 200–201; Thought Attack on, 198;
    tips for, 202
Caterpillar Inc., 36
Caterpillar Logistics Services, Inc., 36
Caterpillar Tractor Company, 35–36
Cerner Corp., T•N•T 1
Chairs for meetings, 173–174
Challenging the status quo, 180, 182–183
Chambers, John, 217
Change Lab Planner, 235–236
Charles, Ray, 43
Checklists: catalyst, 201; expanding your perspective, 144; turbocharging
    the environment, 175
Churchill, Winston, 89, 152, 221
Cisco Systems, 217
Claremont Institute, 122
Clarification, 200
Claw Your Way to the Top (Barry), T•N•T 9
Clement, George, 162
Clement Communications, Inc., 162
Clichés, 110
Cold War, 220
Coleco Industries, 24
Collins, Jim, 64
Common insight, 190, 246
Communication: developing meaningful communication, 85; for
    follow-up, 142; hidden communication, T•N•T 15. *See also*
    Mastering the conversation
Computing mind, 246
Conditioned responses, breaking through, T•N•T 7
Connections, power of, 34–35
Conversation. *See* Mastering the conversation
Conversation of possibilities, 186, 189–190, 246
Conversation of realities, 186, 191–192, 246
Coors Brewing Company, 27
Corning Inc., 173–174
Corporate Portraits, T•N•T 8
Corpus callosum, 159–160, 246
Cosmic fishing, 154–156

Council of Logistics Management, T•N•T 28
Courage: for breaking habits, 100–101; courage paradox, 99; definition
    of, 247; importance of, 63, 100; in Thunderbolt Thinking Model,
    101, 226; tips for developing, 102
Courage to Create (May), 182
Creative Brain (Herrmann), 149
Creative freedom, 157
Creative thinking, 65, 186, 189–191, 246
Crest Microfilm, Inc., 164
Criteria, agreed-upon, 191
Cromwell, Oliver, 205–206
Cross-pollination, T•N•T 22
Crupis, James A., 149–150
Custer's Last Stand, 222

Darwin, Charles, 130
De Gaulle, Charles, 116
Declining returns, 37–39
Deliberation compared with action, 116
Dell, Michael, 46
Deming, W. Edwards, 95
Develop Your Sense of Humor, T•N•T 9
DiPiero, Jim, 111
Discussion technique, 187, 189. *See also* Mastering the conversation
Disney, Walt, 133
Displayed thinking discussion technique, 187, 189, 246
Doublet Manufacturing, Inc., 206–207
Dramowicz, George, T•N•T 26
Draw-a-Brain, T•N•T 10
Draw-a-Picture exercises, 40, 168, 181, 197
Drawing: of brain, 40, 41, 42, 44–45, 81, 148–150, 153, T•N•T 10;
    for capturing brainpower, 148–150; of catalyst, 197; of God, 150;
    for liberation from stuckness, 39–41; of meetings, 168, 181;
    One Picture or One Thousand Words, T•N•T 19
Dumb questions, asking, 133–134
Dyslexia, 42

Eastman Kodak Company, 28
Eating, 163–164
Edison, Thomas, 46, 172
Educational experience, 199
Effective thinking, 246
Eggs-straordinaire, T•N•T 27
Einstein, Albert, 22, 29, 34, 37, 46, 57, 80, 91, 94, 97, 100, 105, 108,
    116, 121, 131, 132, 134, 148, 151, 161, 163, 174, 180, 190, 196,
    200, 208, 217, 224, 228, 232, T•N•T 16
Electronic newsletter, 209
Ellington, Duke, 172
Emotional Intelligence (Goleman), 82–83
Energy, 160
Environment. *See* Turbocharging the environment
Equitable Companies Incorporated, 173–174
Exhaustion from trying to keep up, 35–36
Expanding your perspective: by challenging assumptions, 133–134;
    checklist for, 144; exercise on, T•N•T 6; by following up,
    141–143; by launching yourself from a stuck state, 128–131;
    by maintaining a flexible focus, 134–137; and new avenues of

information, 129–130; overview of, 56, 127–128, 145; by preparation, 137–140; and sensory awareness, 131–133; by strengthening front-end thinking, 137–140; tips on, 145; and writing in notebook, journal, or sketchbook, 130–131
Exposing yourself, 85

F.I.S.H., 155–156, 158, T•N•T 11
Facilitation and facilitator, 196, 198–200
Fantasy associations, T•N•T 3
Fargo Electronics, 209
Farrell, Maura, T•N•T 14
Federal Express, 133
Five-sensing, 131–133, 246
Flash Cap, T•N•T 30
Flexibility: building flexibility, T•N•T 12; and change, 62; of focus, 134–137, T•N•T 12; importance of, 88–89; and nature-of-light paradox, 87; opportunities for, 90; in Thunderbolt Thinking Model, 90, 226; tips for maintaining, 91–92; as zigzagging between activities, 89
Focus: flexible focus, 134–137, T•N•T 12; and narrowing down ideas, 191–192
Follow-up, 141–143
Food, 163–164
Forest paradox, 115
Forum Corporation, 81–82
Franklin, Benjamin, 134
Fringe, use of, 43, 46
Front-end thinking, 137–140
Frost, Robert, 67
Fuller, R. Buckminster, 154
Fun. *See* Humor
Future View, T•N•T 22

G.O.D. (Guaranteed Overnight Delivery), 53
Garbage Bag Dump, T•N•T 13
Gates, Bill, 46
Gecowets, George, T•N•T 28
Gelb, Michael, 150
General Electric Company, 122
General Systems Services, 111
Generation of solutions, 155
Germany, 26, 37
Global Survey on Innovation, 68
Globalized trading, 27–28, 36–37
Goals, achievement of, 83
Goleman, Daniel, 82–83
Golson, Benny, 101
Gone with the Wind, 222
Gonzales, Martin, 111
Gordon, Jack, 58
Gridlock thinking, 246
Group process skills, 200
Groups. *See* Meetings; Teams
Gruber, Howard, 89

Habits, courage to break, 100–101
Hammerschlag, Carl, 80–81
Have questions, 134–135
Head Bowling, T•N•T 14
Headlines, USA, 184
Hemingway, Ernest, 172
Hemispheres of brain, 151–156, 158–159, 247
Herrmann, Ned, 149, 151–154
Hewlett-Packard Company, 111
Hidden agendas, T•N•T 15, T•N•T 21
Hidden Communication, T•N•T 15
High Performance Learning Center, 150
Hill, Napoleon, 82
Holt Manufacturing Company, 35
Honda Motor Company, 28
Honeywell, T•N•T 26
Hot-cold paradox, 103
Hudetz, Joe, 161–162
Human capital, poor investment in, 28–29
Humor: and action, 120; awareness of, 108–110; and catalyst, 201; definition of, 105; development of, T•N•T 9; getting serious about, 106–109; and Head Bowling, T•N•T 14; and hot-cold paradox, 103; importance of, 63, 104, 106–109; library of, T•N•T 9; and meetings, 190, 218; and photo funnies, T•N•T 8; and play, 111–113; and practical joking, 104–105; strategic humor, 106–111, 190, 247; and stuckness, 42–43; and thinking from humorous perspective, 110; in Thunderbolt Thinking Model, 106–111, 226; tips for developing, 108–110, 112–113; and Toys for Thinking, 174–176; of Twain, 191. *See also* Toys for Thinking

IBM, 26
Idea Hatchery, T•N•T 16
Idearial arcticosis, 170–171, 246
If It Ain't Broke . . . Break It! (Kriegel and Patler), 100
II VI Incorporated, 37
Image Storming, T•N•T 17
Images: Image Storming, T•N•T 17; importance of, 150; of meetings, 212
Imagination, 183–185
Incubation: of ideas, T•N•T 16, T•N•T 27; and innovation, 72
Index cards, 191, 192
Industrial Revolution, 29
Inferential Focus, 35
Infrastructure, lack of, 66
Inghilleri, Leonardo, 174
Innovation: building innovative workplaces, 67–76; definition of, 65; formula for, 64–66; Global Survey on Innovation, 68; integrating innovation in three stages, 68–71; performance stage of, 70–71, 73, 75–76; practice stage of, 70, 72, 74–75; preparation stage of, 69–72, 74; self-assessment for, 73–76; strategies for building innovative workplace, 71–73
Insight: and attack thoughts, 155–156; common insight, 190, 246; lack of, 25–26; in Thunderbolt Thinking Model, 50–52
Interconnectedness in brain, 152
International Leadership Center, 149–150
Introductions, T•N•T 20
Iteration in brain, 152
Iverson, Ken, 161
Ivory Soap, 27

Japan, 27, 37
Jobs, Steven, 46

Johnson, Jay, 164
Johnson & Johnson, 156–157, 173–174
Joking. *See* Humor; Practical joking
Journal writing, 130–131

Kanter, Rosabeth Moss, 24
Key Strategies for Success, T•N•T 22
Khrushchev, Nikita, 220
Kieffer, George David, 213–214
King Arthur's Round Table, 219–220
KISS (keep it simple, stupid) principle, 122
Koestler, Arthur, 105
Kriegel, Robert J., 100
Kushner, Malcolm, 105

Langer, Ellen J., 95
Larsen, Ralph, 157
Latecomers to meetings, 207–208
Laugh Connection Newsletter, 104–105
Laughter. *See* Humor
Leader performance at meetings, 210
Left brain hemisphere, 151–153, 158–159, 247
Leonardo da Vinci, 187, 188
Levanon, Isaac, 169–170
Light Touch (Kushner), 105
Limit releasing, 190, 247
Limited, Inc., 119
Linda I. Miles & Associates, 207–208
Little, Arthur D., 68
Logic, 192
Long-range planning, 227–228
Ludwick, Andrew, 164

"Mad as Hell" survey, 213, 215
Mad Hatter's tea party, 222
Magic-carpet fantasy, T•N•T 3
Maguire, Jack, 183
Managing paradox, 93
Marcus Aurelius, 82
Marketing planning session, 228–230
Maryland National Bank, 25
Mastering the conversation: by challenging the status quo, 180, 182–183; and discussion technique, 187, 189; by focusing and narrowing down ideas, 191–192; and imagination, 183–185; by orchestrating the conversation, 192; overview of, 59–60, 179–180, 193; possibility and reality conversations, 186, 189–191; by releasing group creative juices, 189–191; tips on, 190–191, 193; by understanding how conversations flow, 185–186
Mattel Toy Corporation, 107–108
Maturity, 200
May, Rollo, 182
McCormack, Mark, 137, 215
McCrory and McDowell, 131
McDowell, Mike, 131–132
McNellis, Jerry, 187
McNellis Group, 187
Meetings: agendas for, 140–141, 215; anger about, 212–213; barriers in, 170–171, 211; basics of, 213–215; breaks in, 190, T•N•T 23;

building excitement into, 83; chairs for, 173–174; Change Lab Planner, 235–236; characteristics of well-functioning groups, 217–218; definition of, 247; drawings of, 168, 181; follow-up for, 141–143; and humor, 190, 218; images of, 212; latecomers to, 207–208; leader performance at, 210; length of, 161, 207; lessons for, 218–222; and marketing planning sessions, 228–230; myths of, 207; new product or service development sessions, 230; notable meetings in history, 218–222; one-minute meetings, 222; participation in, 220–221; pictograph minutes for, 143; pitfalls of, 211; preparation for, 137–140, 215–216; and providing relief from pressure cooker, 208–209; quality development sessions, 230–231; "Rules of Trust" model for, 216–217; sample agendas for, 140–141; self-assessments on, 210, 213, 214; table for, 219–220; taming the meeting monster, 206–208; team-building sessions, 231–232; Thought Attack on, 169; Thunder Meter for, 210; tips on *not* holding meetings, 209; tips on simplifying, 122; To-Do Chart for, 139; turning meeting room on its ear, 171–174; zero-based meeting attitude, 205–222
Metaphors, T•N•T 4
Metcalf, C. W., 108–109, T•N•T 8
Mexico, 28
Middle East peace talks, 220
Mindfulness, 247. *See also* Awareness
Mindfulness (Langer), 95
Mindlessness, 94–95, 170–171, 247. *See also* Awareness
Mind-mapping, 150
Mink, Michelle, T•N•T 29
Mission development, 226–227
Morin, Christophe, 207
Motorola, Inc., 34, 207
Movie themes, T•N•T 28
Myths of meetings, 207

NakaMats, Yoshiro, 46, 172
Name tags, T•N•T 18
National Round Table of Canada, 220
Nature-of-light paradox, 87
Negative thoughts. *See* Attack thoughts
Negotiation, 200
New product or service development session, 230
Newsletters, 28, 104–105, 209
Newton, Sir Isaac, 27
Nike shoes, 133
Nissan Motor Co., Ltd., T•N•T 25
Nolan, Richard L., 25
Nolan, Norton and Company, 25
Notebook, writing in, 130–131
"Nothing ever happens" mood, 117–123
Nucor Corp., 161

On-the-job Thunderbolting: fast start for, 234, 237; for marketing planning sessions, 228–230; and mission development, 226–227; for new product or service sessions, 230; questions on, 223–224; strategic or long-range planning, 227–228; for team-building sessions, 231–232; and Thunderbolt Thinking Model, 224–226; and visioning, 226–227
110% Solution (McCormack), 137, 215
One-minute meetings, 222

One Picture or One Thousand Words, T•N•T 19

Opportunistic visioning, 27, 191, 247

Opposites, thinking in, 129–130

Paradoxes: courage paradox, 99; forest paradox, 115; hot-cold paradox, 103; managing paradox, 93; nature-of-light paradox, 87

Passion and Thunderbolt SPIRIT, 82–83

Patler, Louis, 100

Patterson, Neal, T•N•T 1

Peavey, Melia, 208–209

Peavey Electronics Corporation, 208–209

Perspective. *See* Expanding your perspective

Philippines, 32

Photo funnies, T•N•T 8, T•N•T 24

Pictograph minutes, 143

Planning: marketing planning session, 228–230; for meetings, 137–140, 215–216; strategic or long-range planning, 227–228

Play, 72, 111–113. *See also* Humor

Play-Doh exercises, T•N•T 5, T•N•T 12, T•N•T 26

Poe, Richard, 56

Point-to-point thinking, 192, 247

Popcorn, Faith, 28–29, 131, 161, 172

Popcorn Report, 28

Possibility conversations, 186, 189–191, 246

Practical joking, 104–105. *See also* Humor

Preparation for meetings, 137–140, 215–216

Price Club, 180

Principle, search for, 191–192

Professional Convention and Management Association's Network for the Needy, 121

Public Broadcasting System, 31–32

Quality and action, 118–119

Quality development session, 230–231

Questioning: Action Ladder for, 137–138; art of, 134–137; and asking dumb questions, 133–134; and follow-up, 141–143; front-end questions, 137–140; *have* questions, 134–135; and maintaining flexible focus, 134–137; and specific questions developed for meetings, 211; trigger questions as examples of, 136–137; *want* questions, 134–135; *why* questions, 135

Random selection in brain, 155

Ratcheting up your brainpower: and B.A.T. process, 156–158; by blending brainpower, 161–162; and brain hemispheres, 151–156; and bridge between brain hemispheres, 159–160; by capturing brainpower, 148–150; and cosmic fishing, 154–156; by creating a brain trust, 162–163; by feeding your brain, 163–164; overview of, 57, 147–148, 165; tips for, 164. *See also* Brain

Reality conversations, 186, 191–192, 246

Reel to Real, T•N•T 28

Regressive introductions, T•N•T 21

Relativity theory, 132

Releasing of limits, 190

Review cycle, 142

Rico, Gabriele Lusser, 100–101, 160

Right brain hemisphere, 151–154, 247

Riley, Walter, 53

Risk taking, 63, 66

Ritz-Carlton Hotel Co., 174

Robert's Rules of Order, 217

Roddick, Anita, 121, 131, 167, 169, 180

Role playing, 129

Roomatoid meetingitis, 171, 247

Roosevelt, Franklin D., 221

Rotemberg, Julio, 60

Round Table, 219–220

"Rules of Trust" model, 216–217

St. Valentine's Day Massacre, 222

Saudi Arabia, 35

Sayers, Gale, 105

Schoeller, Connie, 148–149

School experience, 199

Schunpeter, Joseph, 91

Self-assessment: innovation, 73–76; "mad as hell" attitude, 213, 215; meetings, 210, 213, 214; spirit, 84; stuckness, 33

Sensory awareness, 131–133, 246, T•N•T 25

Seriousness, terminal, 109

Service development session, 230

Shape of Things to Come, T•N•T 26

Sharp Electronics Corp., 154

Show-and-tell sessions, T•N•T 24

Shulze, Horst, 174

Simplicity and action, 122

Sing-a-Song, T•N•T 29

Singing, 109, T•N•T 29

Situationality in brain, 152

Sketchbook, writing in, 130–131

Skyline Displays, Inc., 39

Smith, Fred, 133

Smith, Julie M., 59

SmithKline Beacham Pharma Inc., 192

Social conscience, 121–122

Solar Press, Inc., 161–162

Solutions generation, 155

Specialization in brain, 151–152

Spelling, 191

Sperry, Roger W., 152

Spill the Beans, T•N•T 21

Spirit: and achieving goals, 83; and action attitude, 84; and attitude, 81–85; and building excitement into meetings, 83; and communication skills, 85; and exposing yourself, 85; importance of, 80–81; and passion, 82–83; self-assessment on, 84; in Thunderbolt Thinking, 51–52, 61–64, 79–85, 223, 225–226

Split-brain theory, 152

Stalin, Josef, 221

Staples Inc., 141–142

Status quo, challenging, 180, 182–183

Stewart, Thomas A., 37, 57

Storyboarding, 247

Strategic humor, 106–111, 190, 247

Strategic planning, 227–228

Stuckness: and awareness, 42–43; definition of, 247; and drawing pictures for liberation, 39–41; exercises for getting unstuck, T•N•Ts 1–30; and exhaustion from trying to keep up, 35–36; and laughter, 42–43; launching yourself from, 128–131; as missed global opportunities, 36–37; as not responding to signals, 34; as not seeing power of connecting pieces, 34–35; in organizations, 23–24; and school experience, 199; self-assessment for, 33; signals for, 32–39, 170–171; and staying unstuck, 47; as suffering from declining returns, 37–39; tips and techniques for, T•N•Ts 1–30; and using the fringe to stay unstuck, 43, 46

Subconscious awareness, 154
Success and awareness, 95–96
Success Magazine, 213–214
Sun Tzu, 133
Synergy, 160
SynOptics Communications, 164

T.L.C. Child Care Centers, Inc., 163–164
Tables for meetings, 219–220
Talvacchio, Anne, 155, T•N•T 16
Teams: and blending brainpower, 161–162; as brain trust, 162–163; and team-building sessions, 231–232
Tension in breaking habits, 100–101
Terminal seriousness, 109
Theft of the Spirit (Hammerschlag), 81
Theme and Tools for Thinking, T•N•T 22
Think and Grow Rich (Hill), 82
Think tanks, 233–234
Thinking skills. See Thunderbolt Thinking
Thomas, Philip, 207
Thornburg, David, 106
Thought Attack: barriers to thinking, 182; brain description, 41; catalyst, 198; meetings, 169
Thought Walk, T•N•T 23
3M, 27
3M Canada, T•N•T 19
Thunder courage, 247
Thunder Meter, 210, 247
Thunder wondering, 190, 247
Thunderbolt innovators, 67–76
Thunderbolt outcomes, 247
Thunderbolt Show and Tell, T•N•T 24
Thunderbolt think tanks, 233–234
Thunderbolt Thinking: advantages of, 22–23; attitudes of, 61–64; author's first experience with, 17–18; and being a catalyst, 60–61; definition of, 247; diagram of, 51; and expanding your perspective, 56, 127–146; five-step format of, 54–61; and flash of insight, 50–52; and getting started, 53–54, 239–240; flow of, 51–52, 53–61, 224–225; how-to-think model, 29–30; and innovation, 64–66; as life-based model, 52–53; and mastering the conversation, 59–60, 179–180; for meetings, 205–222; model of, 49–66, 126, 146, 166, 178, 194, 224–226, 247; need for, 31–46; and on-the-job Thunderbolting, 223–237; and ratcheting up your brainpower, 57, 147–166; signals of need for, 23–29; SPIRIT of, 52, 61–64, 79–85, 225–226; tips and techniques for, T•N•Ts 1–30; transformational shift in, 21–30; and turbocharging the environment, 58–59, 167–177; WHAT of, 50–53, 224. See also On-the-job Thunderbolting
Thunderbolting, 247. See also On-the-job Thunderbolting
Time, lack of, 66
Time frames, shrinking of, 26

Tivoli Systems, Inc., 26
To-Do Chart, 139
Tools for thinking. See Toys for Thinking
Total Immersion: Using Sense, T•N•T 25
Toys for Thinking, 174–176, 196, 198–199, 247, T•N•T 3, T•N•T 5, T•N•T 24
Tracking and monitoring system, 142, 216
Trading, globalized, 27–28
Trance, 157
Trigger questions, 136–137, 232
Trust, rules of, 216–217
Turbocharging the environment: and awareness, 170–171; checklist for, 175; overview of, 58–59, 167, 169–170; tips for, 177; and Toys for Thinking, 174–176; by turning meeting room on its ear, 171–174
Twain, Mark, 191
Twilight learning, 157
Tylenol, 26

United Colors of Benetton, 119, T•N•T 9
Unocal Corporation, 121–122
US WEST Communications, Inc., T•N•T 29
Use Both Sides of Your Brain (Buzan), 150

Visioning, 191, 226–227, 247
Visionus myopius, 170–171
Volcanoes documentary, 31–32
Vulnerability, 63

Walking, T•N•T 23
Wal-Mart Stores, Inc., 91, 119–120, 122
Walt Disney Company, 187
Walton, Sam, 91, 116
Want questions, 134–135
Warm-up exercise, T•N•T 2
Welch, Jack, 122
What They Don't Teach You at Harvard Business School (McCormack), 215
Whole-brain thinking, 149, 201, 247
Why questions, 135
Wilczak, Lynn, 26
Wilson, Valarie, 217
Wilson Sculley Associates, Inc., 217
Wizard of Oz, 116, T•N•T 28
Wondering, 190
Woolf, Virginia, 130
World Trade Center bombing, 26
Writing: on index cards, 191, 192; in notebook, journal, sketchbook, 130–131
Writing the Natural Way (Rico), 100–101, 160

Xerox Corporation, 28

Yamaha, 38

Zemke, Ron, 58
Zigzagging between diverse activities, 89

THUNDERBOLT THINKING ®

VISION

Thinking organizations, worldwide, that sustain Innovation

MISSION

Visionary organizations, who understand the need to harness and drive Innovation, come to us to help them achieve market dominance in the new economy. We help them to systematically integrate Innovation throughout their organization by building a customized framework for sustained Innovation. Along the way, they carve out an Innovation process and align it with their vision, integrate it in their business strategies, embed it in their procedures, and bring it alive in their workplaces.

THUNDERBOLT THINKING® CORE SERVICES

Sustaining Innovation: A multifaceted initiative designed to drive Innovation from the executive level to the front line. It is built on facilitated thinking experiences for leaders and teams in which they develop a model and strategies to sustain Innovation in the workplace.

Thunderbolt Thinking Experiences: Produce innovative ideas for new products and services, strategic initiatives, or team building. Our rigorous thinking process drives organizations to the innovative breakthroughs that set them apart.

Thunderbolt Innovation Center: This initiative helps organizations to create an Innovation center that fosters and develops Innovation by providing a highly visible, readily available resource, open to any person in the organization. The on-site center becomes a place where tools and resources help individuals to practice new ways of thinking as they work through tough business challenges.

THUNDERBOLT THINKING® RESOURCES

- Thunderbolt Thinking® *Book:* Hundreds of powerful strategies, ideas, and exercises transform your work environment into a community for thinking.
- *The Tool Kit:* Filled with field-tested techniques plus the gear to fully enhance Thunderbolt Thinking®.
- *The Jump Start Guide:* Energize your toughest thinking sessions with five Thunderbolt exercises.
- *The F.I.S.H.*™: Keep your creative thinking session positive so ideas flow. The F.I.S.H.™ eats Fatally Inappropriate Slimy Hits.
- *Thunderbolt Guppies:* A whole school of F.I.S.H.™ so everyone on your team can have one!
- *Thunderbolt Brain Floss:* Stay alert, aware, and agile in your thinking—especially on those Bad Brain Days.
- *The Idea Hatchery®:* Solve tough problems with this thirty-day idea log that turns random thoughts into solid solutions.
- *Thunderbolt Thinking® Notecards:* Share an idea, recognize your team, or encourage a peer with twelve colorful notecards.

Thunderbolt Thinking, Inc.
4530 William Penn Highway, #6750
Murrysville, PA 15668
(412) 661-8325
Fax: (412) 661-1119
E-mail: ideas@thunderboltthinking.com
Website: www.thunderboltthinking.com

To access more Thunderbolt Thinking tools, tips, techniques, and resources, learn about our services, or order our products, visit our website at www.thunderboltthinking.com.

ORDER FORM

QTY.	TITLE	PRICE	TOTAL
_____	*Thunderbolt Thinking®* *Electrifying Ideas for Building an* *Innovative Workplace* Paperback (7" × 9", 292 pages) Texas residents add 8.25% sales tax	$16.95	_____
			+ _____
		TOTAL	_____

> **Quantity discounts are available**
> **for training programs**
> **and other company uses.**
> **Call 1-800-945-3132**
> **for information.**

☐ Please contact me about Thunderbolt Thinking services.

☐ Payment enclosed.
Please make checks payable to PSI Fulfillment.

Name _____

Organization _____

Address _____

City _____ State _____ Zip _____

Phone (_____) _____

Signature _____

☐ MasterCard ☐ VISA ☐ American Express ☐ Discover

Card No. _____

Exp. Date _____

To place your order by phone, call 1-800-945-3132, fax to 512-288-5055, or write to PSI Fulfillment, 8803 Tara Lane, Austin, TX 78737.